Armitage's Garden Perennials

ARMITAGE'S GARDEN PERENNIALS

A Color Encyclopedia

ALLAN M. ARMITAGE

Timber Press
Portland, Oregon

All photographs are by Allan M. Armitage.

Published in 2000 by

Timber Press, Inc.
The Haseltine Building
133 S.W. Second Avenue, Suite 450
Portland, Oregon 97204, U.S.A.

Fourth printing 2000

Designed by Susan Applegate

Printed in Hong Kong

Library of Congress Cataloging-in-Publication Data

Armitage, A. M. (Allan M.)
[Garden perennials]
Armitage's garden perennials: a color encyclopedia
by Allan M. Armitage
p.   cm.
Includes index
ISBN 0-88192-435-0
1. Perennials Encyclopedias.
2. Perennials Pictorial works.
I. Title.
II. Title: Garden perennials.
SB434.A755 2000
635.9'32'03—dc21   99-30800
CIP

This book is dedicated to my children—

to newly married Laura, whose life keeps getting richer;
to hardworking Heather, whose spirit will never be broken;
to athletic Jonathan, who, without doubt, will capture his dream.

Susan and I have been blessed to watch them grow.

Contents

7

Preface

Some Thoughts of the Author

Gardening is one of those things that gets in one's blood—a thing that is difficult to explain, even to people who have been so transfused. Gardening is one of those abstract activities that means many things to many people. Rock gardens, alpine gardens, bog gardens, butterfly gardens, water gardens, and native plant gardens are nirvana to some and meaningless to others. But all gardeners and their garden themes are tied together by the one glue that binds: the plants. And regardless of the real job they hold, when gardeners get together, the language of plants cuts through all other spoken bologna.

Plants are the common denominator of gardeners. Gardeners love plants, more than water features, or hummingbirds, or silly statues in their garden, and will go to incredible lengths—and expense—to secure them. By definition, gardeners are collectors. Numismatists and philatelists have nothing on gardeners! They encase their precious bounty in secure collections to be occasionally admired and evaluated. Not gardeners; they place their collections in abusive environments and dare them to live, but always with the hope of future glory, if not prosperity.

Gardeners love all plants, but perennials have a special place in the hearts of many, and oh boy, are they collectible! To talk about perennials often inspires passion, but to see them can incite lust and rioting among otherwise conservative, law-abiding citizens. So, to stir things up, I have provided in this book photos of some of my favorite perennials, hoping to share the diversity of plants that can make up a garden. If a picture is worth a thousand words, then I feel I have saved considerable forests.

Come join me as you turn these pages for a magical ride through some of the treasures of the perennial plant kingdom, and the joys of being a gardener. Simply remember the Armitage credo of gardening, "This is gardening, not brain surgery. On balance, gardening should always provide far more pleasure than pain." Have fun.

Acknowledgments

Many thanks to those around me who worked on this tome, especially Jessica Phillips and Amanda Miller. And special thanks to my editor, Franni Bertolino Farrell, whose attention to detail transformed incoherent writing into a readable, enjoyable experience.

Part One
Armitage's Garden Perennials
A to Z

Acanthus

BEAR'S BREECHES

Consider the common names of the plants we buy for our gardens: a bystander would be convinced that we are a bunch of zookeepers, not plant-keepers. Dogwood, pussy willow, and a few other woody plants provide links to the animal kingdom, but perennials are unabashedly animal-friendly. One can hardly grow herbaceous plants and not think animal: do pigsqueak, hogweed, leopard's bane, pussytoes, rattlesnake master, toad lily, and snakeroot ring any bells? Some of those names make sense because the plant actually resembles a particular fauna, but what in the world are the breeches of a bear? Who names these things anyway? I guess it really doesn't matter, since we are growing the plant, not the name. And certainly bear's breeches include some excellent garden plants.

The two common species are *Acanthus mollis*, common bear's breeches, and *A. spinosus*, spiny bear's breeches. Both have similar tall spikes of purple

Acanthus mollis

Acanthus spinosus

Acanthus mollis

Acanthus mollis

Acanthus mollis

MORE →

Acanthus mollis 'Holland's Lemon'

Acanthus spinosus

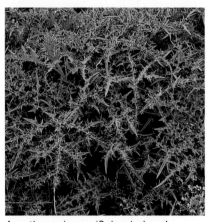

Acanthus spinosus 'Spinosissimus'

and white blossoms, which arise from the leafy plants in late spring. Each white flower on the flower stem is surrounded by a spiny purple bract, which provides color and—when mishandled—considerable pain. Mature clumps provide half a dozen to a dozen spikes of color in late spring, providing a wonderful contrast to the dark green foliage. The two species are best distinguished by their leaves. The leaf of *A. mollis* is much fuller and more rounded than that of *A. spinosus*, which is pointedly pinnately lobed. The common name of *A. spinosus*, spiny bear's breeches, misrepresents the species, as its spiny-looking leaves are not sharp at all.

A number of cultivars have been introduced. As a change from the green leaves of *Acanthus mollis*, golden leaves are the norm in *A. mollis* 'Holland's Lemon'. If you really want spiny in spiny bear's breeches, try *A. spinosus* 'Spinosissimus'. A true man- and woman-eater—it is a well-known fact that many a small pet has inadvertently wandered into a patch of breeches, never to be seen again. Now explain that common name one more time. Full sun, zones 6 to 10.

Achillea

YARROW

The genus *Achillea* is named for the Greek warrior Achilles; one species, *Achillea millefolium*, also known as woundwort, was said to have staunched the wounds of the great warrior's soldiers. The yarrows are a diverse group and provide many fine garden plants. Most are easy to grow, offering excellent foliage, years of color, and flowers useful for both fresh and dried arrangements.

Without doubt, *Achillea filipendulina* (fernleaf yarrow) and its hybrids are among the most welcome of all plants for the spring and summer garden. They are prized for their color and form, as an herbal plant for their fragrance, and as cut flowers for their outstanding longevity. Fernleaf yarrow has large (about 3" across), flat yellow flowers atop 3–4' tall plants. The compound leaves are somewhat fernlike, thus accounting for its common name. Several cultivars, such as 'Gold Plate' and 'Parker's Variety', have been developed, but few differences in appearance or garden performance are obvi-

Achillea 'Coronation Gold'

ous. All these yarrows can be cut and brought inside fresh or hung upside down for dried flower arrangements. Wait until the flowers are fully opened before cutting, otherwise they won't persist more than a single day.

Many yellow-flowered yarrows look alike, but several of the better cultivars offer the gardener additional choices. Most are hybrids, in which *Achillea fili-pendulina* is one of the main parents, and are vigorous and usually more compact. The grand dame is *Achillea* 'Coronation Gold', developed in 1953 to commemorate the coronation of Queen Elizabeth of England. Bearing large yellow flowers and handsome gray-green foliage on 2–3' tall plants, she has lost little of her original popularity with her subjects. As a garden plant or as a cut flower, 'Coronation Gold' is outstanding and should continue to be a mainstay among garden-

ers. Yellow-flowered hybrids that are shorter and more soft in tone than 'Coronation Gold' have also been popular. 'Moonshine', for one, has been a bright standby for many years. 'Anthea' is just a youngster compared to the previous cultivars but is rapidly being accepted by gardeners. The combination of full pale yellow to sulfur-yellow flowers on a 2' tall frame has made 'Anthea' one of my favorites. 'Martina' provides yet another excellent yellow

Achillea 'Moonshine'

Achillea 'Coronation Gold'

Achillea 'Anthea'

Achillea 'Coronation Gold'

MORE →

Achillea 'Anthea'

Achillea millefolium

Achillea 'Martina'

Achillea millefolium 'Colorado'

Achillea millefolium 'Rose Beauty'

and bears many flowers, but the flowering stems are not quite as erect as those of 'Anthea'. All cultivars are reasonably easy to locate in American nurseries. Full sun, zones 3 to 8.

Common yarrow, *Achillea millefolium*, is as plentiful as turf in some gardens and indeed can double as a ground cover. The plants spread like wildfire throughout the season, their finely cut green foliage quickly filling in large areas. Flowers occur as corymbs in spring and early summer, and although they can be used as fresh cut flowers, they persist for only two or three days, not nearly as long as the flowers of *A. filipendulina*.

The many selections of *Achillea millefolium* guarantee that the gardener will suffer no shortage of colors. 'Rose Beauty' provides lovely rosy hues; I love the deep desert reds and roses of 'Colorado', and for bright colors, 'Paprika' or 'Nakuru' work well. Some of the hybrids associated with *A. millefolium* also do well: both 'Appleblossom' and 'The Beacon' ('Fanal'), which have large pastel and bright rose-red flowers, respectively, spread quickly. Some of the newer hybrids are true breakthroughs in color: for oohs and aahs, nothing beats the earth tones of 'Terra Cotta' and 'Fireland'. They are similar, each rising to a height of 3' ('Fireland' may be a little taller). These

Achillea millefolium 'Nakuru'

should prove as popular as any of the cultivars already introduced. As cut flowers, the hybrid yarrows derived from *A. millefolium* are not quite as good as *A. filipendulina*, but I have seen outstanding arrangements with *Veronicastrum*, *Limonium*, and other perennials. All cultivars prefer good drainage and full sun. Hardy in zones 3 to 8.

As a substitute for snuff, *Achillea ptarmica*, sneezewort, probably works quite well, if one is still into that sort of thing; however, the flowers have myriad other uses. They are excellent cut flowers, acting as fillers in cottage bouquets, and the white double flowers are easy to use in the garden, combining well with almost any hue. Plants are generally at their best in northern areas or gardens where cool summer nights are the norm. The leaves are not

Achillea millefolium 'Paprika'

Achillea 'The Beacon' ('Fanal')

Achillea 'Appleblossom'

Achillea 'Terra Cotta'

Achillea arranged with *Veronicastrum* and *Limonium*

Achillea 'Fireland'

MORE →

Achillea ptarmica

Achillea ptarmica 'The Pearl' ('Boule de Neige')

Achillea ptarmica 'Ballerina'

Achillea ageratum 'W. B. Childs'

Achillea sibirica 'Kiku-San'

cut like other species but rather are thick and dark green, with entire margins. In general, plants are 1–2' tall but under good conditions can easily grow to 3' in height. Most selections of *A. ptarmica* have similar flowers, so using the old-fashioned 'The Pearl' ('Boule de Neige') or 'Perry's White' is about the same as choosing 'Angel's Breath' or 'Ballerina', except that these last two are somewhat more compact and shorter. Full sun, hardy in zones 3 to 7.

Achillea ageratum 'W. B. Childs', the white double-flowered Childs's yarrow, is a similar plant, with flowers that are almost identical to those of *A. ptarmica*; it differs from sneezewort, however, by having dissected leaves. Full sun, hardy in zones 2 to 8.

Tough as nails, with white to pink flowers and thick, lobed, dark green leaves, *Achillea sibirica*, the Siberian

Achillea sibirica leaf

Achillea sibirica 'Kiku-San'

yarrow, is beginning to find its way into American gardens. Plants are clump formers; unlike *A. millefolium*, they don't spread, nor do they have the girth and height of *A. filipendulina*. This outstanding yarrow will become a mainstream plant as people discover its ornamental and landscape attributes. Little has been done in the way of selection, however. 'Kiku-San' has creamy white flowers with the faintest pink in the blooms. Full sun, hardy in zones 2 to 8.

Aconitum

MONKSHOOD

Classic plants for the late summer and fall garden, the genus *Aconitum* adds bold accents to northern gardens. Flowers are usually in shades of blue or purple, but ivory, yellow, and bicolors can also be found. For certain, monks-

hood is poisonous (it is also known as wolfsbane), but for most intelligent people, that is not a problem. Simply don't eat the plants—any part of them. Don't worry about your pets: most dogs and cats are smarter than the average gardener. All monkshoods do far better in the northern United States and Canada than in the South.

One of the most popular of the purple- and blue-flowered species is *Aconitum carmichaelii*, azure monkshood, which grows 4–6' tall and has thick, dark green leaves that are divided about two-thirds of the way to the midrib. In late summer to early fall, dozens of individual hooded flowers make up each 5–6" long flower spike (the hood on the flower is responsible for the common name of the genus). Some cultivars of *A. carmichaelii*, also known as late-flowering monkshood, are among the latest of the genus to flower. They include the selection 'Arendsii', which I believe to be one of the finest. Its large deep blue flowers are held on compact well-branched 3' tall plants. For even more height (up to 6'), 'Barker's Variety',

'Kelmscott Variety', and variety *wilsonii* may also be planted.

Aconitum napellus, common monkshood, has handsome blue flowers that open a little earlier than those of *A. carmichaelii*, but as far as gardeners are concerned, there is little difference between the two species; 'Carneum' is

Aconitum carmichaelii var. *wilsonii*

Aconitum carmichaelii 'Arendsii'

Aconitum napellus

MORE →

Aconitum napellus 'Carneum'

Aconitum napellus

a beautiful pink-flowered selection. *Aconitum ×cammarum* is a wonderful strong-growing hybrid of *A. napellus*, with erect stems approximately 4' in height; its selection 'Bicolor' provides flowers in an exotic combination of azure blue and white. Place all monkshoods in partial shade and moist soils. Hardy in zones 3 to 7a.

How about a yellow wolfsbane? or white? There is more to this genus than blue and purple flowers. In yellow wolfsbane, *Aconitum lamarckii*, large racemes of yellow flowers are formed above light green, deeply divided leaves. Stems regularly fall over other plants, but so what? The soft yellows complement just about any other color and fit well into many gardens, even though they may be a little lanky. Cool temperatures, full sun, zones 3 to 6. *Aconitum lamarckii* is a native to Eu-

Aconitum lamarckii

Aconitum ×cammarum 'Bicolor'

Aconitum reclinatum

Aconitum septentrionale 'Ivorine'

rope, but our native species, *A. reclinatum*, white wolfsbane, provides the same effect with a little better weather-tolerance. Plants enjoy full sun and are hardy in zones 4 to 7.

The yellow and white wolfsbanes grow well in areas of cool summer temperatures, and West Coast gardeners can succeed with them all. A wonderful plant I always enjoy seeing is 'Ivorine', a selection of the little-known species *Aconitum septentrionale*, which bears white to light yellow flowers. It is well worth spending some time over the winter trying to locate this cultivar in catalogs. Hardy in zones 4 to 6 (occasionally 7).

Adiantum

MAIDENHAIR FERN

The realization that ferns are as garden-worthy as their flowering perennial counterparts has rekindled the love affair with the common green plant of grandmother's day. Of course, anyone interested in ferns quickly appreciates their remarkable diversity of color, size, and form. One of the most distinctive groups is the maidenhair family, consisting of the northern and southern maidenhairs.

Only gardeners who live in the southern third of the country are for-

tunate enough to appreciate the beauty of *Adiantum capillus-veneris*, the southern maidenhair fern, in their gardens. The light green fronds are doubly or triply divided and arch over on thin wiry stems. The stems appear in the spring in the form of thin horse-shoes; however, the pinnae (individual "leaflets") are so numerous that a dense planting is achieved under favorable conditions. The pinnae are small, only about an inch long, and

shaped like a fan. Plants require mild winters, basic soils, and excellent drainage and are not nearly as easy to grow as many of the coarser ferns commonly found at retailers. They are at their best tumbling from containers and raised beds, or arching over walls; they don't do well in acid conditions, and in areas of pine or oak growth, lime should be added. Native throughout the South Temperate Zone and subtropical regions in Europe, Africa,

Adiantum capillus-veneris

Adiantum capillus-veneris

Adiantum pedatum

MORE →

Adiantum pedatum

Adiantum pedatum subsp. subpumilum

Adiantum pedatum 'Imbricatum'

India, China, Japan, the Americas, and Australia. Reliably cold hardy in zones 7 to 10.

Southern maidenhair fern may be little known in the garden, but *Adiantum pedatum*, the northern maidenhair fern, does not suffer from any such lack of recognition. The wimpy looking fronds of the plant are put forth in the spring, but as temperatures rise, the grayish pinnae can be seen forming an almost perfect horseshoe on the ends of the unique black stems. As the plants mature, they top out at about 12" tall, and the half-inch-long pinnae change from gray to light green. The dark color of the stems is continued in the branches of the horseshoe, making this fern one of the most distinctive and easily recognized in American gardens. Plants move around freely in loose soils, and a few plants can quickly form significant colonies. The distinctive shape and garden "feel" of the lacy, airy fronds and black stems, combined with its toughness, have made this a most useful, must-have fern for the shady, moist woodland garden. As with *A. capillus-veneris*, lime is useful for best growth but seems to be less important for northern maidenhair fern than for its southern cousin.

It is hard to beat *Adiantum pedatum* for overall garden performance, but those who wish to walk on the wild side of maidenhair ferndom might want to try some of the variations on the theme of this species. 'Imbricatum' has crowded stiffly erect fronds that are rather blue-green; its long sweeping foliage make it appear almost shrublike. The opposite is true in subspecies *subpumilum*, in which the fronds are dwarf and congested; the plants grow in a 6–9" tall mound. Partial shade, good drainage, performs well in zones 2 to 7.

Ajuga

BUGLE WEED

Some plants simply perform too well for their own good, and bugle weed is one of them. Of the forty species known, only *Ajuga reptans* is used extensively, although a couple of others (*A. genevensis*, *A. pyramidalis*) are gaining momentum. Without doubt, common bugle weed is by far the most diverse, having undergone extensive breeding and selection. One of the strengths of bugle weed is its ability to colonize large areas of the garden. Many a gardener has started out tucking in a few plants only to turn around a few years later to find a sea of the stuff. Plants creep relentlessly into turf when positioned near it. A word has been coined to describe the result of such restlessness: "buglelawn."

Ajuga reptans, common bugle weed, is deservedly popular for its ability to settle large areas of the garden. Planted as small rosettes of foliage, it quickly searches out new ground. Not all selections of this ground cover are as fast growing, and intelligent cultivar selection can help curb the appetite for territory. Common bugle weed is grown mainly for the colorful foliage, but a large planting of the purple-blue flowers can be breathtaking in the spring.

Two of my favorite cultivars are 'Burgundy Glow', with multicolored foliage, and 'Catlin's Giant', with big dark green leaves and large spikes of blue flowers. Those desiring dark bronze leaves will be well satisfied by either the excellent 'Bronze Beauty' or 'Atropurpurea', while 'Silver Beauty' may be grown for its handsome variegation on the leaves. Partial shade, hardy in zones 3 to 9.

Another fine garden plant is Geneva bugle weed, *Ajuga genevensis*, with its light green wavy leaves and handsome

Ajuga reptans 'Burgundy Glow'

Ajuga reptans

MORE →

Ajuga reptans 'Bronze Beauty'

Ajuga reptans 'Catlin's Giant'

Ajuga reptans 'Atropurpurea'

Ajuga reptans 'Silver Beauty'

Ajuga genevensis 'Pink Beauty'

flowers. 'Pink Beauty' is the best available selection, producing good-looking flowers on moderately aggressive plants. Partial shade, hardy in zones 4 to 9.

Allium

ORNAMENTAL ONION

One of the reasons I enjoy gardening so much is that, having no self-imposed boundaries as to what plants may be deemed ornamental, I am free to welcome any and all comers, fruits and vegetables, sweet potatoes and herbs, to the ornamental landscape. Ornamental onions are not particularly tasty, but their beauty is seldom questioned, at least by the bold and inquiring gardener. Most members of the large genus *Allium* are bulbous and easily planted in spring or fall.

Allium christophii, Persian onion, produces deep purple flower heads 10–12" in diameter, among the largest of any onion. Each head consists of hundreds of star-shaped flowers suspended atop a 1–2' tall stem. Flowers open in the spring and persist for about three weeks. The flower is the most obvious part of the plant, not only because of its size but also because only two to three leaves are produced. This is a lovely onion, persist-

Cut flowers of *Allium giganteum* and *Achillea* 'Coronation Gold'.

ent and long-lived in many areas of the country. Full sun, not great in hot climates; performs best in zones 4 to 6 but is hardy in zones 4 to 8.

I have tried at least a dozen different onions in the Armitage garden, and *Allium* 'Globemaster' is absolutely one of the best. The three to four leaves emerge in early spring and soon a fat flower bud or two can be seen at the base. The flowers force their way through the foliage and emerge as 6" wide lavender softballs. Even the seed heads are ornamental, persisting for weeks after the flower has passed on. Great plants, about 3' tall, perennial as any onion I have grown. A couple of other interesting hybrids are out there; if you can't find 'Globemaster', give 'Beauregard' a try. Full sun to partial shade, hardy in zones 4 to 8.

Allium karataviense (Turkistan onion) and *A. giganteum* (giant onion) are the Mutt and Jeff of the onion world. These two species are obviously onions (just smell the leaves) but differ in flower color, leaf color, and height. The two gray-green leaves of *A. karataviense* lie on the ground and are mottled with purple. Through the base of the leaves emerge fat flower buds, which then give way to perfectly round silver-lilac flower heads on 4–6" tall scapes.

Compared to these dwarfs, the 6' tall *Allium giganteum* is an absolute behemoth. The gray leaves, which are themselves obvious, emerge early but die back even before the flowers are fully developed. The flowers consist of hundreds of purple flowers arranged in neat 4" wide globes, although interesting anomalies occur occasionally. Both species are excellent cut flowers; *A. giganteum* is a staple in the cut flower trade and may be purchased at all good flower shops.

Allium christophii

Allium christophii

Allium 'Globemaster'

Allium 'Globemaster' seed heads

Allium 'Beauregard'

MORE →

Allium giganteum with cowlick

Allium giganteum

Both *Allium karataviense* and *A. giganteum* are summer dormant, prefer full sun, and are cold hardy to zone 4; *A. giganteum* is more tolerant of heat and humidity. Persistent for about two years only.

Anemone

As a gardener, I admit to a certain degree of laziness. Okay, so sometimes I could admit to a lot. Being a tad lazy, I am always on the lookout for plants that can deliver good looks in as many seasons as possible. A few genera flower at different seasons, but one of the most rewarding has to be the genus *Anemone*. This great group of plants

Allium karataviense

Allium karataviense in bud

Allium giganteum

consists of spring flowerers, which arise from tubers (like a potato), and fibrous-rooted plants, which mostly flower in the fall, with one or two spring and summer bloomers thrown in. From the time the snow is melting to the time the snow is falling, anemones are a gardener's companion. Cut flowers, shade and sun lovers, and heights from ankle to waist, this fine genus offers something for everybody, especially lazy gardeners like me.

Often in the late fall, I have my trowel in one hand and the tubers of the Grecian windflower, *Anemone blanda*, in the other—and confusion as to which end is up. With real plants, any dummy knows to plant the green part up, but anemone tubers simply look like shriveled-up brown things. You could put them in a pail of water overnight and allow them to plump up to about four times their original size; this is fascinating to watch, but it will still be impossible to tell which way is up. Simply dig a shallow hole and throw the swollen things in. It doesn't really matter which end is up; the plants will find the proper orientation. Put about a hundred tubers around the garden, preferably in groups of at least twenty. They are so cheap, you can do this without spending your entire year-end bonus. Once you have tossed

them in their respective trenches, you can expect wonderful springtime flowering—unless the squirrels, chipmunks, gophers, voles, or dogs get at them. That is why you plant a hundred. The flowers, consisting of 1–2" wide daisies in colors of blue, purple, red, white, and pink, are held over finely cut, ferny foliage. Single or double-flowered plants are available. They are only about 8" tall, but if they naturalize, they are outstanding components of the woodland garden. If they don't naturalize and become food for your garden fauna, you have not spent a great deal of money. Full sun is best, but woodland conditions are

fine. Full sun to partial shade, hardy in zones 4 to 7.

The only real difference between cultivars is flower color, such as the blue flowers of 'Atrocaerulea' and 'Blue Star', the bicolors of 'Radar', and the white flowers of 'White Splendor', to name but a few.

Another tuberous species, even more ornamental than the Grecian windflower, is *Anemone coronaria*, the poppy anemone. Equally confusing as to head and tail, equally destined for a plunge in the water bucket, and equally tempting to hungry creatures, poppy anemones are nevertheless so beautiful that they have become an

Anemone blanda 'Atrocaerulea'

Anemone blanda 'Radar'

Anemone blanda 'Blue Star'

Anemone blanda 'White Splendor'

MORE →

Anemone coronaria 'Mona Lisa Red'

Anemone coronaria 'Mr. Fokker' (De Caen series)

Anemone coronaria 'Mt. Everest' (St. Brigid series)

important cut flower in the greenhouse and garden. Flowers are about 2" wide, and stems may be up to 18" long. Flowering occurs in early spring. Great garden show and a great cut flower. Plant in full sun, and protect from critters if possible. Hardy in zones 6 to 9.

Variety is available in the long-stemmed Mona Lisa and Cleopatra series; the shorter double-flowered De Caen series; and the semi-double- to double-flowered St. Brigid series. All selections are offered both in single colors and, more commonly, as mixes.

Regardless of how excited one gets about the spring flowerers, the crowning jewels of the anemone family are the fall-flowering Japanese species *Anemone hupehensis* and *A. tomentosa* and the hybrids of *A.* ×*hybrida*. When one thinks *Anemone*, one usually thinks of these. And with good reason! *Anemone hupehensis* includes some excellent 3–4' tall selections, such as the durable 'September Charm' and the rosy red semi-double flowers of 'Prinz Heinrich' ('Prince Henry'). Plants of *A.* ×*hybrida* are actually hybrids of several species, but they have

become well adapted to American gardens, particularly those in the West and North. Provided with a little shade and ample moisture, plants can reach 5' in height and 3' across. The flowers begin to open in late summer to early fall and remain in color for three to five weeks, depending on temperatures. Single, semi-double, and double flowers in white, pink, rose, and lilac can be found. Some of my favorites are the semi- to fully double pink-flowered 'Kriemhilde' and the single pink 3" wide flowers of 'Max Vogel'. If I had but one to choose, however, I would probably show my true populist colors and go with the old-fashioned but timeless single white flowers of 'Honorine Jobert'. So much for keeping up appearances!

Southern gardeners who have had less success in establishing the hybrids should use the indestructible *Anemone tomentosa*, the grapeleaf anemone, with its pale pink or white flowers in late summer and early fall. The toughest of all its selections is 'Robustissima': handsome, adaptable to sun or shade, and disease and insect free. Plants bear fine 2" wide mauve-pink

Anemone coronaria 'Sylphide' (De Caen series)

flowers in late summer. I grow them in full sun in the University of Georgia Horticulture Gardens, where they remain in a fairly compact clump, but in the shady Armitage garden, plants move around with abandon and fill up space in no time. The hybrids are hardy in zones 4 to 7, *A. tomentosa* in zones 5 to 8.

Gardeners cannot live by tubers alone. Some of the finest garden plants are the fibrous-rooted species, such as

Anemone hupehensis 'Prinz Heinrich' ('Prince Henry')

Anemone ×*hybrida* 'Kriemhilde'

Anemone hupehensis 'September Charm'

Anemone ×*hybrida* 'Max Vogel'

MORE →

the spring-flowering snowdrop anemone, *Anemone sylvestris*. I love this plant for its habit of unfurling beautifully clean white flowers with yellow stamens in early spring. In fact, in areas of late winters, one can often see them piercing the snow, thus its common name. The 2" wide flowers are only part of the delight of this 1–2' tall

Anemone ×hybrida 'Honorine Jobert'

Anemone tomentosa 'Robustissima'

Anemone tomentosa 'Robustissima'

Anemone sylvestris

Anemone sylvestris

plant, since after flowering, the woolly fruit persists into the summer. On the downside, it can be outrageously aggressive, reseeding freely where it is happy. It is happier in the North than in the South, where inconsistent winters and hot summers take their toll. Some gardeners consider it a bit of a weed. Not me. I accept anyone's snowdrop anemone weeds with pleasure. Full sun, hardy in zones 4 to 7.

Aquilegia

COLUMBINE

Almost anywhere gardening is enjoyed, columbines are among the best-known and most popular garden plants. The Armitage garden would be but a shell of itself without columbines welcoming spring. Since we may choose from more than sixty-five different species of columbine and all sorts of named varieties, including one or two in the garden should not be difficult. The cultural requirements for all columbines, whether they originate from the East Coast, West Coast, Europe, or Asia, are essentially the same: partial shade and reasonably rich well-drained soils.

The plants are distinguished from most other genera by having petals with spurs, ranging from those with spurs over 4" long (*Aquilegia chrysantha*, the golden columbine) to those with spurs that are essentially nonexistent, such as some of the double-flowered and even triple-flowered cultivars of granny's bonnet, *A. vulgaris*

('Treble Pink'). Spur size and shape are helpful clues to the identity of many of the species. The spurs of the alpine columbine, *A. alpina*, and fan columbine, *A. flabellata*, are hooked (like a fishhook) while those on the Rocky Mountain columbine, *A. caerulea*, are

Aquilegia alpina

Aquilegia chrysantha var. *hinckleyana*

Aquilegia alpina

Aquilegia vulgaris 'Treble Pink'

Aquilegia flabellata 'Alba'

MORE →

Aquilegia flabellata 'Alba'

Aquilegia ×hybrida

Aquilegia caerulea

Aquilegia ×hybrida 'Cardinal'

Aquilegia caerulea

Aquilegia ×hybrida 'Blue Jay'

Leaf miner damage on Aquilegia

Aquilegia ×hybrida 'Lavender and White'
(Biedermeier strain)

Aquilegia ×hybrida 'Music Yellow'

nearly always straight. *Aquilegia alpina* has some of the finest blue flowers and as a bonus—and even though it is native to the cool mountains of Austria—it tolerates heat as well as any species. *Aquilegia flabellata* normally has lavender flowers but is usually found in its white variant, 'Alba'; the blue cast to the foliage, the plump flowers, and the low stature make this selection a favorite among columbine lovers. The fine blue-and-white flowers of *A. caerulea* persist for years, especially in areas of cool summers. The leaves, which always occur in threes (ternate), are unfortunately susceptible to the bane of all columbines, the leaf miner. Leaf miners burrow just beneath the surface of the foliage, leaving scars like a crazed gopher. All species seem to be fair game for these marauding tunnelers, although some plants, in some years, fare better than others.

Columbine flower colors vary tremendously, especially in the selections of *Aquilegia ×hybrida*. As a seed-propagated mix, these hybrid columbines can be striking, providing a gala for the color-starved eye in the spring. The Song Bird series is particularly good, furnishing such choices as the brilliant red of 'Cardinal' and the fine blue of 'Blue Jay'. The Biedermeier strain is far more compact and comes in single colors, bicolors ('Lavender and White'), and a mix. The Music series is outstanding, particularly 'Music Yellow'. *Aquilegia vulgaris* also provides a wide range of color, flower size, and flower shape; the double and triple flowers of its Barlow family, Pink, Blue, and Nora, are not only different from normal flowers but are flamboyant to boot. Speaking of which: while large gaudy columbines appear to be the norm, one of my favorites has always been the delightful red-and-yellow flowers of *A. canadensis*, the Canadian columbine. Just like citizens of that northern neighbor, the plants of this species are quiet, conservative, and do their job without bluster.

Columbines are notoriously promiscuous, and natural hybridization occurs with ease. The resulting seedlings are usually as handsome as any of the parents, leaving many a gardener puzzling over their provenance. Plants can remain in flower for three to six weeks, depending on how long the cool temperatures of spring persist. Partial shade, zones 3 to 8.

Aquilegia vulgaris 'Blue Barlow'

Aquilegia vulgaris 'Nora Barlow'

Aquilegia vulgaris 'Pink Barlow'

Aquilegia canadensis

Aquilegia canadensis

Arisaema ringens

Fruit of *Arisaema ringens*

Arisaema

JACK-IN-THE-PULPIT

Perhaps it's a guy thing: it seems that only men are intent on collecting plants in the genus *Arisaema*. I know I have always had a deep admiration for the foliage and flower details of our native Jack-in-the-pulpit, *Arisaema triphyllum*, but once I looked beyond the native Jack, a whole world of crazy collectibles opened before me. Of course, only other guys seem to be selling them. All the Jacks are terrific for shady spots and moist areas.

When confronted with *Arisaema ringens* (cobra Jack) or *A. sikokianum* (gaudy Jack), some people take a step back, walk around the plants, and mutter something intelligent about plant diversity. Most of us just say wow! The flowers of *A. ringens* consist of a thin but wide purple membrane, or spathe, that became known as the "pulpit." Within the pulpit hides the creamy white spadix (a narrow fleshy stalk), better known as Jack. This peculiar arrangement of flowers was dubbed by some observant fellow as Jack-in-the-pulpit, and that common name applies to nearly all plants in the genus. The 2–3' tall plants produce only two or three leaves, each made up of three glossy green leaflets.

Arisaema sikokianum bears much smaller leaves, often mottled or occasionally variegated, along with highly visible flowers. The spadix ends in a shiny white bulbous tip poking out of the maroon spathe. Not only is this a stunning species, but the hybrids involving *A. sikokianum*, such as the unnamed cross between it and *A. takedae*, are equally stunning.

These Japanese Jacks—*Arisaema ringens*, *A. sikokianum*, and *A. takedae*—all require shady, moist conditions and flower in early spring, much ear-

Arisaema sikokianum

Arisaema sikokianum

Arisaema ringens

lier than our native Jack. All perform well in zones 5 to 7.

The specific epithet of *Arisaema triphyllum* refers to the three ("tri") leaflets ("phyllum") found on the plant; however, plants are highly variable, often consisting of five or occasionally four leaflets. The same variability occurs in the average height (1–3') of the plants. The flowers, which occur in spring to early summer, consist of a spadix surrounded by a purple spathe. The plants multiply by small corms, which, if planted in the spring, will flower the second year. The corms, which can become quite large, were cooked and eaten by Native Americans; early settlers knew the plant as Indian turnip. Partial shade, hardy in zones 4 to 8.

Other *Arisaema* species are being offered by mail-order nurseries for collectors and shade gardeners. Little needs to be said about the makeup of these other Jacks; they differ only in the size, shape, and color of the spathe and in the overall dimensions of the plants. I think that the candy Jack, *Arisaema candidissimum*, with wonderful white spathes blushed in pink,

Arisaema sikokianum × *A. takedae*

Arisaema triphyllum

Arisaema candidissimum

Arisaema triphyllum

Arisaema candidissimum

MORE →

Arisaema consanguineum

and bloody Jack, *A. consanguineum*, a huge member with deeply cut leaves and blood-red spathes, are outstanding. But as soon as I recover from their beauty, I fall in love with the deep purple spathes of *A. fargesii* and the elegant long-necked *A. japonicum* (*A. serratum*). I am content with my regular Jack-in-the-pulpits, but I was fortunate to have planted *A. sazensoo*, the Japanese cobra Jack, in the Armitage garden. I was in seventh heaven, until I saw the unbelievable elegance of *A. tortuosum* in Kew Gardens in England. Arisaemas should not be planted or viewed by people with heart problems—one touch, one glimpse of any of these is enough to give one cardiac arrest. Plant them shallowly in moisture-retentive yet well-drained soils, rich in organic matter, in the shade garden. Hardy in zones 5 to 8.

Arisaema fargesii

Arisaema sazensoo

Arisaema japonicum

Fruit of *Arisaema tortuosum*

Arisaema tortuosum

Artemisia

Many members of the genus *Artemisia* are great plants, their gray hues providing a cool contrast to a sea of green or calming down neighboring (not to say "screaming") colors. Not all artemisias are long-lived perennials; a few often leave us after two or three years. The good selections, however, are worth every square inch of space.

Artemisia ludoviciana (white sage), a mainstay in older gardens, was the most commonly used large artemisia for gray foliage. Seldom is the species sold, but the main selection, 'Silver King', may become an unwelcome guest in gardens. Although they look terrific the first few years, plants are aggressive and difficult to remove. This vigorous nature makes them one of the most popular cut stems for fillers in arrangements, but in the garden, they develop into dozens of in-laws who bring the great aunts and second cousins with them for a visit and never go away. The leaves are almost entire, not cut like *Artemisia* 'Powis Castle'. Flowers are few and insignificant. They grow 3–5' tall and 3–4' wide and combine well with almost everything. Other than their roaming tendencies, they are fine plants. Full sun, hardy in zones 4 to 9.

Many other cultivars of *Artemisia ludoviciana* are out there, including 'Latiloba', whose similar entire leaf margins are distinctly lobed near the ends. Plants grow about 2' tall and as wide. Much more obedient. Another low grower is 'Valerie Fennis', whose silvery gray entire foliage, although absolutely wonderful in the spring, often melts out in the summer, partic-

Artemisia ludoviciana 'Latiloba'

Artemisia ludoviciana 'Silver King'

Artemisia ludoviciana 'Valerie Fennis'

Artemisia ludoviciana 'Valerie Fennis'

MORE →

Artemisia 'Powis Castle' trained as a standard

ularly in the South. She looks great again in the fall. The ugly yellow flowers put forth only detract from the foliage. Remove them or ignore them. Full sun to partial shade, hardy in zones 4 to 8.

Artemisia 'Powis Castle' is a terrific plant in many parts of the country. The evergreen, deeply cut gray leaves impart an airiness to the garden, and the plants provide a focal point for the eye. In fact, it is probably one of the first plants to draw one's eye—a garden designer's blue ribbon winner. Plants may be used to define a wall or introduce a garden bed and may even be trained as a small upright Powis

tree. Left to its own devices, this hybrid grows 2–3' tall and equally wide. As it matures, the stems become woody (like a shrub) and may get lanky and untidy. If necessary, cut back in spring as new growth becomes active. Don't cut back in the fall. Full sun, hardy in zones 6 to 8.

Artemisia 'Huntington Gardens', a closely related plant with divided gray

Artemisia 'Huntington Gardens'

Artemisia 'Powis Castle'

Artemisia schmidtiana 'Nana' ('Silver Mound')

Artemisia 'Powis Castle'

Artemisia schmidtiana 'Nana' ('Silver Mound') as a container plant

leaves, can reach 3' in height. I find that it is more persistent than 'Powis Castle' but has the same look. Full sun, hardy in zones 6 to 8.

One of the best-sellers in the perennial trade, *Artemisia schmidtiana* has been a mainstay in northern gardens for years. The only available cultivar is 'Nana', a dwarf selection known as the silvermound artemisia (it is also sold as 'Silver Mound'). Plants produce tightly compact 1' tall mounds in the spring and early summer, making it a gardener's dream. In rock gardens and in containers, they are beautiful; however, in many gardens, in the South as well as in the North, plants often melt out in the centers as temperature and humidity rise. This is a rather ugly scene after hard summer rains. Plants are woody, like *Artemisia* 'Powis Castle', and evergreen in milder climates. I recommend this beautiful plant in the northern tier of States and southern Canada but not in the South. Full sun, hardy in zones 3 to 8.

Aruncus dioicus

Aruncus

GOATSBEARD

Consisting of only two species, and few cultivars, the genus *Aruncus* could hardly be commended for its wide diversity, but both its species are highly ornamental and useful garden plants, which, once established, live to ripe old ages. Male and female flowers occur on separate plants (that is to say, plants are dioecious), but garden performance is not affected by gender.

With a grand explosion of upright

flower stems consisting of hundreds of small white flowers in late spring, *Aruncus dioicus*, common goatsbeard, tops out at 4–6' in height. Diminutive fruit may be formed on female plants, but their slight size and show are not missed if male plants are used. The alternate leaves are bipinnately compound and doubly serrated. I have always enjoyed the vigor and sheer size of the plant, and I admire plants in the Northeast, Midwest, and Northwest. Unfortunately it languishes in the South, so the Armitage garden is beardless. Full sun, zones 3 to 7.

Aruncus dioicus

Aruncus dioicus

MORE →

Aruncus dioicus 'Kneiffii'

Aruncus dioicus 'Kneiffii'

The deeply filigreed dark green leaves of 'Kneiffii', a smaller cutleaf selection, render it a far more delicate plant. Its flowers are less showy, however, and although horticulturally interesting, the plant is not nearly as eye-catching as the species. I also like the feathery flowers of 'Zweiweltenkind' ('Child of Two Worlds'), which is not quite as coarse and a little easier to use.

Aruncus aethusifolius, dwarf goatsbeard, is the antithesis of its grand and, some would say, overbearing cousin. Similarities between the two species include the dark green compound leaves and tiny white flowers, which are held above the plant. *Aruncus aethusifolius*, however, is far more useful for small areas and rock gardens, attaining but 1–2' in height. One

to three flower stems are produced in late summer, and although the flowers are reasonably handsome, they don't provide a long-lasting show, persisting only for two to three weeks. Even worse, they brown out quickly after flowering. Actually, the foliage is the best part of the plant, handsome throughout the

Aruncus 'Southern White'

Aruncus aethusifolius

Aruncus 'Southern White'

Aruncus dioicus 'Zweiweltenkind' ('Child of Two Worlds')

Aruncus aethusifolius

season regardless of the presence or absence of flowers. Full sun to partial shade, well-drained soils, zones 3 to 7.

A wonderful hybrid between the two species was given to me recently by Richard Lighty of the Mount Cuba Center for the Study of Piedmont Flora in Greenville, Delaware. I placed it in the trial gardens at the University of Georgia (zone 7b)—where goatsbeard has always done poorly at best—and it thrived. Plants are intermediate in height and demonstrate remarkable hybrid vigor, performing well in both heat and humidity. I believe it should be listed as *Aruncus* 'Southern White'. Full sun to partial shade, zones 3 to 7.

Asarum arifolium in bud

Asarum arifolium in flower

Asarum

WILD GINGER

Wild gingers occur throughout the world, but most of those that enliven our gardens hail from Asia and North America. They are handsome, ornamental, and a great deal of fun: handsome and ornamental for their deep green and mottled leaves and fun because of the "little brown jugs" (and some not-so-little jugs) of flowers borne beneath the foliage. All the gingers grow well with woodland species, such as *Mertensia*, *Trillium*, and *Podophyllum*. New species and selections are rapidly filling in shady, moist areas of American gardens.

Great variability occurs in our native *Asarum arifolium*, arrowleaf ginger. The dark leaves are in the shape of an arrow and may be mottled or entirely green, even evergreen, although the winter foliage looks dull and somewhat beaten up. In spring, well before the new leaves emerge, tan flower buds form, providing a glimpse of the fun to come. Fresh, light green spring leaves then emerge, and the silver mottling,

if present, shows up as they mature. Finally, the buds give way to the jugs themselves. Crawl around on your hands and knees and peak under the leaves to find these elusive flowers—it's great fun. This belly crawl is a great equalizer of plant explorers, young and old, rich and poor. Shade and moisture are necessary, hardy in zones 4 to 8.

Asarum canadense, Canadian ginger, is a wonderful spreader, covering the ground with great enthusiasm. Its light green kidney-shaped leaves, 3–5" wide, are totally deciduous, disappearing in the fall and reappearing in early spring. They unfurl at the same time as the brownish red flowers, which

Flowers of *Asarum canadense* (left), *A. arifolium* (middle), and *A. shuttleworthii*, another wild ginger native from Virginia to Alabama and Georgia

Asarum arifolium

MORE →

41

Asarum splendens

Asarum yakushimanum

Asarum yakushimanum in flower

occur at the base of the leaf stems. The three sepals on the flowers are almost red and curled back on the jug. Arguably the best ground cover of the available gingers, and while it can become a bit of a nuisance, it is easy enough to divide and pass along to neighbors. Leaves are larger and plants more aggressive in the North than in the South. With shade and moisture, plants are excellent wherever they are grown. Hardy in zones 3 to 7.

Two relatively new gingers from the Orient provide yet more choice for collectors of the genus: *Asarum splendens* and *A. yakushimanum*, the Japanese gingers. *Asarum splendens* has silver-speckled green foliage and the usual flower jugs. The leaf variegation is

cleaner than on some of our native species and immediately draws the eye. Plants are slow to grow compared to *A. arifolium* or *A. canadense* but eventually form a compact colony. Outstanding—and available. Hardy in zones 6 to 8.

Asarum yakushimanum bears shiny dark green leaves and extraordinarily large (up to 2" wide) brown flowers. The leaves can be 6" long with short petioles, and plants make a tight compact clump in the Armitage garden. They are slow to get going, but once established, grow reasonably quickly. Different, and a must for the collectors and lovers of this group of plants. Shade and moisture needed, hardy in zones 6 to 8.

Asarum canadense in flower

Asarum canadense

Asarum canadense

Aster

I love the fall, but I must admit, both my garden and I are a little tired by mid September. I mean, gardening is great and all that, but people who tell me how lucky I am that I can garden almost the entire year must be from Connecticut. The coolness of fall rejuvenates me after enduring the heat and humidity of the summer: the annuals are pooping out, the hostas are starting to turn yellow, and I just want to go hiking in the mountains. Then, just when I'm ready to plow up the whole place, the asters explode.

The genus *Aster* is immense, bearing species from China, Japan, and Europe, but it is best known for those species from the eastern United States, in particular our native species, the New England aster, *Aster novae-angliae*, and the New York or Michaelmas aster, *A. novi-belgii*. A couple of other natives are also well worth trying, such as the white wood aster, *A. divaricatus*, and the climbing aster, *A. carolinianus*. Some people still look upon asters as weeds? What are they thinking?

Most asters behave rather normally, for asters—sprawling over, growing up, or making big clumps of flowers. But what about one that climbs all over everything? *Aster carolinianus* doesn't actually climb over anything, but it has so many stems, going in so many different directions, that it can be trained to scale the highest wall or, with its own kudzu-like cunning, can totally obliterate your marigolds, which is probably a good thing. Get a strong trellis, a reinforced wall, or a circle of 4' tall galvanized steel fencing to support this wonder, which can grow 9–15' tall and 3–4' wide. The pink to lavender flowers open in mid October and can be cut down to the ground in the spring if it gets too rollicky for its own good. Hardy in zones 6 to 9.

While the asters named after New England are perhaps the best known, many other fine asters hook me on fall gardening just as much. I love our native wood aster, *Aster divaricatus*, with its small white flowers and 1–2' long purple stems. This is one of the few asters for which partial shade is desirable, so tuck it in with astilbes, hostas, or bergenias, or under baptisias. It does not want to stand up tall; in fact, it looks much better sticking out from under these other plants, where its September flowers can be shown off but its lanky stems are hidden. Even though the plants can look rather weedy in the summer, they are well worth the wait. Plants may be cut back in midsummer, but no later than 15 July. Full sun to partial shade, zones 4 to 8.

Aster novae-angliae and *A. novi-belgii* started out as ditch weeds and

Aster divaricatus

Aster carolinianus

Aster carolinianus

MORE →

pasture plants and may still be enjoyed as such, but they are also valued for their persistent flowering, tough garden demeanor, and outstanding performance in a flower arrangement. Horticulturally speaking, little separates the two species: the New England asters do have rougher, hairier leaves than the New York asters, but extensive breeding has made even these slight

Aster divaricatus

Aster novae-angliae 'Alma Potschke'

Aster novi-belgii 'Professor Kippenburg'

Aster novae-angliae 'Alma Potschke'

Aster novi-belgii 'Winston S. Churchill'

Aster novi-belgii 'Winston S. Churchill'

differences even more subtle. Both of these native plants had to go to England and Germany in the early 1900s for "finishing" before they were acceptable to American gardeners. They came back with names like 'Alma Potschke' (3–4'), 'Professor Kippenburg' (9–12"), and 'Winston S. Churchill' (2–3'). But the aster craze has not been dormant in this country. Selections such as 'Harrington's Pink' (3–5'), 'Purple Dome' (18–24"), 'Wood's Purple' and 'Wood's Pink' (9–12"), and 'Hella Lacy' (3–4') were all developed by American gardeners. Dozens of cultivars, in a rainbow of colors, are available, ranging from 8" to 6' tall and generally growing 2–4' wide. But I recommend only those that are of short to medium height (less than 4') for most gardens. The tall cultivars are beauti-

ful but require support—unless sprawling is a desired trait in your garden. Asters also make fine cut flowers; for example, 'Elta', an *A. novi-belgii* hybrid, persists for five to seven days when a preservative is used. Full sun or afternoon shade; if plants are shaded, even medium forms will need support. Hardy in zones 4 to 8.

Some asters, like the wood asters, are sprawly wonderful things, but if you are not into sprawl, you might want to try *Aster tataricus* (Tatarian aster), a tall late-flowering aster from Siberia. Flowering at the same time as the fall sunflowers and toad lilies (*Tri-*

Aster novae-angliae 'Harrington's Pink'

Aster novae-angliae 'Purple Dome'

Aster novae-angliae 'Purple Dome'

Aster novae-angliae 'Hella Lacy'

Aster 'Elta' arranged with anemones

MORE →

cyrtis spp.), they are the dominant element in the late September and early October garden. The leaves, which emerge in the spring, look like big bunches of green chard and remain so until late in the summer, when the 7' tall stems begin to erupt with hundreds of light lavender flowers with yellow centers. The good thing about this species is that plants multiply rapidly; the bad thing is that plants multiply rapidly. If you feel kind, give a gift that keeps on giving.

A smaller offspring of this big mama, called 'Jin-Dai', is only about 4' tall, but I like Big Mama just the way she is. Full sun is best; plants in partial shade will be taller and sprawl more. Stake, or plant them through *Vernonia*, *Baptisia*, or some other large specimen for some neighborly support. Hardy in zones 4 to 8.

Astilbe

How useful does a group of plants have to be to make it a must-have for all gardeners? Some would argue that the moist, partially shady conditions needed for *Astilbe* eliminate it from such a list. I would argue, however, that the great choice of species and the impressive collection of cultivars put the genus on the must-try list, at the

Aster tataricus

Astilbe ×*arendsii* 'Venus'

Aster tataricus

Astilbe ×*arendsii* 'Cattleya'

very least. As landscapes and gardens mature, shade becomes more of an issue, and plants that offer colorful flowers in shady conditions will continue to be in high demand.

The choice of cultivars in the hybrid group *Astilbe ×arendsii* is almost endless, making choosing an astilbe only slightly less daunting than choosing a hosta, daylily, or peony. All require soils rich in organic matter and should be planted in areas that remain consistently moist. They are comfortable on streambanks but do not want to be in standing water. Many a scene at Longstock Water Gardens in England, where carex and *Astilbe ×arendsii* 'Venus' share the edge of the pond, remain well etched in my mind. Since most of our gardens are not crisscrossed by ponds or creeks, the next best thing is irrigation. Find a spot under high shade, provide organic matter if necessary, and water as needed. It is impossible to say which cultivars are best—to each his own! In my travels, I have always been impressed with 'Cattleya', a 3' tall pink-rose flowerer that also brings the Armitage shade alive. Great red color comes from 'Bonn' and 'Montgomery'; 'Gladstone' and 'Bridal Veil' provide handsome whites. 'Europa' and 'Elizabeth Bloom' are excellent soft pinks, while 'Rheinland' and 'Amethyst' are rosy to deep pink.

Astilbe ×arendsii 'Gladstone'

Astilbe ×arendsii 'Bridal Veil'

Astilbe ×arendsii 'Montgomery'

Astilbe ×arendsii 'Cattleya'

Astilbe ×arendsii 'Bonn'

MORE →

All these hybrids are terrific, but I am also truly enamored with our wonderful but little-known native *Astilbe biternata*, whose large white flowers and dark foliage some people have confused with *Aruncus*. Why such a superb native plant is so difficult for gardeners to obtain is baffling. Partial shade, hardy in zones 4 to 8.

Astilbe chinensis, the Chinese astilbe, has always seemed a rather staid cousin of the more flashy hybrids in the family. The common selection 'Pumila' is only about 1–2' tall, and its deep purple compact flowers don't contrast particularly well with the dark green leaves. It has many fans, however, including this fellow. Plants perform much more like ground covers than the *A.* ×*arendsii* hybrids and are great low-maintenance plants. Lots

Astilbe ×arendsii 'Europa'

Astilbe ×arendsii 'Elizabeth Bloom'

Astilbe ×arendsii 'Rheinland'

Astilbe ×arendsii 'Amethyst'

Astilbe biternata

Astilbe chinensis 'Pumila'

of moisture is necessary for good growth, although they are quite tolerant of temporary drought. The stodgy image of 'Pumila' has been chipped away with the appearance of other good cultivars. 'Finale' has light pink flowers, and 'Visions', an outstanding selection, sports a little more rose color in the flowers.

Astilbe chinensis var. *taquetii* has been grown in American gardens for years. The common selection is 'Superba', the hairy plants of which rise to 5' in height and produce long columnar panicles of purple flowers. A great plant for early summer flowering, sure to catch the eye. The rich gene pool of the variety can be found in newer cultivars such as 'Purple Lance', with purple-red flowers, growing 4–4½' tall. All prefer moisture

with a little shade—lots of shade in the South. Hardy in zones 4 to 8.

The most ornamental foliage of the astilbes occurs in *Astilbe simplicifolia*, the star astilbe, which offers dark glossy green leaves arranged in compact clumps. Never reaching more than 2' in height, plants are perfect for

Astilbe simplicifolia 'Sprite'

Astilbe simplicifolia 'Sprite' seed heads

Astilbe chinensis 'Visions'

Astilbe chinensis var. *taquetii* 'Superba'

Astilbe chinensis 'Finale'

Astilbe chinensis var. *taquetii* 'Purple Lance'

MORE →

Astilbe simplicifolia 'Dunkellanchs'

Astilbe simplicifolia 'Hennie Graafland'

Astilbe simplicifolia 'Willy Buchanan'

Astrantia major

the front of the garden or around a small pond. The inflorescences are much more open than other astilbes, providing a light, airy look when in flower. Even the final stage of seed production is ornamental, providing another few weeks of pleasant viewing. The best-known cultivar is 'Sprite', whose shell-pink flowers have proven outstanding for many years. Other cultivars, such as 'Hennie Graafland' and 'Dunkellanchs', are similar to 'Sprite', but 'Willy Buchanan' is set apart by its dwarf habit (less than a foot tall) and light pink flowers. As with other astilbes, moisture and partial shade are conducive to good performance. Hardy in zones 4 to 8.

Astrantia

MASTERWORT

A few plants have such nonsensical names that I cannot wait to get a look at the thing to see what part of it inspired the choice. If sneezewort has to do with sneezing, then what about masterwort? Gardeners are unlikely to be enamored with the name, nor are they likely to find the name attached to a plant at their local garden center. Common name aside, however, the genus *Astrantia* can do great things for partially shaded areas, particularly if water can be provided regularly.

The large, rather weird, 2–3" wide, white to pink flowers of *Astrantia*

Astrantia major

major, great masterwort, occur in early to mid spring. Short papery bracts stick out beneath the flowers, like rounded collars on a shirt. The deep green leaves are shallowly parted into three to seven divisions. Spreading by seed and stolons, the 2–3' tall plants, where comfortable, form an impressive display. Unfortunately for many gardeners, they are only comfortable in cool climates and abhor hot, humid summers. Several outstanding cultivars have been collected, however, and should be tried by adventurous gardeners. My favorite for sure is 'Margery Fish', a.k.a. 'Shaggy' for its greatly elongated collar of bracts, a truly shaggy mane. I first saw 'Ruby Wedding' many years ago and was pleased to see rosy red flowers had been selected from the species. 'Lars' is even darker and makes an impressive garden display. Those who enjoy weird flowers on variegated leaves should try 'Sunningdale Variegated'; the variegation disappears with summer temperatures, which is just as well. Astrantias are best for the West Coast or in zones 5 to 7a.

The good news is that the pink-flowering species *Astrantia maxima*, large masterwort, is the most handsome of all the masterworts. The bad news is that very few nurseries offer it for sale. The flowers are rose-pink, and the leaves are usually only three-parted. It is more difficult to propagate, and not enough gardeners have tried it to have any confidence in its hardiness limits. Find a few (they are out there), plant them, and let's get this plant in more gardens. Plants perform best in partial shade and are probably hardy in zones 5 to 7a as well as on the West Coast.

Astrantia major 'Margery Fish' ('Shaggy')

Astrantia major 'Sunningdale Variegated'

Astrantia major

Astrantia major 'Ruby Wedding'

Astrantia major 'Ruby Wedding'

Astrantia maxima

Astrantia maxima

Athyrium

Having grown up in Montreal in a garden-challenged family, I thought that everyone used ferns simply to cover the dirt. Wherever he could around our little semi-detached, Dad stuck in ferns—boring, never-changing green things that blackened at the first touch of frost. Nevertheless they were great for us boys, whose interest in hockey and baseball far exceeded our interest in garden maintenance. My eyes have opened, however, and my mind has expanded. Eureka, I like ferns. Age does have some value.

Athyrium filix-femina, lady fern, is a boring, never-changing green thing. Ah, but this is a boring, never-changing green thing with style and class, and better than that, this lady is tough as nails. She is deciduous, blackening at the second touch of frost, but her early croziers (ferns have such neat words associated with them—makes one sound intelligent) give rise to beautiful feathery fronds. The rachis (midrib) and stipe (petiole) are often pink or red, providing wonderful contrast to the green pinnae (see what I mean?). Plants stand upright and make handsome airy clumps. This is probably the most variable of all the ferns. I rather like the plumose feathery cultivars ('Plumosum', for instance), but others have been selected because they are, among other miscellaneous atrocities, crested ('Linearis'), both crested and plumose ('Plumosum Cristatum'), dwarf ('Minutissimum'), and round-pinnae'd, like a necklace ('Frizelliae'). Their main function is to provide curiosity, like a car wreck. Although these aberrations do reduce the boredom factor a little, they don't hold a candle to the species. Provide shade and moisture, hardy in zones 4 to 8.

The antithesis of a boring green thing, *Athyrium nipponicum*, the Japanese painted fern, provides toughness, style, and technicolor fronds. This plant makes fern growing a lot

Athyrium filix-femina

Athyrium filix-femina

Athyrium filix-femina 'Linearis'

Athyrium filix-femina 'Linearis'

more exciting. The colors on the main cultivar, 'Pictum', are indescribable—that is, I don't know how to describe them. Someone else took a stab, calling it "a metallic gray suffused with reddish or bluish hues"—which hardly narrows the field. Suffice it to say the fronds are a pastel blend of many lovely colors. Where conditions are to their liking, plants routinely spread themselves around. They tolerate heavy shade but are at their best in morning sun and prefer moist, rather than wet conditions. 'Ursala's Red' describes a selection with more red on the rachis, but it is not so different that one could consider it any better than the species itself. Hardy in zones 3 to 8.

Athyrium filix-femina 'Minutissimum'

Athyrium filix-femina 'Plumosum Cristatum'

Athyrium filix-femina 'Frizelliae'

Athyrium nipponicum 'Ursala's Red'

Athyrium nipponicum 'Pictum'

Athyrium nipponicum 'Pictum'

Baptisia australis with *Heuchera* 'Raspberry Regal'

Baptisia australis seed heads

Baptisia

FALSE INDIGO

I always enjoy a good story, and the history of the blue false indigo, *Baptisia australis*, makes for good reading. This blue-flowered species was one of the very first plants to be subsidized by the English government: the farmers in the colonies of Georgia and South Carolina grew it as a row crop to supplement the true indigo plant (*Indigofera*) for the British empire. The false indigos come in three main colors—blue, white, and yellow—but new hybrids and selections are bringing this fine plant into mainstream gardening. Great plants, great stories, great fun.

Baptisia australis is an excellent "last forever" plant; yet much to the chagrin of retailers, it looks like a stick in a pot when first purchased. Don't fret: plant that stick and soon enough, your friends will no longer be laughing. Plants take time to establish, but after a couple of years in the garden, they flower profusely and take on their classic form and substance. Plants, 3–4' tall and equally wide, look terrific by

themselves or towering over other spring flowerers, such as *Heuchera* 'Raspberry Regal'. Flowers make excellent, albeit rather ephemeral, cut flowers for local occasions. After flowering, fat brown pods are formed. As the seeds within them mature, they come loose from the pod walls, and the whole pod becomes a miniature tambourine. Few insects and diseases bother the plant; however, they do collapse in the late fall, and the first frost turns everything about them black and mushy. Plants will continue to perform for at least ten years. Full sun is necessary for best performance; keep them out of poorly drained soils. Hardy in zones 3 to 8.

Several cultivars and hybrids can be found. A hybrid involving *Baptisia*

Baptisia 'Purple Smoke'

Baptisia 'Purple Smoke'

Baptisia australis

australis is 'Purple Smoke', whose smoke-colored stems and flowers make it truly unique. This is a winner. The dwarf (2' tall) species, *B. minor*, is outstanding and resembles its big brother in every way except size.

The Armitage garden is a mecca for *Baptisia*, and several representatives of the genus fight for recognition among the oaks and weeds. Unfortunately, the oaks are not interested in the garden below, and more and more shade covers the site. Fortunately, *Baptisia alba*, the white false indigo, is far more tolerant of partial shade than the blue false indigo. Plants are ornamental from early spring, when the black stems emerge, and on through the spring and summer, with their many clean white flowers and light green foliage. In late summer and fall, the upward-facing "pea pods" are the legacy of the spring and summer flower

fling, but in 'Pendula', the pods are (you guessed it) pendulous. I don't recommend shade, although these plants certainly brighten it up. Well-drained soils are necessary, hardy in zones 5 (perhaps 4) to 8.

Blues and whites are wonderful, but the yellow indigos cannot be ignored.

Baptisia minor

Baptisia alba

Baptisia alba in the Armitage garden

55

MORE →

Baptisia alba 'Pendula'

Baptisia alba 'Pendula' seed heads

Baptisia viridis

Brightening up the sunny garden, forming interesting fruit, and offering decent foliage, they are sort of the lost sisters of the more popular white and blue versions of *Baptisia*. Their flowers were no less important to Native Americans, who also used them for coloring and dye. I enjoy the small foliage and flowers of *Baptisia tinctoria* (wild yellow indigo) and the bright bold foliage and flowers of *B. viridis*, while the creamy yellow color of *B. sphaerocarpa* provides subtlety seldom seen in this bold genus. Full sun, hardy in zones 4 to 8.

Baptisia sphaerocarpa

Baptisia tinctoria

Bergenia

PIGSQUEAK

Slow to become embraced in the mainstream American garden, pigsqueak is nevertheless offered by most perennial plant catalogs, so somebody must be buying it. If you want to impress your garden friends, rub a leaf of this plant between your thumb and index finger. If you are talented, everyone will soon hear the pig squeak. Be sure to practice on your own before you make a fool of yourself in public.

Bergenia ciliata, fringed bergenia, is a wonderful little-grown plant that can make even a nonbeliever like me want to take home a pigsqueak. Like other bergenias, the light green leaves are the best part of the plant, the organs that make it unique. They are densely pubescent (hairy) with small hairs

Bergenia ciliata

Bergenia ciliata

(cilia) surrounding the leaves. Plants look best in rock gardens or where the leaves can be admired close up. Consider the white flowers, flushed with rose, a bonus; the plants don't flower as well or grow as vigorously as common bergenias. Plant in partial (preferably afternoon) shade and protect from drying winds. Hardy in zones 5 to 7.

In my opinion, making the pig squeak is the best reason to purchase *Bergenia cordifolia* (heartleaf pigsqueak) and its hybrids, but thankfully for the breeders and sellers of bergenia, my opinion doesn't count for much. The 12" tall plants have glossy green leaves that can act as ground covers where shade and slightly moist conditions are found. The early spring flowers rise 8–12" above the leaves in early spring and persist for weeks if temperatures remain cool. Flowers are generally red or pink, but white is also available. The early flowers are often damaged if late freezes occur. In warmer areas of the country, plants are evergreen (actually "ever-bronze") but get badly battered in subfreezing temperatures. In the North, snow mercifully puts them out of view. On the West Coast, they are as perfect as bergenia can be, which is not saying too much. The bronze foliage in the fall and spring is one of the main selling points for gardeners. Partial shade, hardy in zones 4 to 8.

Amply demonstrating the diversity of bergenias are the many cultivars and hybrids of *Bergenia cordifolia*; *B. purpurascens*, purple pigsqueak, with its outstanding deep purple foliage; and others. 'Abendglocken' ('Evening

Bergenia 'Abendglocken' ('Evening Bells')

Bergenia 'Ballawley'

Bergenia cordifolia

Bergenia cordifolia in winter

Bergenia purpurascens

Bergenia 'Ballawley'

MORE →

Bells') and 'Bressingham Ruby' provide almost equally dark foliage in the early spring. 'Ballawley' and 'Pugsley Purple' (is that not an appropriate name for a pigsqueak?) have fine green foliage, while the flowers of 'Distinction', 'Morning Red', and 'Profusion' provide a strong hint as to why some people absolutely love this group of plants. That I am not one of them does not diminish my appreciation when I see *Bergenia* growing well.

Boltonia

Late summer can be a bit of a low time in the garden, sandwiched as it is between the fireworks of summer and the last hurrahs of autumn. Several transition plants, including the ubiquitous yellow daisies, are up to the challenge; one of the best of these is yet another daisy, white as snow and persistent from year to year.

When you put *Boltonia asteroides* in the garden in the spring, plant its selection 'Snowbank'. You might want to add some orange zinnias or some dwarf red cannas at its feet to provide a little contrast, although the flowers comport comfortably with almost any-

Bergenia 'Bressingham Ruby'

Bergenia 'Distinction'

Bergenia 'Profusion'

Boltonia asteroides 'Snowbank'

Bergenia 'Morning Red'

Boltonia asteroides 'Snowbank'

Boltonia asteroides 'Pink Beauty'

thing. And since it grows 3–4' in height and equally wide, give it plenty of room. The small bluish green leaves are sufficiently handsome even when no flowers are present, but when the one-inch-wide white flowers appear in late summer and fall, the appropriateness of the cultivar name is readily apparent. Plants persist for years if placed in full sun and given reasonable drainage; in too much shade, they will require support and do not flower as freely. Full sun, hardy in zones 4 to 8.

'Pink Beauty' is a cousin of 'Snowbank', with many pale pink flowers in late summer and fall. More open and lanky, and not as good a plant, but worth a try for its flowering time and color.

Brunnera macrophylla

Brunnera macrophylla 'Variegata'

Brunnera macrophylla

HEARTLEAF BRUNNERA

I thought the only place I would see outstanding plantings of *Brunnera macrophylla*, heartleaf brunnera, would be in places like Ireland or England, where such plants seem to grow in woodlands and stream banks like weeds. Not true, as a trip to Old Westbury Gardens on Long Island or Gardenview Horticultural Park in Strongsville, Ohio, will attest.

"Look at the forget-me-nots" is probably the first thing you'll think when you see the plants in flower.

The wonderful little blue flowers with small yellow centers look for all the world like forget-me-nots, but the deep green heart-shaped leaves give away the plant's true identity. Where summer temperatures are cool, leaves can be 3" long or more, and plants make a beautiful ground cover in moist, shady soils, holding their own against real forget-me-nots in the same site. Together the plants look like two youngsters holding hands on a pleasant afternoon. *Brunnera macrophylla* is not for everybody—consistent moisture is essential, otherwise the margins of the leaves turn brown. But for the somebodies, it is terrific. The rest of us will continue to plant, pamper, and enjoy its brief visits to our gardens. Plants do well in zones 3 to 7a.

Trying to collect some of the outstanding cultivars of this species is a challenging and occasionally expen-

Brunnera macrophylla

Brunnera macrophylla 'Variegata'

MORE →

Brunnera macrophylla 'Langtrees'

Campanula carpatica 'White Clips'

Campanula carpatica 'Kobalt Bell'

sive activity. Much of the variegated leaf of 'Variegata', the best of the available selections, is taken up with creamy white, and 'Langtrees' has silver white spots. 'Hadspen Cream' offers another variegated look and is highly sought after, a condition only intensified by low supply. The variegated forms are exceedingly difficult to propagate and difficult to establish, and therefore expensive to buy. Obviously, they must be good. Enjoy them if you can find them.

Campanula

BELLFLOWER

The genus *Campanula* offers so many species, cultivars, and varieties that any gardener, north or south, will never run out of plants to try. The species generally bear blue, lavender, or purple flowers, but many other hues, such as white, rosy red, and pink, have been selected. As to habit, the bellflowers offer something for almost every gardener, from upright 4' plants with large flowers to 6" rock garden subjects. The only drawback to the

genus is that it is more appropriate for northern climates; southern gardeners have to struggle to find taxa that perform south of zone 6.

Among the low growers is *Campanula carpatica*, the Carpathian bellflower. Standing only 9–12" tall, this bellflower has some of the biggest, most colorful flowers, relative to the size of the plant, of any campanula. The bell-shaped flowers can be up to 2" across and are copiously produced in early to mid summer. Provide full sun and good drainage, and place them around some rocks or near the front of the garden. This species is native to eastern Europe, and plants are not tolerant of high temperatures and high humidity. I have had little success with them south of zone 6 in the eastern United States, but they can be produced in zones 7 and 8 on the West Coast. They are terrific in the northern Plains states, the Midwest, and Canada.

The Clips series ('Blue Clips', 'White Clips') and the Wedgewood series ('Wedgewood Blue', 'Wedgewood White') are excellent small-statured plants with large flowers. For some of the deepest blue flowers, try 'Kobalt

Campanula carpatica 'Blue Clips'

Bell'. *Campanula carpatica* var. *turbinata* is lower growing and produces large (again, relative to plant height) blue flowers; its selection 'Isabel' is an interesting plant with deep violet saucer-shaped flowers. She looks particularly good when growing among yellow flowers such as *Sedum*.

Both *Campanula portenschlagiana* (Dalmatian bellflower) and *C. poscharskyana* (Serbian bellflower) offer similar low-growing habits (6–9" tall), handsome blue to purple flowers, and absolutely unpronounceable botanical names. Both are exceptionally good plants for the rock garden or for tum-

bling over hillsides and containers. For the North American gardener, there is little to choose between them; usually one takes whatever can be found at the nursery or in the mail-order catalog. The bell-shaped flowers of *C. portenschlagiana* separate it from the star-shaped flowers of *C. poscharskyana*,

Campanula carpatica var. turbinata

Campanula carpatica var. turbinata 'Isabel' with Sedum

Campanula portenschlagiana

Campanula portenschlagiana

Campanula portenschlagiana 'Resholt's Variety'

Campanula portenschlagiana 'Resholt's Variety'

MORE →

but otherwise the species are similar in habit and color. The color ranges from lavender to purple, depending on location, and flowers open in late spring. When not in flower, the plants make good-looking clumps of dark green foliage, or they can be hidden by bigger plants as summer progresses. *Campanula portenschlagiana* performs well in zones 4 to 8, *C. poscharskyana* in zones 3 to 7. I find both species more heat tolerant than most others in the genus, having been successful in the Armitage garden.

The species are just fine in and of themselves, but for *Campanula portenschlagiana*, 'Resholt's Variety' is the best vivid blue, while the deeper purple flowers of 'Bavarica' provide a more somber effect. For *C. poscharskyana*, the range of choices is expanded by 'Blue Gown' and 'Stella', with blue-

Campanula portenschlagiana 'Bavarica'

Campanula poscharskyana

Campanula poscharskyana

Campanula poscharskyana 'Blue Gown'

Campanula lactiflora 'Alba'

Campanula lactiflora 'Loddon Anna'

Campanula lactiflora 'Loddon Anna'

Campanula lactiflora 'Pritchard's Variety'

and-white and vivid violet-blue flowers, respectively. The cultivars are more difficult to find and really no better than the species.

Campanula lactiflora (milky bellflower) and C. latiloba (delphinium bellflower) are totally different in habit than the low growers just mentioned, often reaching 4' in upright height, with flowers opening in mid to late summer. Campanula lactiflora produces hundreds of small lavender or white flowers on many-branched plants in midsummer. Among the best selections of it are 'Pritchard's Variety' and 'Superba', both with flowers in the lavender to purple range. 'Alba' is an excellent choice for clean white flowers, but my favorite is 'Loddon Anna', with soft pale pink flowers on sturdy 4' tall stems. But beware: all can reseed prolifically, and the resulting offspring may be any color. For best results, provide full sun or some afternoon shade and reasonably well-drained soils. Hardy in zones 5 to 7.

The delphinium bellflower, Campanula latiloba, is so named because the blooms are held close to the flowering stem, like the flowers of a delphinium. They are large (up to 2" long) and borne on the 3–5' tall plants in midsummer. The species itself is nowhere to be seen, but its variously hued selections 'Alba' (white), 'Hidcote Amethyst' (an interesting mauve-purple), and 'Highcliffe' (deep blue) provide some happy alternatives for the campanulite. They are most successful on the West Coast but may also be found growing in gardens in zones 5 to 7. Full sun or afternoon shade. Neither of these upright bellflower species do well in areas of hot summers and are seldom grown successfully in the southern half of the country. The low growers are more forgiving of heat and humidity than the upright forms.

Campanula lactiflora 'Superba'

Campanula latiloba 'Alba'

Campanula lactiflora 'Pritchard's Variety'

Campanula latiloba 'Hidcote Amethyst'

Campanula latiloba 'Highcliffe'

Canna

CANNA LILY

The cannas are back! Like an endangered creature slowly making its way back into the mainstream population, canna lilies have returned from relative obscurity to become a rising star in today's gardens and landscapes. In some communities, cannas are an important landscape plant for road medians or public parks, attesting to their toughness. The diversity in the genus had been limited to the point of being boring, with green-leaved, red-flowered plants dominating the choices. With the surging interest in cannas, however, all sorts of new (or rediscovered) leaf colors are finding their way to American gardens. The new cultivars are no more cold hardy or disease or insect resistant than their predecessors, but their new colors are readily embraced, and the need for large bold plants in the garden have made them more prominent in the landscape.

It took me a while to say nice things about the rather gaudy leaves of *Canna* 'Bengal Tiger' ('Pretoria'), but I have come around and actually like the plant. By themselves they are tough on the eye, but when they are sited in combination with other sun lovers, few complaints are ever heard. Two other new kids on the block are the

Canna leaves in a garden border

Canna 'King Humpert'

Canna 'Wyoming'

Canna 'Bengal Tiger' ('Pretoria')

stunning 'Tropicana' ('Phaison') and 'Panache', with foliage and flowers, respectively, to die for, while the variegated foliage of 'Stuttgart' is also becoming popular. 'Stuttgart' is an anomaly among cannas, preferring partial shade rather than full sun. The bicolored flowers of 'Cleopatra' are most interesting (some descriptions may not be so kind), but the plant is one of the toughest, growing through drought and flood. Others that I think are impressive are 'King Humpert', as well as good old 'Wyoming', whose bronze leaves and orange flowers continue to be popular. Yellow flowers can be found in 'Richard Wallace' and 'Independence'. All these hybrids are big, 3–5' tall, but 'Tropicana Rose' and 'Pink Sunburst' are genetic dwarfs, less than 3' tall. 'Pink Sunburst' grows much more robustly and wider than 'Tropicana Rose' and is an outstanding choice for the smaller garden.

I'm not sure the heated love affair with cannas will continue, but as long as new cultivars that perform well in the landscape are introduced, they should be around for a while longer.

Full sun, winter hardy in zones 7 to 10; the addition of winter mulching may allow overwintering into the southern end of zone 6 as well. Further north, treat them like dahlias: lift in the fall and replant in the spring.

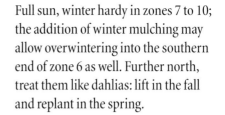

Canna 'Richard Wallace'

Canna 'Panache'

Canna 'Tropicana' ('Phaison')

Canna 'Cleopatra'

Canna 'Pink Sunburst'

Canna 'Stuttgart'

Canna 'Pink Sunburst'

Centaurea cyanus

Centaurea dealbata 'Steenbergii'

Centaurea hypoleuca 'John Coutts'

Centaurea hypoleuca 'John Coutts'

Centaurea

CORNFLOWER, KNAPWEED

If Julie Andrews were walking the highways of America rather than the hills of Switzerland, she undoubtedly would have broken into song about the roads being alive with the blue of bachelor's buttons, or something equally euphonious. Well, maybe not . . . But the annual bachelor's button, *Centaurea cyanus*, does so consistently paint the roadsides (invasively so in the Midwest) that it seems to be a perennial, even though it in fact reappears annually from seed. But other fine members of the genus are perennial and, the bachelor part notwithstanding, well-behaved members for the garden. The base of the flowers of all cornflowers consist of shingle-like papery structures called involucre bracts, whose orientation and color often account for a significant part of the flower's beauty.

With 2" wide rosy purple flowers held above the mid-green cut leaves, *Centaurea dealbata*, the Persian cornflower, makes an impressive display from early to mid summer. Place the 2–3' tall plants in full sun in front or near the middle of the garden. They dislike hot, humid conditions and therefore perform better in the North than in the South. Flowers can be cut when just a little color is showing and will persist inside for an additional five to seven days. Cultivars of different parentage have appeared on the market, including selections of a similar species, *C. hypoleuca*. From the gardener's perspective, they are similiar in garden habit, garden performance, and even color. Full sun, zones 3 to 7.

'Steenbergii' is one of the many rose-purple selections of *Centaurea dealbata* found in mail-order catalogs and garden centers. The plants are more compact and often have a white center in the flowers. Another well-known cultivar (which may in fact be a hybrid with other species) is *C. hypoleuca* 'John Coutts'; its flowers are produced more readily and are more compact than other offerings. All are similar in appearance, but if I had a choice, I'd recommend John for your garden.

With a common name like Armenian basketflower, *Centaurea macro-*

Centaurea dealbata 'Steenbergii'

cephala cannot be all bad. I first saw the cut flowers of the species in the window of a Dutch florist shop, alongside stems of lilies and baby's breath, and was immediately impressed. The 3" wide yellow flowers, which are produced on 3–4' tall plants in late spring and early summer, are bright and beautiful but kind of messy-shaggy.

In fact, they can look terrific one day and awful the next. (It is apparent that I am easily impressed.) Even the flower buds are handsome, surrounded by brown, papery bracts that add ornamental value to the flower. Not very good in the South. Plant in full sun, zones 3 to 7a.

Centaurea montana, mountain bluet, offers fine blue flowers and almost black involucre bracts. Very aggressive in the North, where many an unsuspecting gardener has planted a couple of them only to see them become legion. The 2" wide flowers produce long petals around the outside of the bracts, and weedy as they may be, they are amazingly handsome.

Three cultivars of *Centaurea montana*, though difficult to find, are worth looking for. 'Alba' produces many white flowers; the larger blue flowers of 'Grandiflora' and the creamy white blossoms of 'Ochroleuca' are sufficiently different to make the search worthwhile. Full sun, zones 3 to 7.

Centaurea macrocephala

Centaurea macrocephala

Centaurea macrocephala

Centaurea montana

Centaurea montana

Centaurea montana 'Alba'

Centaurea montana 'Grandiflora'

Centaurea montana 'Ochroleuca'

68

Cephalaria gigantea

Cephalaria gigantea in bud

Cephalaria gigantea

Cephalaria gigantea

TATARIAN CEPHALARIA

A well-grown clump of *Cephalaria gigantea* is a "come-hither" planting. Sited at the center or back of the garden, with lesser subjects at its feet, this 6–8' plant dominates center stage. The large (4–8") compound leaves are usually light to mid green; however, as large as the plants are, blooms are the main reason for its inclusion. The primrose-yellow flowers, which begin as great meaty flower buds, are about 2" across and held on wiry stems well above the foliage. They look suspiciously like the yellow-flowered scabious, *Scabiosa ochroleuca*, only much

taller and coarser. Plants do poorly in hot, humid climates and are best suited to the North and Far West. Full sun, well-drained soils, zones 4 to 7.

Cerastium

SNOW-IN-SUMMER

When the landscape plan calls for plants that supposedly look like snow in the summer, some people roll their eyes and scratch their heads over the intelligence of landscape designers. Such plants do exist, however, and the one that answers that call best is *Cerastium tomentosum*, whose combination of leaves, flowers, and habit have made it a popular plant in many gardens. In the spring (not the summer), the silvery gray leaves flow over rocks, making marvelous foils for more colorful plants at the front of the garden. The plants, covered with half-inch-wide white flowers, may not be quite like a snowbank but at least come close to snow-in-spring. Flowers occur as temperatures warm up and daylengths lengthen, persisting for four to six weeks, depending on temperature. In areas of little snowfall, the plants are "ever-gray" and quite handsome in the off-season. The foliage, like that of artemisias and lamb's ears, are excellent softeners of the garden border.

Cephalaria gigantea

Cerastium tomentosum

Drainage becomes more important the further south one gardens. With poor drainage, plants melt out south of zone 7a, but are still useful in that area in raised beds or containers. Full sun in the North, afternoon shade in the South, excellent drainage required. Hardy in zones 3 to 7.

A couple of other species, such as *Cerastium buisseri* (also known as snow-in-summer), may be found, but they offer few obvious differences. Plants have similar white flowers but are less vigorous, which may be a plus for gardeners in places where *C. tomentosum* becomes too aggressive. Hardy in zones 3 to 6.

Cerastium buisseri

Cerastium tomentosum

Ceratostigma willmottianum

Ceratostigma willmottianum

Ceratostigma willmottianum 'Forest Blue'

Ceratostigma

LEADWORT

I was taught that the term "wort" means "to heal": liverwort heals the liver, lungwort heals the lung, and so forth. Obviously something went wrong here. All the same, the leadworts—healers or not—provide excellent plants for the late summer and fall garden.

The two species seen in American gardens are remarkably different. *Ceratostigma plumbaginoides* (trailing leadwort) is only 6–9" tall. Plants produce blue flowers, a half-inch to an inch across, in late summer and fall, and are one of the toughest little ground covers available. Without flowers, one hardly even notices the plants most of the year, but as days shorten and temperatures start to cool down, they perk up and put on their best blue dresses. The leaves are small (less than an inch in length) and are dark green most of the year, turning reddish as plants get older. They grow best in full sun and, with good drainage, are almost indestructible. This species per-

forms well in zones 5 (4 with protection) to 8.

Neither well known nor widely grown, *Ceratostigma willmottianum* (Chinese leadwort) is certainly worth a try as more plants become available. Growing to 2' in height, it puts forth its handsome blue flowers for about six weeks in late summer. Chinese leadwort is not as tough and adaptable as trailing leadwort, but it has its compact habit to recommend it, and the blue flowers do well with anything white or yellow. 'Forest Blue' is widely adaptable and provides an excellent upright habit. Full sun to partial shade, hardy in zones 7 (perhaps 6) to 9.

Ceratostigma plumbaginoides

Ceratostigma plumbaginoides

Chrysanthemum

What this noble name has been subjected to! The genus, which represented dozens of fine garden plants throughout the world, was unceremoniously stripped of its name and thrown out on the street with but a few family members still clinging to its legs. *Chrysanthemum*—which had included the pot chrysanthemum, fall garden mum, Marguerite daisy, yellow and gold, pyrethrum daisy, ox-eye daisy, nippon daisy, and the ubiquitous shasta daisy—ended up with a couple of annual plants after the smoke had cleared. What a debacle. And now that people and the industry have finally accepted the change in some of the names, it appears as if the names will revert to the originals.

Some of the flowers of *Chrysanthemum coccineum* (*Tanacetum coccineum*) are so bright, it appears as if new paint were applied to the flowers, hence the common name, painted daisy. The 2–3" wide flowers appear in late spring and early summer over the light green, deeply cut, fetid foliage, which last property makes this species, also known as pyrethrum daisy, an excellent pest repellent. Plants may grow 3' tall and are notorious for their need for support. If cut back after flowering, they may return a second flush.

Some wonderful selections of *Chrysanthemum coccineum* exist, but they are not terribly easy to come by. 'James

Kelway' is an old favorite, with bright red flowers atop 3' stems; 'Brenda' is similar in color but shorter, usually around 2' in height. 'Eileen May Robinson' is another terrific old-fashioned daisy with single pink flowers. Double flowers can be admired in 'Shirley Double', while other cultivars such as 'Bressingham Red' add color, handsome leaves, and cut flowers to this diverse group of plants. They are cold hardy in snow-covered zone 4 (occasionally to zone 3) but are not happy in the heat and humidity of a zone 7 summer. Full sun, good drainage.

Fall is the time for pot mums, sold by the dozen for a buck and a half each

Chrysanthemum coccineum 'James Kelway'

Chrysanthemum coccineum 'James Kelway'

Chrysanthemum coccineum 'Eileen May Robinson'

Chrysanthemum coccineum 'Eileen May Robinson'

MORE →

at the local box store. Colorful, cheap, useful, and boring. They perform better in the pot at K-Mart than they do in the garden. *Chrysanthemum* ×*koreanum* (*Dendranthema* ×*grandiflorum*) and other late-flowerers are outstanding, however, and ought to be used more. They are known as Korean hybrids or by their cultivar names, such as 'Ryan's Daisy', 'Hillside Sheffield', and 'Apricot Single'. 'Ryan's Daisy' is about 18–24" tall; 'Hillside Sheffield' and 'Apricot Single' are only about 12" high. Gazillions of flowers in late fall, before frost. Can be propagated by the shovelful, any time. Save your dollar and a half and buy something useful. Great plants! Full sun, zones 3 to 8.

The handsome variegated evergreen foliage of a well-grown specimen of silver and gold, *Chrysanthemum pacificum* (*Ajania pacifica*) always brings praise. The white margins are clean and crisp. Under satisfactory growing conditions, plants of the small slightly serrated leaves make a 3–4' wide clump in a single growing season. Height is only about 15", but its leaf color combines well with many neighbors, such as artemisias or dusty miller. Its other claim to fame is the appearance of dozens of round fuzzy balls of yellow flowers late in the season. Very late—as in November in the Armitage garden, hopefully before frost in more northern sites. Not really being a fan of small fuzzy round flow-

Chrysanthemum coccineum 'Brenda'

Chrysanthemum coccineum 'Shirley Double'

Chrysanthemum coccineum 'Brenda'

Chrysanthemum coccineum 'Bressingham Red'

ers, it took me a few years to think of them as something other than a distraction to the leaves. But now they are as anticipated as flowers of the spring and summer, with the added bonus of wondering if they will open before the frost gets them. Cut plants back if necessary in spring, not fall. Excellent

drainage is an absolute requirement; site the plants on a slope if possible. Full sun, hardy in zones 5 to 9.

Chrysanthemum ×superbum (*Leucanthemum ×superbum*), commonly known as the shasta daisy, has been, is, and forever shall be one of the more popular perennials in the American landscape. They are in front of every gardener in every outlet in every spring—easy to grow, easy to pronounce, and as comfortable as an old shoe. That many of them fall apart in a year or two seems not to make the slightest difference. Nearly all shastas are clothed in white, whether in single, semi-double, or fully double attire.

All sorts of choices are available to the shasta connoisseur. The double fringed flowers of 'Aglaia' are absolutely gruesome; those of 'Wirral Supreme', not nearly as scary. Personally,

Chrysanthemum ×superbum 'Aglaia'

Chrysanthemum 'Ryan's Daisy'

Chrysanthemum 'Hillside Sheffield'

Chrysanthemum 'Apricot Single'

Chrysanthemum pacificum with *Artemisia* 'Powis Castle'

Chrysanthemum pacificum

Chrysanthemum pacificum

MORE →

I'll take single-flowered shastas any day—perhaps 'White Knight', with its lovely single white petals around a yellow center, or 'Snow Lady', an All-American award winner that flowers the first year from seed. 'Polaris' is large, and 'Snow Cap' is the best of the compact forms. If you are having problems with foliage falling apart after flowering, try 'Becky'. She bears fine white single flowers, but unlike the fine lady she was named for, she has the toughest demeanor of any shasta I have tried. In general, plants stand 18–30" tall and require full sun and well-drained soils. Rainy, humid climates are not to their liking. They do reasonably well in zones 4 to 9. Cut back after flowering in warmer areas of the country.

Chrysanthemum ×superbum 'Wirral Supreme'

Chrysanthemum ×superbum 'Becky'

Chrysanthemum ×superbum 'Snow Cap'

Chrysanthemum ×superbum 'Becky'

Chrysanthemum ×superbum 'Polaris'

Chrysanthemum ×superbum 'Snow Lady'

Chrysanthemum ×superbum 'White Knight'

Clematis

A large group of ornamental vines and a few non-viners make up this popular genus. The incredible popularity of the vines is due to their relative ease of culture and diversity of color, flower size, and form. Many a postal carrier has cursed a clematis while trying to wedge mail into a mailbox surrounded by a beanstalk that could support a young Jack. However, a couple of non-vining forms are equally satisfying, if not quite as spectacular, and deserve to be used much more widely.

Big and sprawling, *Clematis heracleifolia* (tube clematis) is non-vining and shrublike in its habit. The ends of the stems produce dozens of tubular flowers, making for showy inflorescences in late spring and summer. The large compound leaves are up to 12"

long, and if the plant is overfertilized, the leaves will almost obscure the flowers. Flowers range from light to dark blue. The plant's main drawbacks are ranginess and leafiness; support tends to make the plant less rangy. Plants may be cut back in late summer if the foliage declines. *Clematis heracleifolia* can be more weedy than useful—but when in its prime, it is a showstopper. Full sun, zones 3 to 7.

'Côte d'Azur' and 'Wyevale Blue' are the most common offerings and differ only slightly from the species. 'Robert Briden' has a touch of blue on the mostly creamy white flowers.

Clematis integrifolia (solitary clematis), one of the big-time sleepers in herbaceous perennials, is a non-vining member that produces solitary flowers of deep blue and opposite entire leaves. A definite must-have plant, it has been obscured in the marketplace by the

omnipresent vines but is well worth a place in the sunny garden. The numerous thin, 3' tall stems should be supported as they grow, otherwise they flop on the ground. The flowers begin in late spring and continue for six weeks, then off and on throughout the season. Under good garden condi-

Clematis integrifolia

Clematis heracleifolia (right) and *C. integrifolia*

Clematis heracleifolia 'Robert Briden'

Clematis integrifolia

Clematis heracleifolia 'Côte d'Azur'

Clematis heracleifolia 'Wyevale Blue'

Clematis integrifolia seed heads

MORE →

Clematis integrifolia 'Alba'

Clematis integrifolia 'Rosea'

Clematis "mailboxensis"

tions, flowers go on to produce fluffy seed heads into the fall. Plants offering white ('Alba') and rose-colored ('Rosea') flowers are occasionally seen—they provide a nice splash of color, but I'll take the wonderful deep blue of the species any day. Full sun, zones 3 to 7.

Vining *Clematis* species and hybrids are everywhere—and with good reason. Where their roots are cool and their foliage is in sunshine, they can be as vigorous and colorful as any plant in the garden. The best support for many of the vines is through shrubs and trees, where they can climb to their heart's content and, in general, make any woody plant look better. In the Armitage garden, nary a shrub escapes from this twining nightmare.

The hybrids are most easily found, but let's not totally ignore the species. I love the tubular flowers of *Clematis texensis*, the Texas clematis, one of the best species for southern gardeners, replete with rose-red blossoms in the spring and summer and stunning fruit later on; 'Duchess of Albany', the most popular selection, has similar flowers but is even more vigorous. I plant the winter clematis, *C. cirrhosa*, for its combination of glossy evergreen leaves, small-flowering chalices, and cottony fruit. I have learned my lesson about planting the beautiful but self-seeding thug *C. terniflora* (*C. maximowicziana*; sweet autumn clematis): one needs to experiment with such explosive plants. After a few springs of removing seedlings from all over the place, I practice the creed of "rip out and replace" with this species.

Interspecific hybridization has re-

Clematis ×*jackmanii*

Clematis texensis seed heads

Clematis texensis 'Duchess of Albany'

sulted in a number of well-known hybrids that many gardeners prefer to the large-flowered hybrids. Most gardeners have heard of Jackman's clematis, *Clematis ×jackmanii*, which is as good as ever. When I can find *C. ×durandii*, with its deep blue leathery flowers, I jump at the opportunity.

But regardless of my obvious preference for more subtle forms, it is the large-flowered hybrids that attract the attention of most gardeners. With

flowers 1–4" wide, and in sufficient colors for everyone, the 8–15' tall vines can cover trellises, holly bushes, clotheslines, and mailboxes with ease. I intensely dislike hybrids with double flowers, such as 'Duchess of Edinburgh' and 'Proteus' (I plant them in the Horticulture Gardens for others to see), but most others can be quite ornamental. The choice depends on color desired and the number of woody plants one can find to grow

Clematis cirrhosa

Clematis cirrhosa seed head

Clematis cirrhosa in winter

Clematis texensis 'Duchess of Albany'

Clematis ×durandii

Clematis terniflora

MORE →

them over. So few shrubs, so many cultivars. 'Nellie Moser' is one of the most popular, available in almost any garden shop, but the hybrids also bring blues ('Elsa Spath', 'Madame Chalmondeley', 'Pearl d'Azure'), pinks ('Pink Champagne'), whites ('Huldine', 'Miss Bateman'), and rose-colored flowers ('Madame Julie Correvon', 'Ville de Lyon'). They all have their moments, and these moments don't end with the flowers. The fuzzy fruit of the hybrids is highly ornamental and provides almost as much value as the flowers—a better reason than ever to buy a few more hollies and spireas and slap a few vines over them. Full sun, zones 3 to 8.

Clematis terniflora

Clematis 'Duchess of Edinburgh'

Clematis 'Nellie Moser'

Clematis 'Huldine'

Clematis 'Proteus'

Clematis 'Elsa Spath'

Clematis 'Miss Bateman'

Clematis 'Madame Chalmondeley'

Clematis 'Ville de Lyon'

Clematis 'Pink Champagne'

Clematis 'Pearl d'Azure'

Hybrid *Clematis* seed heads

Clematis 'Madame Julie Correvon'

Colchicum autumnale with Rudbeckia fulgida

Colchicum autumnale

Colchicum

AUTUMN CROCUS

The autumn-flowering genus *Colchicum* is known as the autumn crocus, but unlike *Crocus*, its members have six stamens rather than three. The corms can be quite large (up to 4" long) and need to be planted as soon as they are received from the mail-order nursery. They are expensive, relative to many other bulbous plants, but once established, they provide exotic entertainment in the garden for many months. Many a head has been scratched in the spring when straplike leaves emerge, only to disappear in a few weeks. Then, in late summer and fall, the single or double flowers appear, only about 6" tall and in cloaks of pink and rose. Colorful though they are, they can also be unkempt and uncooperative. Albeit handsome, few flowers stand upright for any length of time, and a single rainfall can make them look like wet mangy dogs. Pink dogs, of all things.

Colchicum autumnale, C. speciosum, and *C. byzantinum* are the most common species, but most of the garden plants are hybrids. Although colchicums often disappoint gardeners by

Colchicum speciosum

Colchicum naturalized

having too rapid a flowering time in the fall and too short a life span, cultivars like 'Autumn Queen' and 'Waterlily' can be outstanding, particularly when planted with *Rudbeckia* and other fall flowerers. Plant in shady areas and in well-drained soils. Hardy in zones 4 to 7 (8 on the West Coast).

Colchicum byzantinum

Colchicum 'Autumn Queen'

Colchicum 'Waterlily' with *Rudbeckia hirta*

Coreopsis

No matter how hard we try to abuse this group of native plants, they seem to come back for more, in every box store, catalog, and garden center each spring. Along with shasta daisies and columbines, year after year, the genus *Coreopsis* remains one of the top ten perennials sold. The bright yellow flowers of most of its members, along with its willingness to put up with most any garden soil, have made it a favorite. That it is easy for producers to grow, looks good in a container, and appears in every gas station from coast to coast also tends to keep it around. Indeed coreopsis is common, but don't expect all plants that carry the coreopsis label to perform equally well.

One of my favorites is *Coreopsis auriculata* 'Nana', a 12–15" tall selection known as mouse-ear coreopsis. Tough and well behaved, it explodes with bright yellow flowers in early spring. Its small size is made up for by the intense color of the 2" wide blooms. The leaves are spoon-shaped—somewhat like a mouse's ear, I am told. It is a

Coreopsis auriculata 'Nana'

lovely plant in the front of the garden or in a container, and it looks particularly good with concrete frogs. Not long-lasting, perhaps three years if drainage is good, but most coreopsis are similarly disposed: good drainage is a must. Full sun, zones 4 to 9.

One of the mainstays of the beginning gardener and landscaper looking for something bright and easy to grow is *Coreopsis grandiflora*, common coreopsis. In full sun, plants can be spectacular for the first year or two, but by the third year they will usually need dividing or they crash on all sides. This is not a problem unless a person doesn't look forward to such fun. Which is most of us. The other chore

Coreopsis auriculata 'Nana'

81

MORE →

in keeping these plants happy is to remove the dead flowers as soon as possible. The more seed produced, the shorter the useful life of the plant.

Numerous cultivars and hybrids have been selected—all yellow, all quite similar, all requiring removal of spent flowers to do their best. 'Early Sunrise' is relied on in the industry for its ease of production and propensity to stay in flower; plants are about 2' tall. 'Goldfink' bears 2" wide single flowers, and 'Sunray' provides double flowers; both are approximately 2' tall. A similar species, *Coreopsis lanceolata*, has been refined in such good cultivars as 'Brown Eyes', which plants are a little taller than the type but equally handsome. Full sun, good drainage, zones 4 to 9.

Yellow, yellow, yellow—is there any other color out there? With coreopsis, the answer—at least for northern gardeners—is yes, in the form of the pink-flowered *Coreopsis rosea*. More of a spreading plant than an upright grower, plants are only about 9–15" tall. Rose-pink flowers, three-quarters of an inch wide, cover the plants in the spring

Coreopsis grandiflora 'Sunray'

and early summer. Unfortunately, plants are weak and leggy south of zone 7 in the East (fine in zone 8 on the West Coast), although 'American Dream' is a little more vigorous and slightly more heat tolerant. I have seen plants look terrific in Cleveland but awful in Memphis. Full sun, zones 4 to 7.

Coreopsis verticillata, threadleaf coreopsis, is the tough guy of the group, providing classic yellow flowers, reasonably strong stems, and persistence of flower and plant in the sunny garden. The leaves are cut into "Edward Scissorhands" leaflets, and plants are almost as good-looking in

Coreopsis grandiflora

Coreopsis grandiflora 'Sunray'

Coreopsis rosea

Coreopsis grandiflora 'Early Sunrise'

Coreopsis lanceolata 'Brown Eyes'

leaf as in flower. One of the brightest of the available cultivars is the large-flowered 'Golden Showers', but the best-performing selection is 'Zagreb', a 15–18" tough guy with golden yellow flowers. 'Zagreb' may be as good as it gets, but 'Moonbeam' is as popular as it gets. The number-one seller in many areas of the country, its soft light yellow flower color goes well with most other flowers in the garden. Full sun, zones 5 to 9.

Coreopsis verticillata

Coreopsis verticillata 'Golden Showers'

Coreopsis rosea

Coreopsis verticillata 'Zagreb'

Coreopsis verticillata 'Zagreb'

Coreopsis verticillata 'Moonbeam' with *Salvia*

Coreopsis verticillata 'Moonbeam'

84

Corydalis

So many corydalis, so few known! This genus is as diverse as any, including plants with white, yellow, and blue flowers. They are mostly thought of as rock garden subjects, but some species are quite common in any garden, rock or otherwise. The ferny leaves, one of their more enchanting characteristics, are charming even when no flowers are present. All require excellent drainage (as in rock gardens) and prefer partial shade or morning sun.

Corydalis cheilanthifolia, ferny corydalis, is seldom seen in American gar-

dens, but it just might be worth a try. Plants are large, relative to other species in the genus, growing up to 15" tall. The pinnately cut leaves resemble the lip fern (*Chelianthes*—thus its specific name) with many yellow flowers arising from the blue-gray rosette. I have had no success with this plant in the Armitage garden, but what else is new. Gardeners in the Midwest have been luckier than I. Partial shade, excellent drainage, and cool summers are recommended. Hardy in zones 3 to 6.

Corydalis flexuosa, blue corydalis, is an extraordinary plant, and where it is happy, on the West Coast or in the Midwest, it rates the inevitable oohs

and aahs. But the Armitage garden is like hell on earth for this plant, where the oohs and aahs are replaced by "where did it go?" (The guy who tends the Armitage garden is like a starving man salivating about food he can never have but wanting it all the same.) The fernlike foliage is often smoky gray, and the flowers are blue to purple. I have seen it look particu-

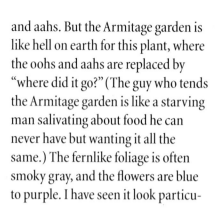

Corydalis flexuosa 'Blue Panda'

Corydalis flexuosa 'Blue Panda'

Corydalis cheilanthifolia

Corydalis cheilanthifolia

Corydalis cheilanthifolia

Corydalis flexuosa 'China Blue'

84

larly handsome in containers, where soil conditions can be more easily controlled. Plants go summer dormant, faster in warm summers than cool, but reemerge the next spring (except in my garden).

Several similar cultivars are offered. 'Blue Panda', the most common, is a good selection, being bluer than 'China Blue' or 'Père David', with their smoky blue and lavender-blue flowers, respectively. Partial shade, excellent drainage, zones 5 to 7.

The easiest, brightest, and most vigorous of the corydalis for most gardeners—*Corydalis lutea*, yellow corydalis —can be found bounding and jumping from rock to rock in gardens in the Northeast, Midwest, and Northwest. Small, plentiful yellow flowers cover the ferny green foliage on 9–15" tall plants. The bounding and jumping is the result of the copious viable seed produced; it flies everywhere, and where it lands on receptive soil, more yellow corydalis will soon emerge. Slightly better in the North than South. 'Alba', a white variant of the species, is worth a try if you get tired of yellow. Partial shade, good drainage, zones 5 to 7.

Crocosmia

Excellent plants for an exotic look, crocosmias boast many 8–15" long straplike leaves and colorful lily-like flowers. Up to a hundred flowers occur on stems held well above the foliage. Crocosmias have made the transition from the bulbous world to the mainstream garden world. Cultivars may be found in bulb catalogs as well as general plant catalogs, which speaks highly of the widespread performance and popularity of this group of plants.

Recent breeding and building up of material means numerous cultivars are now offered, all hybrids involving *Crocosmia crocosmiiflora*. The most popular is 'Lucifer', whose scarlet-red flowers blaze through the summer; she

Corydalis lutea

Crocosmia 'Lucifer'

Corydalis lutea

Corydalis lutea 'Alba'

Crocosmia 'Bressingham Blaze'

MORE →

Crocosmia 'Lucifer'

Crocosmia 'Spitfire'

Crocosmia 'Rowallane Yellow'

Crocosmia 'Citronella'

has been fashionable for years and her intense color combined with her vigor and ease of cultivation will keep her near the top of the crocosmia list for years to come. 'Bressingham Blaze' and 'Spitfire' are known by their large orange-red flowers and vigorous habit; they light up the flowers around them. Some of the better, brighter choices occur in the yellows; I like 'Citronella' but I really fancy 'Rowallane Yellow', from Rowallane Garden in Northern Ireland. All crocosmias are terrific for cut flowers as well.

Full sun for all cultivars. Wet soils result in rotting roots; container planting is useful to improve drainage. Spider mites are a common problem, especially if plants are stressed. Hardy in zones 5 to 8.

Crocus

"Hey Doc, which way is up on this bulb, anyway?" So wondered one of my brighter students after first being introduced to forcing crocus in the greenhouse. I had obviously not taught him much, nor had I been successful in teaching him that the crocus was a corm, not a bulb. To this student and most gardeners, however—bulb, corm, rhizome . . . few really care. Planting crocus and other cormy things in the

Crocus chrysanthus 'Blue Pearl'

would go crazy looking at long grass and yellow leaves. Wouldn't work at our house, guaranteed!

Zones 3 to 8, full sun while the leaves are green. Deciduous shade is tolerable, as long as sufficient sun reaches the crocus leaves before the trees re-leaf.

Crocus vernus 'Remembrance'

Crocus vernus 'Pickwick'

Dahlia 'Royal Dahlietta Apricot'

Dahlia 'Parakeet'

Dahlia

If diversity of flower, form, and habit are criteria for special garden plants, then hybrid dahlias are indeed in that special category. These are plants to either love or dislike with passion (hate should be saved for plants that are more deserving). In some areas of the country, they are true no-brainer plants, the mainstays of the summer and fall garden; in others, they require the weekly maintenance chores of stalking, spraying, deadheading, and Japanese beetle–plucking. Yet their beauty is undeniable, and the diversity within the hybrids equals that of chry-

Dahlia 'Coltness' Mix

Dahlia 'Single Salmon'

santhemums or peonies. Offerings such as 'Coltness' Mix', 'Royal Dahlietta Apricot', and 'Single Salmon' are effective as low-growing bedding plants and beautiful to boot, while medium-sized cultivars like 'Scarlet

Dahlia 'Emory Paul'

Dahlia 'Scarlet Beauty'

MORE →

Beauty', 'Parakeet', and 'Pink Michigan' are excellent choices, with stems sufficiently strong that staking may not be necessary. 'Emory Paul', 'Gypsy Boy', 'Good Interest', and 'Fascination' are but a few examples of some of the taller hybrids with huge flowers, in an array of colors and forms that simply blow people away. Tubers must be dug after the first frost in zones 6 and colder but can remain in the ground in warmer areas. In areas of hot, humid summers, diseases and insect pests can make a gardener question their belief in their purchase. Full sun.

By including *Dahlia imperialis*, I

Dahlia 'Pink Michigan'

Dahlia 'Gypsy Boy'

Dahlia 'Good Interest'

Dahlia imperialis

Dahlia 'Fascination'

Dahlia imperialis

certainly am pushing the bubble to bursting: the tree dahlia is a plant that ninety-eight percent of gardeners in the United States cannot successfully grow, but let's pretend anyway. I first saw *D. imperialis* near Auckland, New Zealand, and therefore I resigned myself to the fact that it would seldom be seen over here. My next encounter was outside San José, Costa Rica, and at that time I decided that everyone should at least have a chance to see a photo of this magnificent plant, even if we can't grow it. Then I saw it used as an annual in gardens in California, where it cost the gardener about the same as a small car. The term "tree" is appropriate, as plants can reach 20' in height. The stems are woody and often tinged with a little red. The 2' long pinnately compound leaves are rather hairy above and have petioles about a foot long. Of course, foliage aside, it is the clusters of nodding pink flowers that keep people interested. Go for it, who needs another car anyway? Native to the Tropics, cold hardy to zone 9. Full sun.

Delphinium

My good friend Michael Dirr claims he never met a cheeseburger he didn't like. I have the same feeling about delphiniums, regardless of where I see them. I knew that plants in many colors, sizes, and flower types have been offered, but I never had the opportunity to see their forces aligned until I wandered into a cultivar trial at Wisley

Gardens, England. It was almost enough to make me renew my vows to the Commonwealth and Queen. Unfortunately, we see about ten percent of the available taxa in the United States, but it is nice to know that interest in this Old World plant has not diminished. Delphiniums are also an outstanding cut flower and an important crop for the cut flower growers here and abroad. Cultivars such as *Delphinium ×belladonna* 'Volkerfrie-

Delphinium elatum hybrids on trial at Wisley

Delphinium ×belladonna 'Volkerfrieden'

Delphinium 'Barba Blue'

Delphinium 'Blue Bird'

MORE →

Delphinium 'Butterball'

den' and the *D. elatum* hybrid 'Barba Blue' have been selected for their cut flower attributes.

Delphiniums can be as beautiful in Atlanta as they are in Montreal, but the term "perennial" must be discarded if one is to grow them in the South. It is simply necessary to accept that delphiniums are annuals there (plant in October, enjoy in early spring, and pull out in June), and two- or three-year perennials elsewhere. In the South, plant at least a full one-gallon plant in October, otherwise insufficient rooting will occur by spring. In the North, plant either in the spring or in September.

A wide range of *Delphinium* species have been used in breeding; some of the more common hybrids, most often involving *Delphinium elatum*, are mixtures sold under the names of Round Table series, Mid Century hybrids, and Connecticut Yankee series. It is worth spending the time, however, trying to locate named cultivars in shades of deep blue ('Blue Bird', 'Molly Buchanan'), light blue ('Blue Dawn', 'Skyline'), lavender ('Ann Page', 'Blue Jade'), or yellow ('Butterball', 'Sun

Delphinium 'Blue Dawn'

Delphinium 'Blue Jade'

Delphinium 'Molly Buchanan'

Delphinium 'Skyline'

Delphinium 'Sun Gleam'

Gleam') for next spring's garden. Dwarf selections (*Delphinium grandiflorum* 'Tom Thumb') and those with outrageous scarlet flowers (*D. nudicaule*) are also great fun to try. All delphiniums, from dwarfs to six-footers, love cool summers and cold snow-covered winters for best perenniality.

The older cultivars are grown from seed and are tall and vigorous. With the many newer selections, there seems to be no end to the colors and sizes of this fine plant. Full sun, good drainage, zones 3 to 6 in the East, zone 8 on the West Coast.

Delphinium grandiflorum 'Tom Thumb'

Delphinium nudicaule

Dianthus

PINKS

I never realized that the plants I knew as dianthus were so closely linked to my wife's sewing hobby. Most of the pinks I had encountered were pink or red (a few were white), therefore the common name made perfect sense to me. I know very little about sewing, so when I learned that the common name had been granted because the petals of several species look like they were cut with pinking shears, I was cut down to size.

With about three hundred species of *Dianthus*, it should not come as any surprise that many people find a few of them better-than-average garden plants. By far the best-known member of this large genus is the carnation, *Dianthus caryophyllus*; millions of stems a year, of dozens of cultivars like 'Red Sims', are cut from farms in South America and shipped to your downtown florist. (They travel a long way to get to your table, so don't be too surprised if they are not as fresh as you would like.) But if you ask a hundred

gardeners what their very favorite dianthus is, more than eighty of them would respond, without hesitation, "sweet William," *D. barbatus*. It's hard to understand how such a beautiful plant could be named after William, duke of Cumberland, best known for brutally crushing a handful of revolts against the English in the mid 1700s. "Sweet" is not exactly the name William would have chosen for himself. But these biennials have been around for a long time and will surely be popular for years to come. They are easy to identify by their unique flower buds and clusters of flowers in an array of colors. *Dianthus barbatus* blends like

Dianthus barbatus 'Indian Carpet' in bud

Dianthus barbatus 'Indian Carpet'

93

MORE →

Dianthus barbatus 'Messenger Mix'

'Messenger Mix' and 'Indian Carpet' are outstanding, and every now and then one can find a cute dwarf like 'Roundabout Picotee' to compare against cut flower selections such as 'Tall Cutting Mix'. Sweet Williams persist for only two years but occasionally reseed to provide some long-term guests. Provide full sun and well-drained soils. Hardy in zones 3 to 8.

The other plant that would come up in the aforementioned survey would be the maiden pinks, *Dianthus deltoides*, a much more perennial plant with hundreds of flowers over thin grasslike leaves. They initially flower in the spring, but if the flowers are removed when spent, blooms will continue into late spring and even early summer. 'Brilliant' and 'Red Maiden' are two fine selections with rose to red flowers, and 'Zing Rose' has deep scarlet flowers. All maiden pinks prefer full sun and hate wet soils. Hardy in zones 3 to 8.

Some of the most effective plants belong to the cheddar pinks, *Dianthus gratianopolitanus*. The cheddar pinks came from the Cheddar district of southern England, where the famous cheese is made in caves. An example is 'Bath's Pink', a wonderful pink-flowerer with blue-green foliage. In areas of mild winters, its leaves are evergreen and bring needed color to the winter scene. These pink cheese balls cover ground, hang over walls, and are almost indestructible; they flower their heads off in early spring, then simply look good the rest of the

Dianthus barbatus 'Roundabout

Dianthus deltoides 'Brilliant'

Dianthus deltoides 'Red Maiden'

Dianthus barbatus 'Tall Cutting Mix'

Dianthus deltoides 'Red Maiden'

Dianthus deltoides 'Zing Rose'

year. A similar and arguably better selection is 'Mountain Mist', with its pink flowers and even bluer leaves; it needs more cold than 'Bath's Pink' and won't flower in the deep South. Another fine plant is 'Firewitch', with rosy flowers over foliage more green than blue; it is much more rounded, not nearly as prostrate as the previous two cultivars, and also tends to flower on and off throughout the season, being one of the best return-flowerers in the genus.

The previous selections are terrific, but so are 'Tiny Rubies' and 'Baby Blanket', both of which offer deep pink

Dianthus gratianopolitanus 'Bath's Pink'

Dianthus gratianopolitanus 'Mountain Mist'

Dianthus caryophyllus 'Red Sims'

Dianthus gratianopolitanus 'Bath's Pink'

Dianthus gratianopolitanus 'Mountain Mist'

Dianthus gratianopolitanus 'Firewitch'

MORE →

double flowers topping out on 6–8" tall plants. Unlike 'Bath's Pink', they do not spread around at all but rather form small clumps. I can think of nothing better than eating cheese, drinking wine, and watching the cheddar pinks flower. Full sun is necessary. Hardy in zones 3 to 8.

Dianthus gratianopolitanus 'Tiny Rubies'

Dianthus gratianopolitanus 'Baby Blanket'

Dianthus gratianopolitanus 'Baby Blanket'

Dicentra

BLEEDING HEART

The genus *Dicentra* contains woodland, garden, and vining members, all shade tolerant, with flowers in shades of white, pink, red, or yellow—a popular old-fashioned group of plants that appeals to almost all gardeners.

Perhaps because our native fringed bleeding heart (*Dicentra eximia* in the East, *D. formosa* in the West) is a homeboy rather than a guest, people tend to consider it a little too common. Many novice gardeners look at it and don't see as romantic a plant as *D. specta-*

Dicentra 'Bacchanal'

bilis, from Japan, but in fact, it offers the gardener a great deal more. First, our native species don't go summer dormant, and second, they offer much more diversity than the imports. If one visits the open glades of an eastern or western forest, fringed bleeding heart is likely much in evidence.

Green leaves with pink flowers are the norm, but breeders in Europe and the United States have provided us with leaves of green to bronze and flowers of white, purple, pink, and red; some may be selections of *Dicentra eximia* or *D. formosa*, or hybrids between the two species. 'Bacchanal' has deep rose flowers; 'Boothman's Vari-

Dicentra 'Boothman's Variety'

Dicentra 'Luxuriant'

ety' and 'Luxuriant' are excellent plants with light rosy red flowers; and white flowers can be enjoyed on 'Langtrees' and 'Snowflakes'. Many other cultivars, equally handsome, are also available. Partial shade (that is to say, morning sun) is recommended, but too much shade results in few flowers. Hardy in zones 3 to 8.

Want a plant that stops people in their tracks? Try *Dicentra scandens*, a climber with hundreds of yellow lockets of flowers. They meander through shrubs or up a trellis, growing vigorously from dozens of twining stems. Plants grow about 10' tall, and starting in late spring or early summer, yellow flowers cover the vine. The leaves and flowers of this yellow climbing bleeding heart are much smaller than those of vines like *Clematis*, but the uniqueness and vigor of this plant will more than make up for the effort needed to find it. Plants require more sun than other species of bleeding heart; full afternoon sun should still be avoided. Hardy in zones 6 to 8.

Dicentra scandens 'Athens Yellow' came from seedlings of a plant brought to Athens, Georgia, from Ireland; it has brighter yellow flowers and is more vigorous than the type. Most plants sold are likely this cultivar.

Dicentra spectabilis, common bleeding heart, is a popular garden plant that undergoes a major metamorphosis each year, emerging early in the spring and going dormant in late summer. Gardeners sometimes wonder what they did wrong as they watch plants disappear between June and August, depending on summer temperatures and rainfall. This is a normal part of the growth cycle for this Japanese species. Annuals can be used to cover the soil left bare by plants that have died back. In early spring, plants push through the ground, their compound leaves and flowers already formed. They can make substantial specimens, growing 4' tall and equally wide on well established plantings. The pink to red lockets of flowers, whose hearts are no doubt bleeding, hang down from the flower stems in spring and persist for four to six weeks, depending on temperature.

Dicentra 'Langtrees'

Dicentra 'Snowflakes'

Dicentra scandens 'Athens Yellow'

Dicentra scandens 'Athens Yellow'

Dicentra spectabilis

MORE →

Dicentra spectabilis 'Alba'

The pink-flowered species itself is by far the most common. 'Alba', with its white rather than red hearts and slightly smaller plants, is different but no less beautiful. Place plants in friable, loose soil. Plants tolerate full sun in the North, but prefer afternoon shade in most other areas. The more sun, the more the soil dries out and the faster plants go dormant; on the other hand, too much shade results in few flowers. Hardy in zones 3 to 7.

Dicentra spectabilis

Dicentra spectabilis 'Alba'

Digitalis

FOXGLOVE

Best known for that wonderful old English weed, *Digitalis purpurea* (common foxglove), the genus includes some other outstanding members as well. All are characterized by many flowers held on long spike-like rods in spring or early summer, and slowly but surely, other lesser known members of the genus are strutting their stuff. All the same, at least ten times more *D. purpurea* is sold than all other foxgloves together, the result not only of its availability but also of its functionality and timeless beauty.

The "grandiflora" of *Digitalis grandiflora* (yellow foxglove) means "large-flowered"—a bit of a misnomer. Large they are compared to some foxgloves (such as *D. lutea*, another yellow-flowered species), but they are smaller than those of common foxglove and others. They do, however, have a couple of good characteristics going for them. First, the yellow flowers, with their brown spots within, are rather hand-

Digitalis grandiflora

some, and second, the plants are much more persistent than *D. purpurea* in the landscape. These true perennials should return for at least five years; eight- to ten- year stints are not uncommon. They grow 2–3' tall and tolerate partial shade and moist conditions. Hardy in zones 3 to 8.

The diversity of the genus *Digitalis* never ceases to amaze me, and when I first discovered strawberry foxglove, *Digitalis ×mertonensis*, I was charmed. The rosette of large leaves is darker green than common foxglove and far more ornamental. The large pink to rose-red flowers—like a ripening strawberry, not yet edible—are borne on one side of the flower stem only. Put about three plants together so that sufficient flowers are massed to catch the eye. These 2–3' tall hybrids persist for about two to three years, longer than *D. purpurea* but shorter lived than *D. grandiflora*. Place in partial shade and moist soils. Hardy in zones 3 to 8.

Most of the foxgloves we use in our gardens are native to the European continent and the United Kingdom. A native stand of *Digitalis purpurea*, common foxglove, in Ireland or Scotland is as breathtaking to the American traveler as our stands of asters are to the visiting European. As long as one remembers that *D. purpurea* is a biennial and needs to be purchased either as a one-year-old plant in the spring or planted in the fall to receive sufficient cold, then this species is a no-brainer. The need for a cold treatment is absolute, but since it is so popular, nobody seems to give it much thought. Plants may produce 4' long flower spikes in the spring in any number of colors. In flower, they are awesome, but leaves decline soon after, as

Digitalis grandiflora

Digitalis lutea

Digitalis lutea

Digitalis ×mertonensis in winter

Digitalis ×mertonensis

Digitalis ×mertonensis

MORE →

Digitalis purpurea with tulips

Wild stand of *Digitalis purpurea*

Digitalis purpurea 'Giant Shirley'

Digitalis purpurea 'Alba'

Digitalis purpurea 'Alba'

Digitalis purpurea 'Giant Shirley'

plants die back. In short, plant removal might as well be done sooner than later. All plants are raised from seed.

Separate colors of white, apricot, or yellow flowers can sometimes be found but most cultivars of *Digitalis purpurea* are available as a mixed bag of colors. Some of the best loved are the tall Excelsior Group, the shorter but equally brilliant Foxy Group, and 'Giant Shirley'. The admiration of these noble plants is shared by hundreds of gardeners and millions of bees, both of whom are ever present when the flowers open. While the pharmacological properties of common foxglove are well known, nobody but my hypochondriac friends tucks it in the garden for that reason. Place in partial shade; provide morning sun and moist organic soils. Hardy in zones 4 to 8.

Disporum

FAIRY BELLS

One of the many plants that separates a lover of gardening from a lover of garden design is fairy bells. *Disporum* consists of about fifteen species of shade tolerant woodland-residing plants, native to North America, China, and Japan. The plant I enjoy most is *Disporum sessile*, the Japanese sessile fairy bells. In particular, its yellow-flowered variety *flavum* ranks right up there in my great shade plant list, alongside some of the Jacks (*Aris-*

aema) and gingers (*Asarum*). In the spring, the plants—flowers already formed—rise up out of the ground with a mighty stretch, first unfurling their light green foliage, then showing off their butter-yellow flowers as they emerge from their leafy winter quarters. Sounds pretty impressive, until you realize I am referring to a plant that is only 2–3' tall and 12" wide. Many people who visit the Armitage garden quickly agree with me. Place three plants about 8" apart and you will be rewarded with a stunning sight. The flowers persist for many weeks, followed by round green fruit. Plant in

Disporum sessile var. *flavum*

Emerging stems of *Disporum sessile* var. *flavum*

Disporum sessile var. *flavum*

Disporum sessile 'Variegatum'

MORE →

partial shade; dense shade is tolerated but not appreciated. Avoid heavy clay soils. Hardy in zones 4 to 8.

'Variegatum', a selection of *Disporum sessile*, is not as tall or as vigorous, but its white-and-green variegated foliage is pleasing to the eye. Plants are more stoloniferous and thus spread around more easily than variety *flavum*, but they are only about 12" tall. The flowers tend to blend into the foliage because they too are variegated; the green fruit which follows continues to be ornamental. A fun plant—get down on your hands and knees to admire it fully. Partial to full shade, zones 4 to 8.

Disporum sessile 'Variegatum'

Fruit of *Disporum sessile* 'Variegatum'

Dryopteris

WOOD FERN

So much of the Armitage garden is in deep shade that at first I despaired of ever finding plants sufficiently tough for the area. I quickly realized, however, how lucky I was to have some dense shade because it allowed me to use all sorts of shade lovers, particularly the ferns. And in my research, I found that some of the wood ferns are among the toughest, adaptable, and versatile ferns available to the American grower.

Dryopteris erythrosora, autumn

Dryopteris erythrosora with *Polygonatum*

fern, has some excellent characteristics, including bronze to almost red new growth and an evergreen habit. They tolerate deep shade (where they can be united with other shade lovers like Solomon's seal, *Polygonatum*) but are also adaptable to areas of full morning sun. Plants can grow 2–3' tall and equally wide, making a significant impact in the shaded garden. The large fronds, up to 2' long and 10–12" wide, are the best part of the fern by far, emerging in the spring and tending to stay bronze throughout the summer, resulting in an subtle colorful look, and not just a filler for shade. One of the best selections from the stable of

New growth of *Dryopteris erythrosora*

Dryopteris erythrosora

ferns available to gardeners. Plant in rich organic soils, zones 5 to 9.

Another outstanding tough fern is *Dryopteris filix-mas*, male fern. For years I have used male fern in the deepest shade and worst soil in the Armitage dungeon, and it is the one fern I can count on to return year after year, better than ever. For all its vigor, the planting remains in one spot and does not run all over the place. Nothing colorful, nothing flashy, just a good blue-collar plant. The several plants that have been selected by male fernites, such as 'Barnesii' and 'Polydactyla', generally differ in the shape of the pinnae (leaflets) and tips of the fronds. 'Cristata Martindale' is quite remarkable for a fern gone amok: plants have terminal crests, and the pinnae all curve toward the apex of the frond— it is distinctive and an eye-catcher. Shade, moisture, and reasonable soil help in the performance of the plant, but they are tolerant of drying out and poor soils. Hardy in zones 4 to 8.

Dryopteris marginalis, the marginal wood fern, is not as colorful as others but it is a hardy, useful plant for moderate to deep shade. The "marginal" part of its name comes from the arrangement of the spore cases on the margins of the undersides of the fronds. The fiddleheads (the unfolding fronds) are covered with a golden brown "fur," and the leathery fronds remain evergreen. Plants are about 2' tall and 2' wide. They are better ferns for the North than the South, preferring moist cool climes for best performance. Place in drifts of six to twelve plants in organically rich, moisture-retentive soils. Hardy in zones 4 to 7.

Dryopteris filix-mas

Dryopteris filix-mas 'Barnesii'

Dryopteris filix-mas 'Polydactyla'

Dryopteris filix-mas 'Cristata Martindale'

Underside of *Dryopteris marginalis*

Dryopteris marginalis

Echinacea

CONEFLOWER

"What can I put in the yard that even I can't kill?" I hear this a lot from husbands upon whom severe conjugal stress has been placed. Several correct answers present themselves, depending on the degree of stress or fright I see in the questioner's eyes. One is the coneflower, *Echinacea*, a group of plants for all gardeners, regardless of experience or ability. These purple, pink, and even yellow flowers from the great American midland are easy to recommend and almost indestructible.

Hardly one's idea of a full-size flower but certainly one that gets attention and a guaranteed second look is *Echinacea pallida*, the pale coneflower. The thin pale pink to purple ray flowers take a little getting used to; however,

Echinacea pallida

Echinacea paradoxa

the combination of those flowers and the central disk is quite lovely. Deep green leaves are found at the base, and the flower stems rise to about 3' in height. Plants are not as popular or as persistent as their more famous cousin, *E. purpurea*, but they return for three to five years, asking little in the way of care. Plant in full sun, in almost any soil—include at least three plants, spaced a foot apart, to create a fuller looking group of flowers. Blooms occur in summer. Hardy in zones 4 to 8.

I first saw *Echinacea paradoxa*, yellow coneflower, in the great Missouri Botanical Garden, a must-see garden for anyone in the country. Plants look like common purple coneflower, although not as vigorous, but they have yellowish ray flowers rather than pale pink or purple ones. "This is a paradox," my guide said, and I nodded sagely— then quickly went to the library to look up the meaning of the word. Regardless of how much confusion this plant might elicit, it is handsome and well worth placing in a sunny area of the

garden. Height is only 2–3', and the flowers range from light yellow to merest tinges of sunshine. Not as persistent as *E. purpurea*, but few plants are. Hardy in zones 4 to 7.

"Take your echinacea pill, dear" says my health-conscious wife as she presents me a tidy concoction of *Echinacea purpurea* (purple coneflower), ginkgo, and goldenseal to swallow. I no longer think of my stomach as a functioning organ of digestion but rather as my private botanical garden. On the other hand, after downing onion blossoms and ribs at the local restaurant, who am I to complain about healthy additives?

Medicinal uses aside, can you imagine Lewis and Clark first setting their eyes upon the majestic vistas of grasses and wildflowers and enormous populations of animal life in their journey across the American prairie? How I enjoy reading the accounts of their expedition! Even a trip to the great prairie garden at the Holden Arboretum outside Cleveland or to the natural Midwest area at the

Echinacea purpurea in a prairie

Chicago Botanical Garden fills me with joy and sadness—joy at the incredible diversity of plants that graced the land, mixed with sadness that so few of these areas exist any longer. I thank the visionary leaders of our arboreta and botanical gardens for preserving some of our natural history, and doing it so well.

This historical discourse does have a point, I think. One of the occupants of the great American prairie is *Echinacea purpurea*, the purple coneflower, which has made the transition to the backyard as well as any native plant and better than most. The ray flowers often droop downward off the black central cone, and plants rise in height from 3' in full sun to 4–5' in partial shade. They are best if planted in full sun in almost any soil. I love seeing

them alone or together with lilies or loosestrife (*Lysimachia*).

Numerous selections of *Echinacea purpurea* have made for wider and more horizontally oriented ray flowers and various shades of purple. I don't believe that all these are a great deal better than what Lewis and Clark saw, but they are neater and fuller in flower

Echinacea purpurea 'Bright Star'

than the original and so fit in better with current garden styles. Some of the purplish cultivars include 'Bright Star', with its rosier flowers; 'Bravado', with somewhat larger flowers; 'Magnus', in which the ray flowers are supposed to be more horizontal than

Echinacea purpurea 'Bravado'

Echinacea purpurea 'White Swan'

Echinacea purpurea 'White Lustre' with *Lilium*

Echinacea purpurea 'Magnus'

Echinacea purpurea 'Robert Bloom'

Echinacea purpurea 'White Lustre'

MORE →

those of the species; and 'Robert Bloom', with even larger flowers than most others. (In truth, if all purple cultivars were lined up, I doubt seriously whether one person in a hundred could tell you which cultivar was which; I would be in the group of ninety-nine, that is for sure.) White-flowered cultivars are shorter in habit but easier to mix and match in the garden. 'White Swan' and 'White Lustre', whose subtle differences are found in the color of the cone and orientation of the ray flowers, are both good. Full sun, zones 3 to 8.

Echinops ritro

GLOBE THISTLE

Blue flowers will always occupy an important place in gardens, perhaps because there never seems to be enough of them from which to choose. Provide a vigorous grower with interesting round blue flower heads, and a popular plant arises. I've always enjoyed *Echinops ritro* mixed in with other equally vigorous plants like the coneflowers and sea hollies. The flower heads and leaves are rather coarse and prickly to the touch, thus the common name. They make excellent cut flowers, fresh or dried, but picking them is not a lot of fun. Plants grow to 5' in height and 3–4' across. They attract swarms of bees, so check the flowers before you put your nose too close. They also attract aphids, which can disfigure both leaves and flowers.

A few selections are offered, but they are all similar to each other and if truth be told, similar to the species itself. 'Taplow Blue' is the main listing in catalogs and nurseries and grows 2–3' tall; 'Taplow Purple' is, well, a little more purple. 'Blue Cloud' has somewhat bluer flowers. Plant in full sun, in any reasonable garden soil, zones 3 to 7.

Echinops ritro

Echinops ritro 'Taplow Blue'

Echinops ritro 'Taplow Purple'

Echinops ritro 'Blue Cloud'

Aphid damage on *Echinops ritro*

Echinops ritro 'Taplow Blue'

Epimedium grandiflorum 'Rose Queen'

Epimedium grandiflorum 'Lilafee'

Epimedium

BARRENWORT

A wonderful genus of low growers for the woodland and shaded area of the garden. A few years ago, only two or three species were available but recent explorations in Japan and China and excellent breeding efforts have brought additional species and more interest to this fine group of plants. If you have shade, you should have epimediums.

Epimedium grandiflorum, longspur barrenwort, is easiest to find in nurseries and one of the finest species sold. The deciduous plants have the typical oblique leaves of the genus; the tough good-looking foliage makes them excellent as ground covers under trees and in woodland environments. The flowers are among the largest in the available barrenworts, sporting long spurs on pale pink flowers in early spring. The flowers, which often emerge before or at the same time as the foliage, persist for four to six weeks. While tolerant of deep shade, they perform better in an area with morning sun and afternoon shade.

Similarly, provide moisture when needed, especially if plants are competing with tree roots. They are drought tolerant but not that tolerant.

'Rose Queen' is the most common cultivar of *Epimedium grandiflorum* offered, with outstanding rosy red flowers. The lilac flowers of 'Lilafee' are not quite as large, but they are outstanding when they stand above the foliage. Subspecies *koreanum* has long spurs, like 'Rose Queen', but its flowers are much less pink. Hardy in zones 5 to 8.

The small white flowers of Young's barrenwort, *Epimedium* ×*youngianum*, found in cultivars like its 'Niveum' and 'Milky Way', are the opposite of the splash and size of *E. grandiflorum*

Epimedium grandiflorum subsp. *koreanum*

Epimedium grandiflorum as a ground cover

MORE →

Epimedium ×youngianum 'Milky Way'

Epimedium ×youngianum 'Roseum'

Epimedium ×youngianum 'Niveum'

'Rose Queen'. The light rose flowers of *E. ×youngianum* 'Roseum' also have leaves with rosy red margins in the spring. Smaller in every respect than *E. grandiflorum*, but equally handsome and carefree.

I love *Epimedium ×rubrum*, red barrenwort, for a couple of reasons. In the Armitage potpourri I call a garden, the plants remain evergreen and are even reasonably handsome in the winter, not just plants with leaves that refuse to fall off. The new leaves, which emerge in early spring, are suffused with red, both around the margins and splotched on the bronzy leaf blades.

The red flowers are not large, but they appear in numbers and persist as well as any other barrenwort. *Epimedium ×rubrum* is easy, undemanding, and colorful. For tolerance to shade, it has few equals. As with *E. grandiflorum*, providing an area of morning sun results in even better performance. Hardy in zones 5 to 8.

Let's face it. All barrenworts share many similarities: they are low growing, work well in the shade, and are seldom noticed by those admiring some noble beech or elegant elm. The comments that accompany the other barrenworts mentioned can be dittoed

Epimedium ×youngianum 'Niveum'

Epimedium ×rubrum

Epimedium ×rubrum

here for *Epimedium* ×*versicolor*, the bicolor barrenwort, but with a few exceptions. The flowers are the earliest to emerge, appearing before the foliage. The old leaves are also evergreen but should be removed as soon as you spy the first flower. They only detract from the wonderful yellow flowers, and additional foliage will appear to take the place of what you remove. An exceptionally good plant, tough as nails and reliable. Full to partial shade, moisture is appreciated. Hardy in zones 4 to 8.

Of the several selections of *Epimedium* ×*versicolor* offered, the main one is 'Sulphureum', with flowers ranging from soft yellow to almost butter-yellow. While we are talking about yellow-flowered epimediums, I cannot in all conscience omit one of the most vigorous and reliable of the worts, *E.* ×*perralchium* 'Frohnleiten', with its dark green leathery leaves and wonderful bright flowers. Not only is it outstanding when it is supposed to be, it is the best epimedium for winter foliage. A winner in all respects!

Epimedium ×*rubrum* in winter

Epimedium ×*rubrum*

Epimedium ×*perralchium* 'Frohnleiten' in winter

Epimedium ×*versicolor* 'Sulphureum'

Epimedium ×*versicolor* 'Sulphureum'

Epimedium ×*perralchium* 'Frohnleiten'

Epimedium ×*perralchium* 'Frohnleiten'

Eremurus aitchisonii

Eremurus aitchisonii

Eremurus

FOXTAIL LILY

Eremurus is not a plant for people checking out the petunias at K-Mart but rather a plant for the daring and curious. This most wonderful bulbous specimen is available mainly through mail-order catalogs and specialty nurseries. To see it is to become a believer, and viewing the tall stately candles of white, orange, yellow, and pastels is a great treat. Plants range 3–8' in height, poking through the soil in spring and reaching up and up to flower in late spring and summer. Like a grand fireworks show, the foxtail lilies rocket with momentary greatness, then totally disappear, nothing but an explosive memory. One doesn't usually think of light flowers as an exploding fireworks show, but when the creamy pink-white candles of *Eremurus aitchisonii* and the pure white missiles of *E. himalaicus* or pastels like the Highdown hybrids of *E.* ×*shelfordii* (*E.* ×*isabellinus*) are alight, you may change your definition of fireworks. The yellows of *E. stenophyllus* can easily be categorized as flaming. In most gardens, plants seldom return for more than a year or two, but if they are protected and luck is with you, a few more years of fireworks may be yours. Plant the tentacle-like rhizomes in a large hole, so that the tentacles are not cramped up. They must not be allowed to dry out before planting, and moisture is necessary after planting. Place other plants around them so once they disappear, they will not be missed. Enjoy the show. Full sun, hardy in zones 5 to 7.

Eremurus ×*shelfordii* Highdown hybrids

Eremurus himalaicus

Eryngium

SEA HOLLY

Live near the sea, plant sea oats. Or sea kale, or sea thrift, or simply enjoy the seaside with sea urchins. If you love the salt spray but don't live near the sea, importing sea holly from the Mediterranean coast to the suburban garden may help a little. A number of fine *Eryngium* species can be found, and while not all are even remotely native to a coastline, they are all colorful (usually silver or bluish) and interesting. Many make long-lasting cut flowers, but beware of the prickly blooms —they are much better to look at than to handle.

Some of the largest flowers and most colorful plants in the genus belong to *Eryngium alpinum*, the alpine sea holly. Certainly in northern climes, a blue tinge will appear on the stems and flowers of this species in mid to late summer, when the flowers are at their peak. Even when not at their peak, the immature flowers can be as handsome as the finished product. The plants grow about 2–2¹/₂' tall, and soft bracts extend from the flowers. Soft is relative, however, and even these bracts can provide some unwanted pain. The leaves are coarse and dull green.

Eryngium alpinum 'Amethyst', with lighter blue flowers and stems, is a popular cultivar; 'Blue Star' is probably the most common, with lavender-blue bracts. 'Superbum' has the largest flowers and is an excellent selection. Place in well-drained soils and full sun. Their maritime upbringing makes alpine sea hollies more comfortable in sand than clay. Hardy in zones 4 to 7.

Eryngium giganteum, or Miss Willmott's ghost, is the plant for people who have everything. Named for an eccentric English gardeness, it provides history, surprise, and ornamental value, with large flowers of steely silver rather than blue. These 3–4' tall

Immature flowers of *Eryngium alpinum*

Eryngium giganteum in a border

Eryngium alpinum

Eryngium alpinum 'Blue Star'

MORE →

biennials tend to disappear after flowering, but in areas where the Lady is happy, she will return from seed—if not the next year, then the year after, sneaking up on you like the ghost she is. Unfortunately, Miss Willmott's ghost is not happy in the South and is not often seen even in the East; but she haunts the Northwest with glee.

Eryngium giganteum 'Silver Ghost' is shorter (about 2' tall) and has large heads of gray-white flowers—not quite as ghostly but otherwise differing little from the species. Plant in well-drained soils, or sandy soils in full sun. Hardy in zones 4 to 8.

The genus *Eryngium* is remarkable in its ability to confuse gardeners with flowers and foliage that to most of us look like anything but sea holly. The eastern native *Eryngium yuccafolium*, rattlesnake master, supposedly cures rattlesnake bites or even drives the snakes away. My kind of plant in snake country. The leaves are narrow (like those of yucca), and the small flowers are creamy white and almost without bracts. Plants grow about 3–4' tall.

The foliage of *Eryngium agavifolium*, agave sea holly, looks like an agave and is similar to the rattlesnake tamer, only much more spiny. Both *E. agavifolium* and *E. yuccafolium* are heat tolerant and more amenable to poor soils than other more exotic species. The best part about them is that they are fun to have in the garden: they keep people guessing as to just what those plants want to be when they grow up. Full sun, reasonable soils. Both hardy in zones 5 to 9.

Eryngium giganteum

Eryngium giganteum 'Silver Ghost'

Eryngium agavifolium

Eryngium yuccafolium

Eryngium yuccafolium

Eupatorium

JOE-PYE WEED

To see some of our native plants glowing on their own and complementing other ornamentals makes you proud to be an American; too bad you often have to go overseas to appreciate the glow. This was brought home most clearly when I took a fall trip to the British Isles and admired the Joe-pye weeds towering over our asters and black-eyed Susans. I knew I would see asters and Susans, but I wasn't prepared for all the Joes. About half a dozen species are found in American gardens, and as a group they are attracting converts. Particularly good for the autumn, but some are impressive all season.

"Where did these fall-flowering ageratums come from? That is some bedding plant variety!" That was the first thing I thought when I came upon *Eupatorium coelestinum* (*Conoclinum coelestinum*; hardy ageratum) in a Midwest garden. Since I was supposed to be the expert, I kept quiet and listened as the real expert, the gardener, cursed this "darn weed." That is why experts are experts: they keep their mouths shut and learn from gardeners. The darn weed is pale blue to lavender and grows about 2–3' tall. The lanky growth makes it a little weedy, and more people enjoy it at the edge of the woods rather than in the middle of the garden. It is essentially unnoticed until the flowers appear in late summer and fall, and then it is everywhere. A terrific plant, much more tolerant of heat than most other members of the genus. A white selection, 'Album', is also available. 'Wayside' is a bit more compact and shorter, and does not appear to be as weedy as the species. Partial shade, good moisture. Hardy in zones 6 (perhaps 5) to 10.

Native in much of the eastern half of the country, *Eupatorium purpureum* (Joe-pye weed) is particularly impressive in the Smoky and Appalachian ranges. In the garden, where a little fertilizer and water are provided, I have seen 10' tall backdrops provided by half a dozen plants, each topped with large inflorescences of claret-colored flowers in the fall. They are best in areas with cool summers and consistent rainfall, so unfortunately, the Armitage garden in north Georgia can only offer some puny 3' tall excuses for the species. But when happy Joe-pyes are complementing the asters, the rudbeckias, and the daylilies in the fall, the yard is magically transformed into a garden. Butterflies, bees, and birds swarm about, and they look

Eupatorium purpureum with *Pennisetum*

MORE →

Eupatorium coelestinum

Eupatorium purpureum

Eupatorium coelestinum 'Album'

Eupatorium purpureum

Eupatorium maculatum 'Gateway'

Eupatorium coelestinum 'Wayside'

Eupatorium maculatum 'Gateway'

almost as good as they did when Joe Pye discovered them in the mountains.

Nurseries and catalogs offer similar plants, such as *Eupatorium maculatum*, spotted Joe-pye weed. The main difference is that *E. maculatum* has purple-spotted stems; otherwise, the habit and flowers of the two species are nearly the same. 'Atropurpureum', a purple-leaved selection, provides stunning purple hues from soil level to flower top. If the thought of 8' tall plants in the garden is a little overwhelming, *E. maculatum* 'Gateway', smaller but still a robust 4–5' tall, is otherwise similar to the type. Provide full sun and well-drained soils for both species, hardy in zones 4 to 7.

A fine native plant, *Eupatorium rugosum* (white snakeroot) is beginning to attract a loyal following among adventurous gardeners. Plants grow to 5'

in height and are topped by white flowers in summer and early fall. I have seen excellent specimens in European and American gardens, but some of the best were in the outstanding display gardens at Blue Meadow Nursery in the Berkshires of western Massachusetts. Cold temperatures are no problem, but heat is not appreciated. A most useful cultivar, 'Chocolate', is admired more for its bronze to purple foliage than for its flowers. Plants are only 2' tall and are more shade tolerant than the species. White flowers also appear in late summer. Full sun and reasonable soils are needed. Hardy in zones 3 to 7.

Euphorbia characias subsp. *wulfenii*

Eupatorium rugosum

Eupatorium rugosum 'Chocolate'

Euphorbia characias subsp. *wulfenii*

Euphorbia

SPURGE

So many spurges, so little time! In a genus of nearly two thousand species, where does one start? A glance through some catalogs may get one off the starting block. I certainly have tried a good number, with occasional success, but have killed my fair share as well.

The handsome 4–5' tall upright plants of *Euphorbia characias*, Mediterranean spurge, have blue-green foliage and yellow bracts that are outstanding in early spring. That the species is native to the Mediterranean region should provide a hint as to its range of cold and moisture tolerance, but where winters are reasonably mild (zone 7 south) and soils not waterlogged, plants thrive and reseed with abandon. Although they persist for only two years, another population generally is starting up while others are dying down.

The most common variant, subspecies *wulfenii*, is shorter (3–4' tall) but otherwise quite similar. 'John Tomelson' bears showy bright yellow bracts, and 'Lambrook Gold' has

MORE →

Euphorbia characias 'John Tomelson'

Euphorbia characias 'Lambrook Gold'

bracts so yellow that one is advised to put on sunglasses before viewing them. 'Ember Queen', a variegated selection of the species, is simply a must-have plant. Full sun to partial shade, well-drained soils are essential. Hardy in zones 6 (perhaps 5) to 8.

A relative newcomer to the spurge scene, *Euphorbia dulcis* (chameleon spurge) is represented by the purple-leaved cultivar 'Chameleon', thus its common name. Growing in mounds rather than upright or spreading, it can be beautiful in combination with green or white plants around it. Unfortunately its range of adaptability is rather narrow: it looks poor where too warm and dies where too cold. Worth a try, however, if loose change is rattling around in your pocket. Full sun, reasonable soils, hardy in zones 5 to 7.

Most garden spurges bear yellow bracts but Griffith's spurge, *Euphorbia griffithii*, has red to orange ones. Vigorous growth with thick stems and fleshy leaves make this a winner where it can be grown. Like *E. dulcis*, its range of happiness is somewhat limited in this country. In the Northwest, it thrives; in the Midwest, it also does well; in the South, it dies. 'Fireglow' (with bright orange-red bracts) and 'Dixter' (less red, more orange) are similar to the species. Both are excellent but well mixed-up in the trade. Full sun, well-drained soils. Hardy in zones 5 to 7.

Euphorbia myrsinites, the myrtle spurge, is probably the most reliable of the ornamental spurges. The stems are covered in whorled blue-green leaves and terminate in sulfur-colored

Euphorbia characias 'Ember Queen'

Euphorbia dulcis 'Chameleon'

Euphorbia dulcis 'Chameleon'

Euphorbia griffithii 'Fireglow'

bracts. A great plant, but in areas of the Southeast and Southwest, where it reseeds with abandon, it may be considered both a handsome 6–9" ground cover or a pernicious weed. On the other end of the height spectrum is *E. lathyris*, caper spurge, a fun-to-grow plant with an upright habit, wonderful green flowers, and bluish fruit that resembles capers. Its reputation of discouraging gophers and voles is suspect, but it certainly attracts attention. Great fun! Full sun to partial shade, moist soils. Myrtle spurge is hardy in zones 5 to 9, caper spurge in zones 6 to 9.

Euphorbia myrsinites

Euphorbia myrsinites

Euphorbia lathyris

Euphorbia myrsinites

Euphorbia lathyris

Euphorbia griffithii 'Dixter'

Euphorbia lathyris

Gaillardia ×grandiflora

BLANKETFLOWER

Gaillardia ×grandiflora is one of those plants that doesn't get much respect even though it is tough, colorful, and easily available. Perhaps it is the lack of challenge that makes gardeners shrug their shoulders when asked about blanketflower. Like the good masochists we are, it may simply be too simple. Plants may grow up to 3' tall, but most available cultivars are shorter and more compact, usually extending only 12–18". The daisy flowers are made up of many colors (thus the "blanket" in blanketflower) and may be up to 2½" wide. The drawback to *G. ×grandiflora* is that it is not particularly long-lived: four years is an excellent run, two years is frustratingly normal.

A good many cultivars have been developed. Particularly popular are 'Goblin' and 'Golden Goblin', two dwarf selections. I think 'Goblin' is exceptional, but I have no use for the hideous double flowers of the Lollipop series. Flowers of *Gaillardia ×grandiflora* all have multicolored blooms consisting of crimson, yellow, and burgundy. Hardy in zones 2 to 9.

One of the parents of blanketflower is *Gaillardia pulchella*, an agreeable half-hardy (zone 8) species with multicolored flowers. Its selection 'Yellow Plumes' is a great improvement on the species. Full sun and well-drained soils are necessary. Good drainage is essential, otherwise plants rot overnight.

Gaillardia ×grandiflora 'Goblin'

Gaillardia ×grandiflora 'Goblin'

Gaillardia ×grandiflora 'Golden Goblin'

Gaillardia ×grandiflora Lollipop series

Gaillardia pulchella 'Yellow Plumes'

Gaura

The generic name comes from the Greek *gauros* ("superb"), a probable reference to the flowers of this genus, which consists of about twenty species; but only *Gaura lindheimeri*, our Texas native, has made its way into American gardens. The plants have become popular because they are tough as nails, putting up with blistering sun, terrible soils, and parking lot abuse. The foliage is handsome enough, although half a dozen plants are needed to make a full planting. It is, however, those superb white flowers suffused with pink that entrance gardeners. They are held well above the foliage and wave in the breeze like a swirl of butterflies.

An exciting addition is 'Siskiyou Pink', introduced by Baldassare Mineo of Siskiyou Rare Plant Nursery in Medford, Oregon. The pink to rosy red flowers of this selection make a handsome contrast to the leaves and remain colorful even during the heat of summer. 'Corrie's Gold' is a variegated cultivar with yellow-and-green foliage and white flowers. Full sun is necessary, otherwise no particular needs. Hardy in zones 5 to 8.

Gaura lindheimeri 'Siskiyou Pink'

Gaura lindheimeri 'Siskiyou Pink'

Gaura lindheimeri

Gaura lindheimeri

Geranium ×*cantabrigiense* 'Biokovo Karmina'

Geranium ×*cantabrigiense* 'Biokovo'

Geranium ×*cantabrigiense* 'Biokovo'

Geranium cinereum 'Ballerina'

Geranium

CRANESBILL

Geraniums are a collector's dream, so diverse that they can be collected like fine silver. From prostrate dwarfs to those that scramble through shrubs, from purple to rosy red flowers, geraniums provide something for everyone. As a gardener, I have gone through my "geranium stage of life" and no longer have to try every new (or old) geranium that finds its way into a catalog or the garden center. Now I can waste my money on other groups of plants, trying to find a single good one in a hundred tries. (Finding that one plant is the holy grail of the gardener —the ninety-nine others are quickly forgotten.) All geraniums have palmate (shaped like a hand) leaves, five-petaled flowers, and fruit reminiscent of a crane's bill, hence the common name.

A hybrid from England between the ground cover *Geranium macrorrhizum* and the European native *G. dalmaticum*, the Cambridge geranium (*Geranium* ×*cantabrigiense*) provides aggressive growth with handsome flowers. The purple-violet flowers persist longer than many species because little seed is produced, so the plants remain in flower for many weeks. Plants seldom grow taller than 12", 6–8" being more common.

Geranium ×*cantabrigiense* 'Biokovo', with white flowers tinged pink, is the best-known selection—an excellent cultivar that has done well in many parts of the country. 'Biokovo Karmina' bears raspberry-red flowers. Both are about 10" tall and bear little seed. Full sun to partial shade, hardy in zones 5 to 7.

Geranium cinereum, the grayleaf geranium, is the plant for rock gardeners or those who simply enjoy the more subtle aspects of plant composition. The small leaves of this species are gray-green, and the flowers may be rose-red or pink, usually with a fine pattern of colorful veins in the petals. Given their propensity to die in wet soils and hot weather, they should be placed in areas of exceptional drainage, that is to say rock gardens, where they will fare much better. I think 'Ballerina', with its lilac-pink flowers, and 'Splendens', with deep magenta, dark-centered blossoms, are outstanding. Both stand 4–6" tall and flower early in the spring. 'Laurence Flatman' is similar to 'Ballerina' and has deep venation to the pink flowers. Full sun, excellent drainage. Hardy in zones 5 to 7.

Without doubt, one of the best geraniums for both hot and cool climates is Endress's geranium, *Geranium endressii*. 'Wargrave Pink', the only selection offered, has enjoyed consistently good reviews throughout the country. Plants can grow up to 18" tall and are covered in spring by one-inch-wide, notch-petaled, salmon-pink flowers. One of my choices for the beginning geranium collector. Partial shade, good drainage, zones 4 to 7.

Geranium psilostemon, the Armenian geranium, is a plant that can't fig-

ure out whether it should be a vine or a normal plant—and therefore has become a scrambler. Its long stems, if properly maintained, form shrublike

mounds of light green foliage, 3' tall and equally wide. Like a kid after a playground fight, each magenta flower sports a large black eye. This is a big

Geranium cinereum 'Splendens'

Geranium cinereum 'Laurence Flatman'

Geranium endressii 'Wargrave Pink'

Geranium endressii

Geranium endressii

MORE →

Geranium endressii 'Wargrave Pink'

Geranium psilostemon 'Bressingham Flair'

Geranium psilostemon

Geranium psilostemon

Geranium 'Ann Folkard' with *Alchemilla*

lanky plant, but if supported, it is a people stopper. 'Bressingham Flair' is similar but not quite as big and a little easier to use.

'Ann Folkard', a natural hybrid involving *Geranium psilostemon*, is a true scrambler, growing through and over small shrubs. The leaves are almost chartreuse, and the flowers have similar rose-red to magenta flowers. Where happy, 'Ann Folkard' takes the form of the plant it is growing through. It seems to be happiest on the West Coast, but gardeners in the Midwest and Northeast are claiming success. The South has not been as friendly. Full sun to partial shade, good drainage, zones 5 to 7.

Geranium sanguineum, bloody cranesbill, is the toughest species in the genus. Plants thrive in the North and the South, from the West Coast to the East. When other geraniums let you down, try the bloody cranesbill. The common name sounds like a medieval battle, and it alone makes plants worthy of a little space. Growing about 12" tall, they are covered with magenta flowers beginning in the spring and continuing for six to eight weeks. The leaves are among some of the smallest in this large genus. This cranesbill is not nearly as sexy as many others but makes up for it by its reliability. Selections 'Alan Bloom' and 'Cedric Morris' offer larger flowers than the species

Geranium 'Ann Folkard'

Geranium 'Ann Folkard'

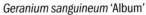

Geranium sanguineum

Geranium sanguineum 'Album'

Geranium sanguineum 'Alan Bloom'

Geranium sanguineum 'Cedric Morris'

Geranium sanguineum 'Glenluce'

Geranium sanguineum 'Minutum'

MORE →

and excellent vigor; 'Minutum' is more dwarf and better suited to sunny rock garden situations.

For me, the magenta flowers of *Geranium sanguineum* are a little hard to take, therefore the white flowers of 'Album', the veined pink flowers of 'Striatum', and the lovely pink flowers of 'Glenluce' are among my favorites. Full sun, reasonable drainage. Hardy in zones 3 to 8.

Geranium sanguineum 'Striatum'

Geranium sanguineum 'Striatum'

Geum

AVENS

Indian chocolate, chocolate root, lion's-beard, old man's whiskers, grandfather's-beard, prairie smoke, cloveroot, and herb bennet are some of the more descriptive common names for members of the genus *Geum*, suggesting that some of them may be hallucinogenic. Regardless, they all beat the heck out of avens (whatever an avens is). At least fifty species of this venerable genus are known but only three or four are consistently offered. The most popular is the Chilean avens, *Geum chiloense*, which is colorful but overrated. A few other species, although more subtle, are outstanding plants for the appropriate situation; I

Geum coccineum 'Werner Arends'

Geum chiloense 'Fire Opal'

enjoy the orange flowers and compact habit of *G. coccineum* 'Werner Arends', especially around *Hakonechloa* and other bright grasses.

Since the plants of *Geum chiloense* are so popular, they must be much better than most of the specimens I have seen. The main cultivars have been in commerce for many years and provide colorful flowers held high above the hairy compound leaves. The excesses of the American climate are tough on most of them, resulting in lots of leaves, few flowers, and short-lived plants. Better performance can be expected in areas of cool summers; the record for these plants is not so good in the heat and humidity of the South and lower Midwest. To be fair, they can look stunning in well-drained but consistently moist soils and cool climes.

Geum chiloense 'Lady Stratheden'

Geum chiloense 'Mrs. Bradshaw'

I have been more a critic than a fan of some of the *Geum chiloense* cultivars for many years. Many people love them, however. The most common selections are 'Lady Stratheden', an 18" plant with buttercup-yellow semi-double flowers, and 'Mrs. Bradshaw', with its scarlet semi-double blossoms. 'Fire Opal' is a brilliant scarlet. Full sun to partial shade, well-drained soils. Hardy in zones 4 to 7.

Geum rivale (Indian chocolate, water avens) is particularly suitable for gardeners who have a boggy area and like the taste of dilute chocolate—although I have a feeling that the chocolate part won't gain the plant many fans. (The thick, brown rootstock may be boiled in water, yielding a brownish liquid that tastes faintly like chocolate.) Regardless of its confectionary

appeal, the plant is wonderful in a cool, moist, partially shaded area. The foliage has seven to thirteen leaflets, and the bell-shaped nodding flowers are usually reddish purple. Even the flower buds are ornamental. I like the white-flowered 'Album', but it is difficult to locate; 'Leonard's Variety' and 'Leonard's Double' are the most common taxa, bearing mahogany-red nodding flowers and deeply cut foliage, in single or double forms, respectively. Terrific in the Northeast and Northwest, but performs poorly in hot, humid summers. Consistent moisture is essential. Partial shade to full sun, hardy in zones 3 to 7.

Geum triflorum is a native American. Its common name, prairie smoke, is derived from the distinctive feathery fruit, which arises from drooping pur-

plish red inflorescences, each made up of two to seven flowers. The 6" long leaves are softly hairy and consist of approximately thirty leaflets. Native to the prairies and the mountains of the West, this 9–12" tall species is icy cold hardy. The flowers of variety *campanu-*

Geum rivale

Geum chiloense 'Mrs. Bradshaw'

Geum rivale

Geum rivale 'Album'

Geum chiloense 'Mrs. Bradshaw' in winter

Geum rivale in bud

Geum rivale 'Leonard's Variety'

MORE →

latum, one of several natural varieties that occur, are more bell-shaped than those of the type. Full sun, consistent moisture, zones 2 to 7.

Geum triflorum

Geum triflorum var. *campanulatum*

Hakonechloa macra 'Aureola' with *Hosta*

Hakonechloa macra

HAKONE GRASS

What a terrific sight! *Hakonechloa macra* (rolls off the tongue, doesn't it?) is a shiny green-and-yellow dwarf grass from Japan that sparkles in the late afternoon sun, bringing alive whatever corner of the garden it calls home. It is only about 9–15" tall, consisting of layers of 4–6" long leaves. The fall flowers, while not colorful, are showy nevertheless; but it is this slow-growing grass's cascading habit, fresh look, and pinkish red fall color that give it its season-long appeal. One of the few colorful grasses at home in partial shade, it consorts freely with the likes of astilbes, hellebores, and hostas.

The golden variegated *Hakonechloa macra* 'Aureola' is particularly handsome, but 'Alboaurea', with white margins on its green leaves, is no slouch either. I like all the cultivars, in fact; I only wish they were a little quicker to grow and more tolerant of the abuse heaped upon them in the Armitage garden. Partial shade, consistent moisture, and compost-laden soils are best. Hardy in zones 6 to 8.

Hakonechloa macra 'Alboaurea'

Hakonechloa macra 'Alboaurea' in flower

Hakonechloa macra 'Aureola'

Helenium

SNEEZEWEED

Obviously someone with hayfever coined the common name for this North American genus. When I am snuffling and sneezing in the fall, I direct my sniffily wrath toward whatever is in flower at the time. Sneezeweed would make me sneeze, which I could verify if I stuck my nose in the middle of a flower, but at that time of year, sticking my nose in the middle of my Hannah dog's coat works just as well. Regardless of its name, *Helenium* offers some fine fall-flowering plants that are real color-makers at that time of year.

Although the genus consists of over thirty species, the cultivars associated with *Helenium autumnale*, common sneezeweed, provide the greatest color and diversity. Its selection 'Rubrum' provides hues in the burnt-orange curve of the rainbow, but it is the hybrids involving this and other species that are special. 'Brilliant' and 'Coppelia' offer additional burnt oranges and other fall tints, while 'Butterpat', 'Gartensonne', 'Riverton Beauty', 'Wyndley', and 'Zinnaeflora' have flowers in various shades of yellow to light orange. With heights approaching

Helenium 'Riverton Beauty'

Helenium 'Zinnaeflora'

Helenium autumnale 'Rubrum'

Helenium 'Gartensonne'

Helenium 'Butterpat'

Helenium 'Wyndley'

MORE →

3–5', the more vigorous cultivars often require staking to keep them from falling over in heavy weather. Cutting them back once during the summer makes them shorter and stronger. Full sun, well-drained soils are best. Hardy in zones 3 to 8.

Helenium 'Brilliant'

Helenium 'Coppelia'

Helianthus angustifolius

Helianthus

SUNFLOWER

A frequent trick question in trivia games: where does a Jerusalem artichoke come from? The surprising answer: from a sunflower. Gets them every time. Jerusalem artichoke, *Helianthus tuberosum*, is a perennial, but by far the best-known species in the genus is the annual sunflower, *H. annuus*, which Kansans adopted as their state flower. That state flower provides oil for cooks and seeds for birders but mainly contributes sunshine to gardens throughout the world. The perennial sunflowers for the garden are equally sunny and beautiful but not nearly as well known. All require full sun, and most are large.

Helianthus angustifolius, the swamp sunflower, is a big plant, growing 5–8' tall and lighting up the fall garden like a spotlight in the night. Plants produce dozens of 1–1½" wide flowers in September and October and continue to do so until frost. The 5–7" long narrow leaves are opposite, entire, and seldom troubled by bugs or fungi. Full sun is

Helianthus angustifolius

an absolute must, resulting in strong stems and many flowers. If grown in shade, plants will stretch to over 8' tall, then fall over. Not a pretty sight. The other drawback to the species is its aggressive nature: it will spread and may soon become a nightmare, a bright, happy-face nightmare, requiring fibbing to friends about why they should be thanking you for the basket of white roots you are a little too eagerly providing. Drainage is not as important as it is to many other perennials. Hardy in zones 6 (with protection) to 8, with reasonably rich soils.

Another large plant, not for the faint of heart, is *Helianthus giganteus* (giant sunflower), a seven-to-twelve-footer that seems to grow about a foot a day. It doesn't spread like *H. angustifolius*, but the clump gets bigger and bigger. The prettiest selection is 'Sheila's Sunshine', with primrose-yellow flowers. Great plant, but get the metal stakes out—it will topple like a pine tree in a storm if not supported. Hardy in zones 5 to 9.

Helianthus ×*multiflorus*, the "many-flowered" sunflower, is another excellent perennial—admittedly without the knockout power of *H. angustifolius* but also without its wandering ways. Flowers appear in summer and into the fall, held above dark green opposite foliage. Unfortunately, Japanese beetles, aphids, and other goodies feel comfortable on this plant. The 3" wide flowers are often double, yellow, and numerous. I enjoy 'Capenoch Star' and 'Morning Sun', both of which offer single yellow flowers; double and semidouble flowers shine on 'Corona Dorica' and 'Loddon Gold'. All are about 3–5' tall. Full sun and well-drained soils are necessary for best performance. Hardy in zones 4 to 8; disease and insect pressure are greater in the South.

Helianthus giganteus 'Sheila's Sunshine'

Helianthus ×multiflorus 'Capenoch Star'

Helianthus ×multiflorus 'Corona Dorica'

Helianthus ×multiflorus 'Morning Sun'

Helianthus ×multiflorus 'Loddon Gold'

Heliopsis helianthoides 'Goldgreenheart'

Heliopsis helianthoides 'Goldgreenheart'

Heliopsis helianthoides

SUNFLOWER HELIOPSIS

Like the late great John Denver said, "Sunshine on my shoulder makes me happy." So does sunshine in my garden, and I enjoy *Heliopsis helianthoides* for the sunny disposition it brings to the garden. Plants grow about 3' tall, and the dark green serrated leaves provide good value even when not in flower. The yellow to golden daisy flowers, 2–2½" wide, are produced at the end of every stem. The good part is their brightness and ease of culture. The bad part is that Japanese beetles, aphids, and other chewing things also enjoy that brightness; however, since gardeners like to share so much, we might as well share with the bugs as well.

Many of the selections of *Heliopsis helianthoides* are hybrids between the species and its variety *scabra*, which provides the coarse feel to the leaves.

Heliopsis helianthoides 'Incomparabilis'

Heliopsis helianthoides 'Summer Sun'

Heliopsis helianthoides 'Mars'

Heliopsis helianthoides 'Ballerina'

Heliopsis helianthoides 'Golden Plume'

The most popular is 'Summer Sun', a 2–3' tall plant with excellent credentials in the North and South. Many other single and semi-double flowerers, such as 'Ballerina' and 'Mars', look similar. My favorite is 'Goldgreenheart', whose green heart is surrounded by golden petals. A little gaudy, but we all need a little shtick. Doubles like 'Golden Plume' and 'Incomparabilis' are useful for those who prefer fuller flowers. Full sun, well-drained soils. Hardy in zones 3 to 9, but better in the North than the deep South.

Helleborus

HELLEBORE, FALSE ROSE

Flowering long before the calendar date of spring, the hellebores come in an assorted mix of flower color, leaf size, and vigor. Although two species dominate the scene, many other fine hellebores are available through specialty nurseries. They are evergreen and produce dozens of flowers with white, purple, or green sepals (their petals are actually inconspicuous nectaries). I couldn't imagine my garden without hellebores; they are as much a part of the coming of spring as the melting of snow.

We are starting to see *Helleborus foetidus* (bearsfoot hellebore), a recently awakened sleeper in the land of hellebores, throughout gardens and landscapes. The compound leaves, which consist of narrow fingerlike leaflets, provide some outstanding foliage, and the small greenish flowers provide a show from February to June. Even the fruit, which forms after flowers have lost their color, provides garden value into late spring or early summer. Planted with small-flowering

Helleborus foetidus

Helleborus foetidus

Helleborus orientalis

MORE →

Helleborus foetidus 'Wesker Flisk'

Helleborus foetidus 'Wesker Flisk'

Foliage of *Helleborus foetidus* (left) and *H. orientalis*

Helleborus orientalis Party Dress series

daffodils, Virginia bluebells, and hepaticas, this hellebore is a no-brainer. 'Wesker Flisk', a selection of the species, has more of a red tint to many of the petioles and leaflets. Even its yellow-green flowers have a slight rouge appearance. Do not fret if you cannot find it, however, as it is not significantly different from the type. Provide afternoon shade and well-drained soils. Hardy in zones 5 to 9.

All the positive statements just made can be repeated in spades for the Lenten rose, *Helleborus orientalis*, the most popular of all false roses. The leaves are much bigger than *H. foetidus*, and the leaflets are not as fingerlike. The flower stems arise from the ground, forming many white, green, or mauve to purple flowers in late winter and early spring, and providing more flower power than *H. foetidus* but

Helleborus orientalis

Helleborus orientalis 'Dusk'

not as subtly. I can think of a few problems that beset the bearsfoot hellebore, but I am hard-pressed to come up with any for the Lenten rose. They persist for years, reseed easily, welcome spring even in the snow, remain in flower and fruit for months, and blend in to the rest of the landscape once their day in the sun is complete. No wonder the supply cannot keep up with demand.

New cultivars of *Helleborus orientalis* appear more and more frequently, but most are seed-propagated and offered as a mix or series. Among the finer selections are 'Dusk' and 'Dark Burgundy', which produce dark purple to almost black flowers; the Party Dress series has some of the most perfect double flowers in the genus. Partial shade and reasonably well-drained soils boost longevity and their ability

Helleborus orientalis

Helleborus niger

to produce seedlings. Hardy in zones 4 to 9.

The white flowers of *Helleborus niger*, the Christmas rose, provide a beautiful sharp contrast to the dark green foliage, making it the "cleanest" looking of the hellebores. More difficult to establish than the previous two species, it nevertheless thrives where conditions are to its liking. Unfortunately, those conditions are more demanding than needed for most other hellebores sold in the country. Try them in different moist, shady locations and leave them alone. Once established, they will reseed and the colony will be well on its way.

A few cultivars have been introduced, but the variations on the species are slight indeed, and *Helleborus niger* itself is equal to any of them. On the other hand, a few outstanding hybrids have been produced using Christmas rose as a parent. Although none are easy to find, that never stopped intrepid gardeners before. *Helleborus ×nigristern*, a handsome cross between *H. niger* and *H. ×sternii*, provides dark green foliage and a pink tinge to the flowers. The finest of all is the Blackthorn Group, which strain stops people in their tracks—an example of what can be achieved by dedicated hellebore breeders. Partial shade and well-drained soil with plenty of organic matter. Hardy in zones 3 to 8.

Helleborus niger

Helleborus ×nigristern

Helleborus Blackthorn Group

Hemerocallis

DAYLILY

All the world's a garden and all the players are daylilies. At least it seems that way. Wherever the sun shines, there resides another daylily. One daylily after another muscles into the gardens of America, each trying to outdo the other; each daylily breeder adds a little pinch of this or a big dollop of that. That daylilies are so popular obviously point to the obvious: they are colorful, available, and essentially trouble-free. They have been bred to within an inch of their lives, providing gardeners with a vast panorama of options: singles, doubles, rebloomers, dwarfs, giants, diploid, tetraploid—the beat goes on and the beat is good. In our pursuit of the next great daylily, however, do not trample upon some of the fine species that parented the hybrids. Species such as *Hemerocallis dumortieri* and *H. fulva*, with the brownish backs to their tepals, and *H. minor*, which helped tame the vigor of the hybrids, are still gardenworthy plants.

Hemerocallis fulva

MORE →

Hemerocallis dumortieri

Hemerocallis minor

Hemerocallis 'Eeenie Weenie'

Hemerocallis hybrids are categorized into various heights (dwarf, low, medium, and tall) and a dizzying array of flower shapes and colors. When I see dwarfs like 'Eenie Weenie' and 'Stella d'Oro', I am more impressed with the long flowering time than the compact habit. The classic selections of 'Hyperion' and 'Golden Chimes' provide tall, vigorous plants in shades of yellow, and another old-fashioned selection is still one of the best deep yellows of all, 'Mary Todd'. But that is just the beginning! I bounce from the pure white of 'Ice Carnival' to whites with yellow centers such as 'Gentle Shepherd' and 'Luminous Jewel', and then to bicolors like 'Pandora's Box' and 'Lady Diva', to reds ('Red Joy', 'Scarlet Tanager'), pinks ('Benchmark', 'China Bride'), pastels ('Tender Shepherd'), and even almost black ('Black Ruffles'). But before I crawl away, exhausted by this DNA tinkering, my eye spies even more unworldly shapes. I see the fringed tepals of 'Atlanta Irish Heart', the obnoxious double flowers of 'Heather Harrington', and the spidery tepals of hybrids like 'Kindly Light' and 'Red Rain'! I run for cover under a stately beech, panting in the shade of a classic, never-changing hardwood. (How did this beech get purple leaves?)

Abundant blooms are produced when daylilies are planted in soils

A hillside of *Hemerocallis*

amended with manure or leaf mold. When plants first emerge in the spring, provide a well-balanced fertilizer to give them a kick start. Plants are heavy feeders and require consistent moisture to be at their best. Of course, they don't appreciate boggy soils, and good drainage is important. So is full sun; too little sun results in few buds, and in some cultivars, buds may not open at all. In essence, when planning a site for your daylilies, choose an area of full sun, provide some fertilizer and moisture in a well-drained area, and get out of the way. Aphids can be a problem, but in general, choosing the right daylily is simply a matter of taste. Hardy in zones 3 to 9.

Hemerocallis 'Gentle Shepherd'

Hemerocallis 'Stella d'Oro'

Hemerocallis 'Hyperion'

Hemerocallis 'Luminous Jewel'

Hemerocallis 'Mary Todd'

Hemerocallis 'Ice Carnival'

Hemerocallis 'Pandora's Box'

Hemerocallis 'Golden Chimes'

Hemerocallis 'Lady Diva'

MORE →

Hemerocallis 'Red Joy'

Hemerocallis 'Black Ruffles'

Hemerocallis 'Scarlet Tanager'

Hemerocallis 'Tender Shepherd'

Hemerocallis 'Heather Harrington'

Hemerocallis 'Benchmark'

Hemerocallis 'Atlanta Irish Heart'

Hemerocallis 'Red Rain'

Hemerocallis 'China Bride'

Hemerocallis 'Kindly Light'

Hepatica

LIVERLEAF

I finally found a nursery that was propagating liverleaf, not just digging it out of the wild. I was ecstatic; I had studied up on this wonderful wild-flower and had long lusted after our two wonderful eastern natives, *Hepatica acutiloba* and *H. americana*. My getting excited over diminutive hepaticas often causes eyes to glaze over, especially when I have to get down on all fours just to admire them. Even my dog has no respect; she walks over them and even lies down on top of them. Never growing more than 6" tall and as wide, liverleaf nonetheless can carpet a woodland area once established. Both species have small white or light blue flowers that are among the earliest to flower in the spring. In the Armitage garden, they emerge in late February and flower through April. They differ mainly in the shape of the three-lobed leaves: the lobes of *H. americana* are rounded, whereas those of *H. acutiloba* are pointed. Foliage is usually bronze to purple in the spring and green by and throughout summer. Most available plants are grown from seed, therefore leaves may be spotted or entirely green. Similarly, flower color ranges from deep blue to white.

Several non-native species have also generated a good deal of interest but are even more difficult to locate. *Hepatica nobilis* is native to northern Europe and is similar to *H. americana*. The plants have larger, bluer flowers, and selections of it have been offered

Hepatica americana

Hepatica americana

Hepatica acutiloba

Hepatica americana

Hepatica nobilis

Hepatica acutiloba

Hepatica nobilis 'Light Blue'

Hepatica nobilis 'Rubra'

MORE →

with red ('Rubra') or light blue flowers. There is something fascinating about hepaticas with atypical flower colors; unfortunately, the effort to stabilize the colors of our native species has not received the same attention. If you can find *H. nobilis* or its selections and live in the North, go for it: they may be expensive, but if they live, they will have been worth every dollar. Similar wallet shedding should be done without a second thought if the blue-flowering *H. transsilvanica* comes up for sale; its numerous handsome large flowers occur in early spring. Outstanding and eye-popping.

Hepaticas are among the many ephemerals that grace our garden in early spring. They are best placed in deciduous shade (under oaks or beeches, for instance) where they can enjoy full sun while flowering, then disappear in the vegetation of later emerging shade plants once the canopy fills in. They enjoy the company of rue anemone (*Anemonella thalictroides*), Virginia bluebells, and trilliums. Hardy in zones 3 to 7.

Hepatica transsilvanica

Heuchera

CORAL BELLS

Every time I open a catalog, I see that someone has developed a new heuchera. If it is not the best coral bell ever, then it would never have been developed, or so the catalog says. But after reading a dozen catalog descriptions, it is apparent that some of them belong in the fiction section of the library. Coral bells are best known for the clusters of small coral bell-shaped flowers atop long stems. They have been around for many years, favorites of our grandmothers. But how many of these things do we really need? I

Heuchera americana

know that I looked at at least forty different ones, and I have barely skimmed the surface. I admit, however, that my curiosity generally gets the best of me and undisciplined as I am, I have to try a couple every year. Despite the many species of coral bells, the majority of the plants we see are hybrids, divided into those with mundane green leaves and colorful flowers (mainly hybrids of *Heuchera sanguinea*) and those with colorful, bronzed leaves and mediocre flowers (mainly hybrids of *H. americana*).

Heuchera americana, the American alumroot, is an excellent garden plant all by itself, reveling in rich soils and moist, shady spots. Growing to about

Heuchera americana with *Hosta*

12" tall when not in flower and up to 3' when the small greenish flowers appear, plants are always noticed by native plant enthusiasts but usually overlooked by everyday gardeners. The evergreen bronze leaves, which are often lined with darker veins, are always more colorful in the cooler months of early spring and fall. In areas of little snow, they even look good when cloaked in ice. They are outstanding in combination with other shade tolerant plants such as hostas; both genera have their moments of beauty and complement each other well.

Breeders have taken advantage of the vibrant leaves of *Heuchera americana* and other species with distinctive foliage, such as *H. micrantha*. With all the hybridization going on, however, we are getting closer to plants with the winning combination of good leaf and good flower. It was difficult to get too excited about the older hybrids, although several cultivars bred for their fine leaves, such as 'Dale's Selection', were immediately accepted by gardeners. Then along came the wonderful bronze-leaved 'Palace Purple', the finest bronze-leaf in its heyday and still an excellent plant; 'Palace Purple' fertilized the heuchera business and soon, like weeds after a rain, all sorts of new hybrids appeared.

A comparison of 'Palace Purple' with cultivars like the shiny dark 'Bressingham Bronze' shows some of the obvious leaf differences. As can be seen in the hybrid names, the breeders are as good at providing interesting names as they are in providing interesting plants. How can you resist 'Smokey Rose', 'Amethyst Mist', 'Chocolate Veil', 'Plum Pudding', 'Whirlwind', or 'Persian Carpet'—all almost as exciting as their names promise. As a group, the Veils ('Chocolate Veil', 'Pewter Veil') are excellent, and 'Whirlwind' has some of the finest foliage of any of them. In areas of little snow, plants like 'Pewter Veil' are nearly as good in the winter as they are in the

Leaves of *Heuchera* 'Palace Purple' (left) and 'Bressingham Bronze'

Heuchera 'Palace Purple'

Heuchera 'Smokey Rose'

Heuchera 'Dale's Selection'

Heuchera 'Amethyst Mist'

Heuchera 'Chocolate Veil'

MORE →

summer. Hard to ask for more. And yet even more choices for the gardener are in the offing, and it is unlikely that the throng will lessen in the coming years.

Plants do well in moist soils and partial shade. Although they will grow well in heavy shade, leaf colors are more vibrant with two to three hours

Heuchera 'Pewter Veil'

Heuchera 'Plum Pudding'

Heuchera 'Canyon Pink'

Heuchera 'Pewter Veil' in winter

Heuchera 'Persian Carpet'

Heuchera 'Fireglow'

Heuchera 'Bressingham Bronze'

Heuchera 'Whirlwind'

Heuchera 'Huntsman'

of direct sun. In general, the flowers of bronze-leaved plants are less exciting than other coral bells and should be removed when they emerge. They will not be missed, and the energy involved in seed production is redirected to foliage production. Plants are generally 2–3' tall and 2' wide, hardy in zones 4 to 9.

Heuchera sanguinea itself can be a little boring. No question that some fine cultivars involving this species are available, but there are now enough corals, reds, pinks, cherries, bicolors, and whites to fill most gardens in America, and it takes a confident fibber to distinguish one named introduction from another. But when they flower in the spring, several can be quite captivating. That I am not a big fan of coral bells does not mean I don't appreciate the rosy flowers of

'Canyon Pink', 'Fireglow', 'Huntsman', and 'Oakington Jewel', or the white blooms of 'June Bride' and 'White Cloud'. But the best of them all is 'Raspberry Regal', the tallest coral bell I have encountered in my trials, with strong stems terminating in dozens of raspberry-red flowers. It is terrific as a garden plant and equally good when the flower stems are cut and used as fillers for larger flowers. Full sun is just fine for this vigorous grower, but some shade is also tolerated. Many flowering coral bells persist only a few years, but 'Raspberry Regal' seems to return year after year. As much as I admire some of the flowering hybrids, I think variegated coral bells like 'Snowstorm' ought to be trashed. I am constantly told how wonderful they are. I don't listen. To each his own.

Plant in partial shade, or in an area with two to three hours of direct light. Consistent moisture is necessary for best flower production. Remove flower heads after blooms are finished to reduce seed production. Plants are about 3–5' tall, hardy in zones 3 to 8.

This brief discussion on *Heuchera* would not be complete without mention of *Heuchera villosa* (hairy alumroot), a little-used native of the southeastern United States. Both

Heuchera 'Oakington Jewel'

Heuchera 'Oakington Jewel'

Heuchera 'Raspberry Regal'

Heuchera 'June Bride'

Heuchera 'White Cloud'

MORE →

the heart-shaped leaves and the small white flowers are hairy, accounting for the common name. The purple-leaved 'Purpurea' is excellent, and one of the newest up-and-comers is 'Autumn Bride'. It has wonderfully wide (6") lime-green leaves, and the white flowers occur in the fall, not the spring as with most of its cousins. Another

choice, for the undisciplined in us all. *Heuchera villosa* requires shade to thrive; too much sun results in a constant wilted look, and any stress to the plant can also cause spotting on the leaves or leaf margin burn. Doesn't sound quite as good as other species, but I still enjoy its fresh foliage and late-flowering tendencies. Plants grow 1–3' tall, hardy in zones 6 to 9.

Heuchera villosa 'Autumn Bride'

Heuchera villosa 'Purpurea'

Heuchera villosa 'Autumn Bride'

Hibiscus

MALLOW

These excellent perennials are thought of as plants for southern gardens, but they grow well into zone 5. The greenhouse hibiscus (*Hibiscus rosa-sinensis*), in all its many colors, is best known as a houseplant and conservatory specimen—probably the reason these plants are believed to have such poor cold hardiness. Garden hibiscus have also been selected in numerous colors and heights, and sufficient choice is available. For this fellow from Montreal, where hibiscus was something only seen in a botanical garden, and a novelty at that, being able to grow a couple outside is indeed a treat.

Hibiscus coccineus

Hibiscus coccineus

Hibiscus coccineus, swamp hibiscus, is a marvelous little-known plant whose 3" wide blood-red flowers are as colorful as any greenhouse hibiscus seen in florist shops. The many stout woody stems are clothed in dark green leaves, and their erect, stiff habit provides see-through architecture throughout the summer. The many narrow-petaled flowers occur at the top of the 5–6' stems in early summer and continue opening for about six weeks. The leaves are palmately compound and handsome in their own right. After a hard frost, the entire plant dies to the ground in the winter.

Plant in full sun, as shade retards growth and flowering. Constant moisture encourages the flowering and growth of this great plant, but plants grow just fine in normal garden soils. One does not require a swamp to be successful. Hardy in zones 7 to 10.

Hibiscus moscheutos, common rose mallow, is the hibiscus for the North, at least to zone 5, bringing the look of the

Hibiscus 'Lord Baltimore'

Hibiscus 'Disco Belle'

Tropics to Baltimore and Chicago, with woody stems and many summer flowers. Patience is needed for the plants to emerge in the spring; they are often among the last to arise. Once they do, they produce many woody stems and grow 3–4' tall. Everyone loves the flowers, including a squadron of flying pests. In particular, hordes of Japanese beetles flock to its yummy leaves.

Many cultivars (likely hybrids of this species and two or three others) are available, representing nearly all the colors of the rainbow. Some of my favorites are 'Lord Baltimore' and 'Lady Baltimore', an older couple with red and pink flowers, respectively. Others, such as the wonderful pink-flowered 'Anne Arundel', are also

Hibiscus 'Anne Arundel'

Hibiscus mutabilis

handsome. Cultivars with the Disco name, such as 'Disco Belle' and 'Disco White', have enormous flowers (easily 8" across) and are also hardy as far north as Chicago (zone 5b). Garden hibiscus should be placed in full sun; shade results in lanky, tall plants. Most cultivars are hardy in zones 5 to 10.

Like the Jolly Green Giant, *Hibiscus mutabilis* (Confederate rose) rises 8–10' in height in a single year and makes everyone smile. Plants produce multiple strong (an inch in diameter) woody stems with large velvety, lobed leaves. But it is the 2–3" wide flowers that provide the entertainment. They open in the fall, starting in early October and

Hibiscus 'Disco White'

143

MORE →

Hibiscus mutabilis 'Flore Plena'

continuing for as long as two months, or until frost. In the species, the flowers open white or pink, then change to deeper red by the evening (the specific epithet, *mutabilis*, means "changing"). The most common selection is 'Flore Plena', with large double pink flowers; cultivars with red or rose flowers ('Raspberry Rose') can also be found. Place in full sun; partial shade results in even taller plants with a minimum of flowers. Hardy in zones 7 (occasionally 6) to 10.

Hibiscus mutabilis 'Flore Plena'

Hibiscus mutabilis 'Raspberry Rose'

Hosta

What does one do with shade? You can either curse your misfortune or celebrate your good luck. If shade is attributable to the presence of mature hardwoods or conifers, then feel blessed not to have your house in a clear-cut subdivision. If however the shade is cast by a Joe Camel billboard or something equally obnoxious, get rid of whatever stands between you and the sun. Simple Armitage rule of thumb: trees stay, tree products go.

If daylilies are the kings of sun, hostas are the kings, queens, princes, and princesses of shade: they are enjoying an unprecedented period of popularity in American gardens. For some gardeners, they are a gift to brighten up the darkness here and there; for others, they are obsessions, collected like baseball cards, resulting in a crop rather than a garden. I really like hostas, and every now and then I must stop myself from buying the next chartreuse or variegated one, lest my shade become a hosta nursery. In the Armitage garden, however, I have the unwelcome help of deer, voles, bugs, and my Hannah dog, who joyfully chases squirrels indiscriminately. Hostas are noted for their foliage (and visits from Hannah and Bambi certainly result in notable foliage). The

Emerging leaves of a hosta

flowers, reminiscent of lilies, are handsome and quite useful as cut flowers. In fact, some of the most fragrant flowers belong to the fragrant hosta, *Hosta plantaginea*.

As the new leaves push from the soil and begin to unfurl, hosta time begins. Vistas of greens, whites, yellows, and blues appear before one's eyes, color to challenge any garden plant. Hostas differ in habit, and their mature size helps decide their use. Plants may be categorized as small (*Hosta venusta*), ground covers (*H.* 'Francee'), edging (*H.* 'Gold Edger'), background (*H.* 'Sun Power'), and specimen plant (*H. sieboldiana* 'Frances Williams', *H.*

fluctuans 'Variegata'). Foliar choices are abundant: from species hostas to selections to hybrids with names like 'Red Neck Heaven' and 'Royal Stan-

dard', there is no lack of choice. From leaves that may be described as green (*H.* 'Invincible'), bluish (*H.* 'Blue Cadet'), and chartreuse (*H.* 'Sum and

Hosta 'Francee'

Hosta 'Sun Power'

Hosta venusta

Hosta 'Gold Edger'

Hosta fluctuans 'Variegata'

A vista of hostas

Hosta 'Red Neck Heaven'

MORE →

Substance') to the variegations of white-and-green (*H.* 'Antioch'), yellow-and-green (*H.* 'Bright Lights', 'Spritzer'), and white-and-yellow (*H. montana* 'Aureomarginata'), the hosta collector is in his glory. The challenge offered by this plant is to choose one or two cultivars among the hundreds that bombard you each year.

Hosta sieboldiana 'Frances Williams' in a border

Hosta 'Antioch'

Hosta 'Royal Standard'

Hosta 'Blue Cadet'

Hosta 'Bright Lights'

Hosta 'Invincible'

Hosta 'Sum and Substance'

Hosta 'Spritzer'

Although the number of cultivars and their population has risen astronomically, hostas are not trouble-free. They are attacked by insects, voles, moles, slugs, and deer. Nothing is more frustrating than watching a plant disappear because voles have eaten the roots or slugs have torn up the leaves, or walking out in the morning to discover a favorite hosta has been decimated by marauding deer. Such is life in the hosta world.

Plant hostas in partial shade; they tolerate more sun than most people believe. The further north one gardens, the more sun hostas can tolerate. Few do not benefit from some afternoon shade. Keep plants consistently moist or leaf margins become brown. Hardy in zones 3 to 8.

Hosta montana 'Aureomarginata'

Slug damage on a hosta

Woolly aphid on a hosta bloom

A hosta decimated by deer

Hypericum

SAINT JOHN'S WORT

Along with *Echinacea*, Saint John's wort is as often found in the medicine cabinet as in the garden. Its antidepressant properties have long been a part of herbal dosings in Europe, and our stressed-out society has also come to embrace *Hypericum* with a vengeance. The species that is helping to calm and placate is *Hypericum perforatum*, which is seldom grown as a garden plant; however, a number of others are widely planted for their large yellow flowers or ornamental fruit.

Hypericum androsaemum (tutsan) can be a terrific plant in zones 5 to 7 for its upright habit, small flowers, and

Hypericum androsaemum

Hypericum androsaemum

MORE →

Hypericum androsaemum

Hypericum androsaemum 'Albury Purple'

Hypericum androsaemum 'Variegatum'

Hypericum calycinum

Hypericum calycinum

ornamental fruit. They grow to about 3' in height and bear small bright yellow flowers, which are somewhat hidden by the foliage. The flowers are far less noticeable than those of most of its cousins, but the colorful fruit, a deep red, is used as a filler in upscale arrangements. The fruit-laden stem is so much in demand that plants are also grown commercially by cut flower growers throughout the world. Plants do poorly in the deep South but are a great addition in much of the rest of the country. An excellent selection for the garden is 'Albury Purple', which provides good purple foliage and interesting fruit on the same plant. 'Variegatum' has wishy-washy creamy white margins on the leaves, but the variegation is neither crisp nor clean, resulting in a plant that looks like it

Hypericum 'Hidcote'

Hypericum 'Hidcote'

isn't sure what it really wants to be. Plant in full sun to partial shade, zones 5 to 7.

The long stamens in the 2–3" wide flowers of *Hypericum calycinum* (Aaron's beard) look a lot like, well, long stamens, but perhaps Aaron's beard was unusually scraggly. In any case, the bright, beautiful flowers cover the plants in spring and early summer. They are best used as ground covers and can spread rapidly in areas of cool summers and mild winters. The glossy green leaves cover large berms and hillsides, making a splendid carpet. Plants in the South do not withstand the difficult summer heat and humidity and often look ragged by August, but they do return fresh in the spring.

A hybrid involving *Hypericum calycinum* arose at Hidcote Gardens in England and is appropriately known as *H.* 'Hidcote'. Each 2" wide yellow flower is sterile and persists for days on the 2–3' tall plants. Beautiful, but a little temperamental in much of this country. Plant in full sun to afternoon shade, hardy in zones 5 to 7.

Ipheion uniflorum

SPRING STARFLOWER

Blooming their little heads off in early spring, a planting of a few dozen bulbs of *Ipheion uniflorum* today produces hundreds of bluish star-shaped flowers in February to March in a couple of years. The flowers, which are held on 4–6" stems, are slightly fragrant; however, the narrow grasslike, pale green leaves give off the scent of garlic when handled. It is this slightly unpleasant smell that limits more widespread use of this fine species. If you admire them with your eyes rather than your hands, I can think of no reason not to include a few of these inexpensive plants.

Most of what is offered through catalogs is *Ipheion uniflorum* itself, with light blue flowers; however, several selections of the species are available. The most common is the darker blue 'Wisley Blue', which is the best of the easy-to-find cultivars. 'Rolf Fiedler' has larger petals and clear blue flowers on 4" stems, but Rolf does not produce nearly as many flowers as the others. For a surprise, try the white 'Album'. Plant in full sun, zones 5 to 9.

Ipheion uniflorum

Ipheion uniflorum 'Wisley Blue'

Ipheion uniflorum 'Rolf Fiedler'

Ipheion uniflorum (left), *I. uniflorum* 'Wisley Blue' (middle), and *I. uniflorum* 'Rolf Fiedler'

Iris danfordiae

Iris reticulata 'J. S. Dijt'

Iris xiphium hybrids

Iris

So many choices, such a small garden! The Armitage lament about so many wonderful perennials, but never more true than with this immense genus of ornamental plants. From America to Siberia, with stops in Europe, Japan, and China, no place, it appears, has failed to send us irises that have not been welcomed to our gardens with open arms. Most are grown from rhizomes or regular fibrous roots, but a few arise from bulbs or corms. The bulbous irises tend to be early-flowering and short (4–9"), while the bearded irises and other more common forms flower later and are more robust. From Brainerd, Minnesota, to Lafayette, Louisiana, there is an iris that wants to be there.

All the bulbous species (*Iris danfordiae*, *I. reticulata*, *I. xiphium*) and their cultivars tend to be early, short, and ephemeral. The Danford iris (*I. danfordiae*) is only about 4" tall, but its bright yellow flowers stand out at a time when few other plants are in flower. I love to plant them as an annual by my rocks by the pond, since they seldom come back after the first year. Combining them with *Chionodoxa*, *Pushkinia*, and other early bulbs

makes the yellow flowers even brighter. Full sun to partial shade, hardy in zones 5 to 9.

The small bulbs of reticulated iris, *Iris reticulata*, belie the large flowers produced on the 4–6" plants. Occurring in various shades of purple and blue, the flared petals and small standards appear in February and March, before the short leaves expand. After flowering, the leaves shoot up to about 12" long. Some excellent selections of reticulated iris include 'Harmony', 'Cantab', and 'J. S. Dijt'. Individual bulbs may not persist more than about three years, although once established, some may continue to flower for four to five years. Full sun, hardy in zones 5 to 8.

The Dutch irises (hybrids involving *Iris xiphium*) send up their foliage early, but the 12–18" tall flower stems open later than the other bulbous species. In fact, this tall flower is a common and popular cut flower, often seen in your local florist or grocery store, and is excellent for cutting out of your own garden. The Dutch hybrids may be planted in the fall as far north as zone 6b, and persist for two to three years. Foliage appears in late winter or early spring, and flowers of white, blue, purple, and yellow provide rainbows of bloom—beautiful or gaudy,

Iris reticulata 'Harmony'

Iris reticulata 'Cantab'

depending on one's outlook. Cultivars include 'Blue Dream', with dark blue and yellow flowers; the lighter blue 'Ideal' (one of the best for cut flowers and also one of the easiest to obtain); and an outstanding white, 'White Wedgewood'. Full sun, hardy in zones 6b to 9.

If an award were presented to "most popular perennial with too many choices," the bearded iris would be the winner. The "bearded" part refers to the band of hairs on the falls (the drooping petals), and with all colors of the rainbow available and dwarf to tall cultivars for sale, the gardener is hard-pressed to know which one to choose. The leaves are about 2" wide and often tinged with blue. Depending on cultivar, flowers are produced as early as very early spring to mid summer. Al-though leaf diseases and insects are creating more problems in the bearded irises than in the Siberians or Japanese, bearded iris will no doubt continue to be popular, if only by virtue of sheer numbers available.

I was at the Royal Botanical Garden in Hamilton, Ontario, when the bearded were doing their thing, and what a thing it was! That garden is well worth a visit any time, but the panorama of color during iris time is outstanding. Some of my favorite hybrids are 'All Aglow', 'Chensled', 'Cozy Calico', and 'Ecstatic Night', but 'Glittering Amber', 'Lynn Hall', and 'Wild Ginger' aren't half bad either. Full sun, hardy in zones 3 to 10.

The American gardener has lately embraced the flat-topped large-flowering *Iris ensata* (Japanese iris) and its

Cut stems of *Iris* 'Ideal'

Iris 'White Wedgewood'

Iris 'All Aglow'

Iris 'Chensled'

Iris 'Cozy Calico'

Iris 'Glittering Amber'

Iris 'Wild Ginger'

MORE →

hybrids with abandon: the popularity of Japanese irises has increased threefold in the 1990s. The flowers are among the biggest in the genus, and sufficient color choice exists for any combination. Large leaves and immense fruit are also characteristic of this fine group of iris. They tolerate swampy conditions, but normal garden soils are fine assuming they are irrigated in dry times.

The numerous Japanese introductions ('Aichi', 'Aka-fururin', 'Kigari Bi') sound like a cross between someone suffering from a bad cold and samurai battle cries; those bred by American hybridizers have more prosaic names. Japanese-American relations are always enhanced when consumers can choose among such diverse cultivars as 'Pink Frost', with its tinge of pink on creamy white flowers; 'Moonlight', whose purple and white petals always catch the eye; 'Regal', a deep lavender with white streaks on its falls; and

Iris 'Ecstatic Night'

Iris 'Lynn Hall'

Iris 'Pink Frost'

Japanese iris vista

'Rikki-Pikki', the cleanest white of all. Each brings the typical large flat shot of color on 3–4' tall stems. Full sun, hardy in zones 4 to 9.

Iris louisiana, the Louisiana iris, is making a good deal of noise in the iris world, no longer simply content to be an interesting group of plants from the bayous of Louisiana and the Gulf Coast. In fact, the Louisiana irises are actually a complex made up of about five species and the hybrids between them. Narrow leaves on 3–5' tall plants and smooth (not bearded) flowers with drooping standards (the upright petals) typify this group. They love water and require it in serious amounts;

however, bayous are not necessary as long as irrigation can be applied. 'Sun Chaser' and 'Sun Fury' are hybrid crosses of such species as *I. fulva*, with its copper-colored flowers; the dixie iris, *I. hexagona*; and the red to purple flowers of *I. nelsonii*. They are all worth a try. Northern hardiness has not been established, but they are more cold tolerant than they are credited with being. Probably zones 4 to 9. Full sun and consistent moisture are recommended.

Their dozens of colors—all with clean, narrow dark green foliage—make the Siberians a favorite among iris lovers. The leaves are among the

Iris fulva

Iris hexagona

Iris nelsonii

Iris 'Regal'

Iris 'Moonlight'

Iris 'Rikki-Pikki'

Iris 'Butter and Sugar'

MORE →

Iris 'Sun Fury'

best in the iris family, seldom exhibiting disease or insect problems. But of course most gardeners don't purchase irises for their leaves, and choosing among flowers in hues of white, blue, lavender, and yellow should satisfy most of us. Plants grow 2–3' tall and quickly form significant colonies.

Of the many cultivars listed in catalogs, one of the most popular is 'Caesar's Brother', with dark velvet flowers; I also enjoy the whites found in 'Butter and Sugar' and 'White Swirl'. 'Pansy Purple', 'Llewelyn', and 'Sally Kerlin' bring blues and purples to the table, and 'Ruffled Velvet' is just as the name implies. Full sun translates into the most flowers per plant; plants grow well in areas of partial shade but produce few flowers. Hardy in zones 3 to 9.

Siberian iris at Longwood Gardens in Pennsylvania

Iris 'Pansy Purple'

Iris 'Ruffled Velvet'

Iris 'Llewelyn'

Iris tectorum, the Japanese roof iris, offers large flowers of purple or white on short (12–15" tall) plants, making this easy-to-grow roof iris a favorite for the front of the garden. The short raised bristles borne along the midrib of the falls help to identify this species as a member of the crested iris group. The small standards are the same color as the falls. The light green leaves are wider than most of the other irises in the garden, but because they are shorter, they don't take up as much room when flowering is complete. Plants move by above-ground rhizomes and can form a significant colony in two to three years.

The best cultivar of *Iris tectorum* is the white-flowering 'Album'. The yellow streak along the falls contrasts subtly yet effectively with the clean white of the rest of the flower. Variegated foliage and lavender-blue flowers can be found on 'Variegatum'. Partial shade and consistent moisture help performance. Hardy in zones 4 to 8.

Iris 'Sally Kerlin'

Iris tectorum

Iris 'White Swirl'

Iris tectorum 'Album'

Iris tectorum

Kalimeris

JAPANESE ASTER

With persistent double white flowers, cut leaves, and excellent weather tolerance, *Kalimeris pinnatifida*, the Japanese aster, is on the Armitage list of no-brainers for new gardeners. Other than its outstanding performance, I suppose there is nothing particularly remarkable about the plant. It consorts with all sorts of neighbors, including shade tolerant astilbes and sun loving verbena. The 1–2' tall plants start flowering in late spring or early summer and continue to do so until frost. A small piece obtained from a friend will fill out into a wide colony within a year or two.

Another species, *Kalimeris yomena*, is best known for its green-and-yellow selection, 'Variegata'. It is handsome, I suppose, but does not possess the outstanding performance of *K. pinnatifida*. Full sun to partial shade, zones 4 to 8.

Kalimeris pinnatifida

Kalimeris yomena 'Variegata'

Kalimeris pinnatifida with *Verbena*

Kirengeshoma palmata

YELLOW WAXBELLS

This unique species from Japan provides all sorts of subjects for lively conversation: leaves, flowers, fruit, and, not least, debate over how to pronounce the name of the genus. The

Kirengeshoma palmata

Kirengeshoma palmata

opposite palmately lobed leaves are light green, and the yellow drooping flowers are thick and waxy, thus the common name. The interest in the plant continues after flowering, with the appearance of fruit that might have been dreamed up by Stephen King: two to three pointed horns are borne on the inflated capsule. Plants are not the easiest to establish, needing protection from winds and an abundance of organic matter. Moist soils are recommended, but boggy conditions should be avoided. Place in partial shade, or at least shaded from afternoon sun; not recommended for the hot, humid summers of the South. Hardy in zones 5 to 7.

Kirengeshoma palmata

Fruit of *Kirengeshoma palmata*

Kniphofia

RED-HOT POKER

Ever wonder how the various vowels and consonants got together to make up a name like *Kniphofia*? It is one genus I consistently misspell, never remembering if it is "ph" or "f," and in what order. The name begins to make sense, however, when one learns that it was discovered by the German botanist, J. H. Kniphof. (I'm just glad my friend Billy Goidehlpht didn't discover any plants.) Red-hot pokers are so called because the tall spires of flowers are often scarlet or fire-engine red; however, yellows, greens, and pinks are also part of this plant's palette. The sword-shaped leaves form a large tuft of foliage, giving rise to the upwardly mobile spires in late spring or early summer. The most common species is the old-fashioned *Kniphofia uvaria*, whose many flowers still provide good value for the money. Often the flowers at the top are scarlet; the older ones at the bottom of the spike are chartreuse-green, providing a bicolor effect.

The assortment of colors offered to the public has exploded, and the gardener may now choose from selections of *Kniphofia uvaria* or hybrids involving several other species. The vigorous spires of 'Bressingham Comet' and the smaller spikes of 'Atlantia' are among

Kniphofia 'Bressingham Comet'

Kniphofia 'Shining Scepter'

Kniphofia 'Atlantia'

MORE →

my favorites in the red to scarlet range. I have recently become a convert from the red, hot part of the poker to the beauty of the yellow pokers. I love the bright yellows of the large fat pokers of 'Shining Scepter', the smaller 'Sally's

Kniphofia 'Sally's Comet'

Comet', and the classical shape of 'Sunningdale Yellow', which is outstanding even in containers. For a more subdued look, I add the softer yellow of 'Sulphur Gem'. Torn between the "red hot" colors and the yellows? How about burnt orange? 'Kingston Flame' (4–5' tall) and the luminous 'Catherine's Orange' (3' tall) both provide a good number of bright, eye-catching blooms. Full sun, zones 5 to 8.

Lamium

DEAD NETTLE

The lamiums are closely related to the stinging nettles (*Urtica* spp., which are never forgotten by those who have meandered too close to them), but since lamiums lacks the stinging hairs, they were dubbed dead nettles. Low-growing plants for shade, lamiums provide variegation of foliage and reasonable flowers. Two main species are found in landscapes, and both are quite useful for specific uses.

Lamium galeobdolon (*Lamiastrum galeobdolon*; yellow archangel) is one of the finest species for deep, deep shade that I have come across. Its selection 'Variegatum' bears opposite green-and-silver leaves on square stems. Plants are only about 9" tall. The distance between the leaves is considerable, resulting in long stems that cover the ground like a speed skater. The variegated leaves combined with deep yellow flowers brighten up even the darkest location. This is the kind of aggressive plant I like: it takes over areas that no

Kniphofia 'Sulphur Gem'

Kniphofia 'Kingston Flame'

Lamium galeobdolon

Kniphofia 'Sunningdale Yellow'

Kniphofia 'Catherine's Orange'

other plant wants to battle. Several other cultivars have been selected, but for covering ground, 'Variegatum' is the best bet. The compact 'Herman's Pride' has more refined silver markings and the same bright yellow flowers; plants don't spread but rather form handsome clumps of colorful foliage. I have great fun growing yellow archangel in tubs, letting the plants boil over to start another drifting puddle of color at the base. Partial to deep shade, consistent moisture. Hardy in zones 4 to 8.

Many selections of *Lamium maculatum*, spotted nettle, are offered for sale to the American gardener, and while each claims to be better than the one before, they all do the same job: they slowly fill in with astonishing variability of leaf and flower, though they don't trip over themselves in their exuberance to do so. The 6–9" tall plants have opposite multicolored leaves and flowers in shades of pink, mauve, and white. Better in the North than the South, where the humidity often results in leaf spotting problems.

Some of the variation in the species can be seen in 'Chequers', a popular cultivar with green-and-white leaves and deep pink flowers. For mauve to pink flowers and bleached foliage, 'Beacon Silver' has proven tough and popular; the same foliage and white flowers may be found on the aggressive 'White Nancy'. Partial shade, zones 3 to 7.

Lamium maculatum 'Beacon Silver'

Lamium galeobdolon

Lamium galeobdolon 'Herman's Pride'

Lamium maculatum 'Chequers'

Lamium maculatum 'White Nancy'

Liatris borealis

Liatris scariosa 'White Spires'

Liatris

GAYFEATHER

The habit of flowering from the top down on erect spikes makes gayfeathers unique among garden plants. The 3–5' tall, mid to late summer spike of *Liatris spicata* consists of individual button-shaped, aster-like flowers, usually mauve in color but sometimes white or rosy red. There is not a lot of "body" to liatris, and the plant grows much like a lily, with thin grasslike leaves surrounding the central stem. Putting three to five plants together provides a more immediate picture than scattering them.

The commercial cut flower industry long ago discovered that liatris makes an excellent cut flower. Cut the stems when the flower is about a third of the way open and place immediately in a solution of floral preservative for many days of enjoyment. The gayfeathers are native to the midwestern United States and are particularly prevalent in the Great Plains and the Midwest; gardeners in these regions are advised to plant them and get out of the way.

Several other species are also available. I enjoy the full flowers of *Liatris scariosa* and particularly its white selection, 'White Spires'. The short *L. borealis* may not be very tall (approximately 1'), but it is an excellent performer; its opposite in size, *L. pycnostachya*, at 6' tall, is large enough to be used as a weapon. And for something quite un-liatris like, try *L. graminifolia*, whose grasslike leaves demand a double take.

All have their moments in the sun. but it is the common gayfeather, *Liatris spicata*, that is the most available and the most widely grown. Its white-flowered selection 'Floristan White' stands out well, and the slightly shorter, more compact 'Kobold' is also worth a spot in the garden. Full sun, zones 3 to 9.

Liatris graminifolia

Liatris spicata

Liatris spicata

Ligularia

Most species in the genus *Ligularia* work best in a large garden where the daring gardener has lots of room for experimentation. Ligularias take front stage with their large leaves and impressive yellow and orange flowers. They are all moisture lovers and in fact do best, under all circumstances, where water is readily and consistently available. If water is lacking, the plant that looks so plumb and beautiful in the cool morning air looks like a limp rag doll in the warm afternoon sun. I wouldn't plant any ligularia if I didn't have a wet space for it. Not all species are big, brash, and bold; some are rather common looking.

The large rounded dark green leaves of *Ligularia dentata*, bigleaf ligularia, make it a favorite, particularly on the edge of water features such as streams and ponds. The bright flowers are secondary in appeal; it is the attractive

Liatris spicata 'Kobold'

Ligularia dentata 'Desdemona'

Liatris spicata 'Floristan White'

Ligularia dentata 'Desdemona'

MORE →

Ligularia sibirica

foliage that is the charm. Provide consistent moisture and, if possible, keep out of the afternoon sun. It is almost impossible not to have the leaves wilt on warm days, even though the wilting does not seem to cause any permanent damage. Looks lousy, though. Slugs account for shot holes in the leaves, adding to the gardener's dismay. Several cultivars are sold, the best being 'Desdemona', although 'Othello' is similar. Whenever I go to a nursery, they look too similar, making me believe the original plants have since been mixed-up at the production level.

Ligularia stenocephala, narrow-spiked ligularia, offers a much different look: its leaves are triangular to heart-shaped, above which the long slender flower stalks arise. Dozens of small yellow flowers open along the 1–2' long raceme in late spring. An excellent architectural plant where abundant, consistent moisture levels can be maintained. Without consistent moisture, leaves look wilted much of the time.

The only selection of *Ligularia stenocephala* to be found in most nurseries is 'The Rocket', which hoists lemon-yellow flowers on 18–24" long stems. Absolutely outstanding plants where the environment consists of cool nights, warm days, and plenty of moisture. Not recommended for the South. Full sun to partial shade, zones 5 to 8.

Other interesting species of *Ligularia* include *Ligularia macrophylla*, with large, wide sword-like leaves like no other species, and *L. sibirica* (cold hardy to zone 3), with silver backs to its large round green leaves.

Ligularia stenocephala 'The Rocket'

Ligularia stenocephala 'The Rocket'

Ligularia macrophylla

Lilium

LILY

Trying to choose a few lilies is like trying to choose a few daffodils: with so many to choose from, where does one begin? That the choice is so difficult, however, is testament to the beauty and diversity of the genus *Lilium*. From little-known species to the dozens of hybrids, no gardener can complain about a lack of options. All prefer full sun and good soil drainage.

If I had to choose but five species to grow, I could probably get down to about seven or eight—and then pick the final five names out of a hat. I hope that I would choose the gold band lily, *Lilium auratum*, with its prominent gold bands down the length of each white petal. Other variants of this upright lily include the white-flowered 'Opala' and the larger-flowered variety *platyphyllum*. Hardy in zones 4 to 9. I think that if I could grow the Canada lily, *L. canadense*, I would have an entire garden full of them. The pendant golden flowers stop everybody in their

tracks with their classic beauty. Unfortunately, they are difficult to find and do poorly in warm climates. Hardy in zones 3 to 7. Would I pick the orange, nodding flowers of *L. henryi*, Henry's lily? The scarred face (actually raised projections called papillae) and the reflexed petals of the flowers make an impressive picture. They tower to about 6' in height and return year after year. Hardy in zones 4 to 7. As I stuck

my hand in the lily hat yet again, fingers crossed, I would hope to choose the fragrant, exotic regal lily, *L. regale*. On a still evening, nothing can match the sweet smell emanating from the regal lily in the garden. The buds are a soft wine color, and the flowers retain that hue on the outside of the petals but are beautifully white when they open. The combination of buds and flowers is indeed a wonderful picture.

Lilium auratum

Lilium auratum 'Opala'

Lilium auratum var. *platyphyllum*

Lilium canadense

MORE →

Lilium regale

Plants are not particularly persistent, but worth the few years of pleasure they bring to the garden. Hardy in zones 3 to 8. If I lived in a cool climate, I would also hope for the Turk's-cap lily, *L. martagon* or one of its hybrids. The uncommon "turban" look of the flower and the whorled leaves make it fairly distinctive in the garden. Flower color is usually purple-red, but the

Lilium canadense

Lilium henryi

Lilium regale

Lilium henryi

Lilium Backhouse hybrid

Lilium martagon

Lilium martagon 'Album'

white 'Album' is especially handsome. Of the many hybrids involving *L. martagon*, the Backhouse hybrids are among the toughest, and handsome as well. Hardy in zones 3 to 7.

The number of Asiatic and Oriental hybrids now available to the gardener is mind-boggling. From large upright trumpet flowers to graceful nodding blooms, from ten-foot giants to two-foot pixies, the choices are seemingly endless. In general, the flowers and

Lilium 'Dandy'

Lilium 'Amourette'

Lilium 'Campfire'

Lilium 'Acapulco'

Lilium 'Apollo'

Lilium 'Vivaldi'

Lilium 'Casa Blanca'

Lilium 'Enchantment'

Lilium 'Imperial Gold'

the leaves of the Oriental hybrids are larger and plants flower a little later than the Asiatics, but all are worth a try in the garden when the lily fever is upon you. A few of my favorites in the Asiatic group include the bronze-orange color found in 'Amourette'; the virgin white of 'Apollo'; the fiery orange of 'Campfire'; the subtle peach hues of 'Dandy'; the ever-popular 'Enchantment'; and 'Vivaldi', a warm yellow. In the Oriental group, I enjoy the red-pink 'Acapulco' and the white 'Casa Blanca' and have been impressed with 'Imperial Gold'. The soft color of 'Soft Moonbeam' and the short stature of 'Trance' have provided immense enjoyment in the Armitage garden, but my all-time favorite has to be 'Olivia', who returns year after year to lighten up the garden.

Linum

FLAX

Entire oceans of blue can be seen in European farmfields, where annual blue flax, *Linum usitatissimum*, is still grown for the fiber and linseed oil the plants yield, but only a few species of flax are used for gardens. One of the most handsome but seldom seen is yellow flax, *L. flavum* (zones 5 to 7),

Linum flavum

Lilium 'Soft Moonbeam'

Lilium 'Olivia'

Lilium 'Trance'

Linum perenne

with its 2" wide butter-yellow flowers. *Linum perenne*, the perennial flax, is the most common species and with good reason. The tough stems terminate in nodding flower buds, which then turn up to the viewer their beautiful blue hue. 'Album' is a good white selection. A good plant for edges; prefers partial shade in the South, full sun in the North. Great drainage is necessary. Hardy in zones 4 to 8.

Linum perenne

Linum perenne 'Album'

Linum usitatissimum by the acre

Lobelia tupa

Lobelia ×speciosa 'Bee's Flame'

Lobelia

From brilliant reds to handsome blues and purples, lobelias can be impressive. Red is their classic color, found in *Lobelia cardinalis* (cardinal flower), *L. tupa*, and in the red and scarlet hybrids. A good deal of selection and breeding has produced garden choices, only a few of which are improvements on *L. cardinalis* itself.

Ask anyone about *Lobelia cardinalis*, and they will tell you about a beautiful plant, probably growing near some water, with brilliant red flowers. To see dozens growing together in a colony is to have an out-of-body experience. The lipped flowers are held on a long flower stem, and the hummingbirds and butterflies will love them as much as you. Provide full sun if sufficient moisture can be provided, partial shade if plants are growing in normal garden soils. Hardy in zones 2 to 9. Blood lobelia, *L. tupa*, has large matted-red flowers combined with handsome foliage. Plants prefer full sun to partial shade, zones 7 to 8. The hybrids, known as *L. ×speciosa*, include 'Bee's Flame',

'Compliment Scarlet', and 'Scarlet Fan'. All sport brilliant red to scarlet flowers on 3–4' tall plants. Cultural recommendations are similar to *L. cardinalis*. Hardy in zones 5 to 8.

Blue, lavender, and purple are also found in the genus. One common blue lobelia is known botanically as *Lobelia siphilitica* for its supposed efficacy in treating that disease. If the Latin label is difficult for bashful gardeners to ask for by name, they may simply inquire about big blue lobelia. Plants grow 2–3' tall, flower later than cardinal flower, and tolerate partial shade to full sun. Hardy in zones 4 to 8. Several hybrids bear lavender to purple flowers; the best known are other excellent hybrids of *L. ×speciosa*, such as 'Compliment Purple'. The least-known hybrid is probably *L. ×gerardii*, which has many lavender to purple flowers on unbranched stems; 'Vedrariensis' is similar to the hybrid but with dark green leaves tinged with red and dark violet flowers. Long-lived, good looking, and hardy in zones 4 to 8. Full sun to afternoon shade recommended; provide plenty of moisture.

Lobelia ×speciosa 'Compliment Scarlet'

Lobelia cardinalis

Lobelia siphilitica

Lunaria

MONEY PLANT, HONESTY

Lunaria annua is a most common biennial (a plant that takes two years to flower, then dies), with a a common name that refers to the silver-dollar shape of the fruit. The fruit turns translucent over time and may be dried for long-lasting indoor decorations. Where the plants do well, they are lovely, but they also seed every-

Lunaria annua fruit

Lunaria annua

Lobelia ×*speciosa* 'Compliment Purple'

Lunaria annua 'Alba'

Lobelia ×*gerardii* 'Vedrariensis'

MORE →

Lunaria annua 'Variegata'

Lunaria annua 'Variegata'

Lunaria rediviva

where, so that your small plot, conceived as a place to grow a plant or two for dried fruit, soon resembles the Franklin Mint. Their propensity for self sowing results in large colonies in the spring, but if most flowers are removed before the seed is released, the advance can be controlled. The common flower color is lavender, but 'Alba' is even prettier and reseeds true. 'Variegata', with variegated leaves and lavender flowers, is outstanding. Partial shade is best. Hardy in zones 4 to 8.

Another species of *Lunaria* is the shrubby money plant, *Lunaria rediviva*. Much more perennial than its biennial counterpart, *L. rediviva* has finely toothed leaves and fragrant flowers. Other than size, however, the most notable difference between the two species is the fruit. In *L. rediviva*, it is elliptical rather than round as in the more common *L. annua*. They are more difficult to grow, but certainly worth a try if you are already a fan of this genus. Provide partial shade to full sun, well-drained soils. Hardy in zones 4 to 8.

Lunaria rediviva

Lupinus

LUPINE, BLUEBONNET

Seldom is heard a discouraging word about lupines when one sees them in their flowering glory—they are that perfect. "Discouraged" is the word, however, for many gardeners who try to reproduce the Texas bluebonnets in their eastern yard or the English lupines in their Midwest garden. But even two or three fall-planted lupines are a source of sheer delight in the spring garden and can be enjoyed even though they don't look like the planting at Chatsworth in England. The genus is certainly variable; from the awesome light yellow flowers of the California tree lupine, *Lupinus arboreus*, to the blue-flowered northwesterner *L. polyphyllus* and its white-flowered cousin, 'Albus'. Throw in the roses of the annual Mexican lupine, *L. hartwegii*, and it becomes obvious that nature has provided a well-set table.

Of course, sitting at the head of the table are the hybrids, a potpourri of species first popularized by George

Lupinus 'Russell Hybrid Pink'

Russell, an English plantsman, who bred the famous Russell hybrids. Numerous crosses followed including the ivory flowers of 'Blushing Bride', the pink of 'Gina Lombaert', and the wonderful mixtures found in the Gallery hybrids. Additional cultivars are being offered more and more, but the Russells are still the most readily available and therefore continue to be the main game in town. Regardless of the lupine chosen, remember that they love cool weather, hate the combination of heat and humidity, and except for fortunate gardeners in the Northwest and perhaps the Northeast, they will not be as handsome the second or third year as they were the first. Many are easily grown from seed, and nurseries often carry substantial containers of well-grown plants that may be planted out in the fall. If you can find them, go for it. Plant in full sun, well-drained soils. Hardy in zones 3 to 7.

Lupinus arboreus

Lupinus 'Russell Hybrid Mix'

Lupinus 'Blushing Bride'

Lupinus 'Gina Lombaert'

Lupinus 'Gallery Mix'

172

Lychnis ×arkwrightii 'Vesuvius'

Lychnis flos-cuculi

Lychnis flos-cuculi 'Alba'

Lychnis

CAMPION

I was scratching my head the other day, wondering what in the world a name like campion has to do with anything. Except for one of my students, whose last name was Campion and who saw no problem with the name, the rest of us couldn't figure out why anybody would hang that moniker on a plant. Turns out some of these plants grew wild outside Roman stadiums, used for athletic events, like Christians vs. Lions, and garlands of them were used to crown the champion (usually a lion), hence the common name. Several fine annual species are offered, such as the little-known *Lychnis ×arkwrightii* (better known in the hybrid 'Vesuvius') and the wild, ragged *L. flos-cuculi*, ragged robin, and its white variant 'Alba'.

Without doubt, two species of *Lychnis* and their selections reign supreme in American gardens. A native of eastern Europe, *Lychnis chalcedonica*, the Maltese cross, has been a garden favorite for many years. Opposite leaves, swollen nodes, and the five-petaled flowers—with petals shaped like a cross—show its affiliation with the dianthus family, and indeed the

Lychnis chalcedonica

Lychnis chalcedonica

Lychnis chalcedonica 'Flore Plena'

genera are closely related. The common form and color of the flowers is single and scarlet, but double flowers ('Flore Plena'), rose-colored blooms ('Carnea'), and even flowers of puce ('Murky Puce'—now who would name anything "murky puce"?) are occasionally seen. New hues for an old-fashioned plant. Full sun, decent soils, zones 3 to 7.

The other reigning species is the short-lived but explosive *Lychnis coronaria*, rose campion, characterized by magenta to rosy red flowers and gray woolly leaves. It reseeds itself with abandon: individual plants may disappear, but in general, gardeners will find this plant returning year after year. The species has gaudy purple flowers, but several hybrids, in particular 'Abbotsford Rose', subdue the magenta and replace it with bright rose. For more conservative gardeners, a white selection ('Alba') and a bicolor ('Angel Blush') help to make the garden an even more pleasant place for champions. Full sun to afternoon shade, zones 4 to 7.

Lycoris

RESURRECTION FLOWER

Oh, that the fine genus *Lycoris* would have a little more tolerance to cold: its members may presently be enjoyed only by those who garden south of zone 6, although one species goes into zone 5. The foliage of the plants, known as resurrection flowers, emerges in the late winter and spring, then goes dormant in the summer, leaving nothing but bare ground and despondent gardeners, sure that their plants have died. Like magic, however, in late summer and fall, naked stems emerge, as if resurrected, topped with brilliant amaryllis flowers. The stems have given rise to another common name, naked ladies, and some gleeful gardeners like to plant them with *Or-*

Lycoris albiflora

Lychnis chalcedonica 'Carnea'

Lychnis coronaria 'Abbotsford Rose'

Lychnis coronaria 'Alba'

Lychnis coronaria 'Angel Blush'

Lychnis coronaria 'Angel Blush'

MORE →

Lycoris aurea

Lycoris radiata in bud

nithogalum umbellatum—which enjoys many common names. Who says creativity is dead in America?

Brilliant flowers of white (*Lycoris albiflora*) and yellow (*L. aurea*) can occasionally be found, but the large mauve flowers of *L. squamigera* and the fire-engine red of *L. radiata* are the most common. The latter two can multiply rapidly, and passing bulbs

Lycoris squamigera

Lycoris radiata

across the fence is a common occurrence. *Lycoris squamigera* is hardy to zone 6, the others to zones 7 or 8. Full sun to partial shade. All are outstanding.

Lysimachia

LOOSESTRIFE

At last a genus for people who don't want challenges and who enjoy the prospect of plants that live. Loosestrifes are the worst of thugs to the best of plants, and they all bring beauty, character, and the chance of allowing you to shower your neighbors with plants they will have forever. The usual flower color is yellow, but white is common with several species as well. When you plant *Lysimachia*, you are planting the future. Line up your friends now.

An aggressive member of the clan, *Lysimachia ciliata* (hairy loosestrife) has lots of small cilia or hairs along its stem and beneath its leaves, and many yellow flowers are borne at the nodes above the foliage as plants mature. The running root system of this green-leaved species provides plants all over the place. In recent years, the boring green species has been superseded by

Lycoris squamigera

Lycoris radiata with *Nicotiana*

'Purpurea', which is equally aggressive but much more handsome. I can even put up with its traveling ways because its purple-leaved foliage provides terrific contrasts with other plants in the garden—it even makes my bishop's weed (*Aegopodium*) look good. In hot, humid summers, the purple leaf fades somewhat but still remains a muted dark green. In the winter and early spring, it provides color in an otherwise barren landscape. Full sun to partial shade, zones 5 to 8.

Lysimachia clethroides (gooseneck loosestrife) is the reigning king and queen of the roamers, but it is nevertheless a beautiful plant in the right place. The right place simply happens to be an island bed surrounded by concrete. While I can make light of its traveling tendencies, gooseneck is a wonderful plant for filling in large areas and providing handsome white flowers. The many half-inch-wide flowers are arranged on a long, undulating (like a goose's neck) inflorescence. Excellent for cut flowers. That it is a roamer is simply testament to its success. Grows in full sun to partial shade; moist soils are to its liking. Hardy in zones 3 to 8.

A closely related plant but without the roaming habit is another white flowerer, *Lysimachia ephemerum*, up-right loosestrife. I thought this would be the cat's meow when I first discovered its existence, to have a plant with flowers similar to gooseneck (without the neck) but without worrying that it would take over. It does well in areas of the Northwest, not too bad on Long Island, only fair in the Midwest and Southeast. Still a plant worth trying if you're a frustrated gooseneck lover. Hardy in zones 5 to 7.

The common name of *Lysimachia nummularia*, creeping Jenny, includes a strong hint as to what the plant wants to do. Happily, this first-rate plant is a creeper that most gardeners enjoy and encourage. Particularly

Lysimachia ciliata 'Purpurea'

Lysimachia ciliata 'Purpurea' with *Aegopodium*

Lysimachia clethroides

Lysimachia ciliata

Lysimachia clethroides

MORE →

Lysimachia ephemerum

Lysimachia ephemerum

Lysimachia nummularia

Lysimachia nummularia spilling over a window box

Lysimachia japonica 'Minutissima'

Lysimachia japonica 'Minutissima'

good for filling in areas around steps, rocks, or places where people routinely traverse, as stepping on it every now and then does no harm whatsoever. The yellow flowers add a little color, particularly to the green-leaved species; this contrast is lost when one grows the best selection, gold-leaved 'Aurea', whose golden color brightens the spring then fades a little in the heat of summer. Fewer flowers are produced but they are lost in the foliage anyway. Rooting at the nodes between the leaves allows *L. nummularia* to be fairly aggressive, but it is easily pulled out if it gets too rambunctious. I love this plant but am still trying to figure out who Jenny is. Partial shade, zones 3 to 9.

Another wonderful creeping member of the genus is probably my favorite, the short Japanese loosestrife, *Lysimachia japonica* 'Minutissima'. This 1" tall plant, with its tiny leaves and small yellow flowers, is growing between the stones in my little walkway and puts up with the abuse of gullywashers, drought, and the heavy boots of my visitors. Great plant for a specific area. Partial shade, zones 5 to 8.

Macleaya cordata

PLUME POPPY

Macleaya cordata is a plant that needs lots of room—it's perfect for the unsqueamish gardener for whom space is not a problem. I have seen outstanding displays of plume poppies in large containers, on either side of an entrance, where their growth can be controlled. Their lobed leaves, light green above and gray-green beneath, have gained plume poppies quite a following. They are particularly handsome

Lysimachia nummularia 'Aurea'

Lysimachia nummularia 'Aurea'

Macleaya cordata

Macleaya cordata

Macleaya cordata

MORE →

when plants are young, fluttering in the breeze. The small cream-colored flowers are held in long plumes at the top of the plants in early to mid summer. Plants are 6–10' tall, spreading quickly by rhizomes to form large colonies. In fact, they are thugs and a nightmare to remove. When broken, they bleed a yellow sap, a characteristic common to the poppy family. No cultivars are available. Full sun to partial shade, hardy in zones 3 to 8.

Mertensia virginica

Mertensia virginica 'Alba'

Mertensia asiatica

Mertensia

BLUEBELL

Spring is the time of great promise in the garden, with many of us frantically scraping the soil, hoping to rediscover our favorite prizes. I know that spring has sprung when the light green leaves and the blue flowers of *Mertensia virginica*, Virginia bluebell, show themselves in late winter and early spring. I love watching the pink buds evolve from being coiled up like a scorpion's tail to opening to deep pink or blue flowers. Lavender and blue are the normal flower colors, but some plants

Mertensia virginica 'Rosea' with *Ipheion*

Mertensia sibirica

retain their rose-pink flower color until nearly the end of bloom time. The big floppy leaves look a little like donkey ears and get larger as spring progresses. Finally, in early summer, normal summer dormancy is reached and the plants decide to go to bed, leaving the area bare—but that usually presents no problem because by that time neighboring plants have grown over the area. *Mertensia virginica* is a woodland plant, best grown at the edge of a woodland path or by a shaded pond. Few cultivars have been isolated; occasionally a rose-pink ('Rosea') occurs, which looks very nice with other small bulbs such as

Mertensia asiatica

Ipheion. A white-flowered 'Alba' also turns up, but who wants a white blue-bell? Partial shade, zones 3 to 8.

Other interesting species of *Mertensia*, although less vigorous and more secretive, are the compact Asian blue-bell, *Mertensia asiatica*, with incredible blue leaves and light blue flowers, and the full-bodied, tall Siberian blue-bell, *M. sibirica*, which does not go dormant.

Miscanthus

EULALIA GRASS

Of all the grasses used in ornamental horticulture, save those for turf, the grasses of the genus *Miscanthus* are far and away the most popular. An explosion of interest in foliage and an emphasis on low maintenance has drawn the grasses into the mainstream of American gardening. They are particularly useful in commercial and institutional landscapes, where low maintenance is much more important than in the urban or suburban garden. Other species can be obtained, but the main species is common miscanthus grass, *Miscanthus sinensis*.

All eulalia grasses should be grown in full sun, although plants will tolerate some shade. In partial shade, plants are taller and more floppy, requiring a cage to keep them from staggering over everything. They may be enjoyed all winter but should be cut back to the base in spring, as soon as new growth has commenced. Do so with heavy shears or a chain saw—these are not wimpy plants, and in fact are considered invasive in the Northeast, Southeast, and Midwest.

Miscanthus sinensis itself provides a handsome planting in the summer and wonderful bronze foliage and flowers in the winter—indeed, good fall color is a given for all species and cultivars of *Miscanthus*. It is the summer foliage, however, that is the raison d'être of this particular species, and wonderful combinations of foliage and flowers abound. 'Adagio', 'Arabesque', and 'Yaku Jima' are examples of selections with mainly green foliage; for variegated foliage, one can choose 'Cabaret', an introduction with wide

Miscanthus sinensis in winter

Miscanthus sinensis 'Adagio'

Miscanthus sinensis

Miscanthus sinensis 'Arabesque'

MORE →

bands of white, or the narrow-banded, narrow-leaved 'Morning Light', both of which are quickly superseding 'Variegatus', the old variegated standby. Banded foliage is found on cultivars like the upright-growing 'Strictus'. Large flowers and good-looking foliage combine in 'Malepartus' and 'Silberfeder' ('Silver Feather'). Full sun, hardy in zones 5 to 9.

Miscanthus sinensis 'Morning Light'

Miscanthus sinensis 'Malepartus'

Miscanthus sinensis 'Variegatus'

Miscanthus sinensis 'Yaku Jima'

Miscanthus sinensis 'Cabaret'

Miscanthus sinensis 'Strictus'

Monarda

BEEBALM

How much *Monarda* have I given away in the last few years? Fragrant, handsome, and colorful the beebalms may be, but well behaved they are not. Three plants will form a large colony the first year, surround their neighbors the next, and be pulled out the third. In areas where such multiplication is not a problem, however, and where powdery mildew does not make its host too unsightly, beebalm sports many beautiful colors and offers excellent performance. I am not sure where this place is or where these plants are, but I am assured they exist.

Monarda 'Blue Stocking'

Miscanthus sinensis 'Silberfeder' ('Silver Feather')

Monarda 'Squaw'

MORE →

Monarda 'Cambridge Scarlet'

Monarda 'Talud'

Monarda 'Croftway Pink'

Monarda 'Petite Delight'

Several species may be found, but the main player, and one that moves around the garden so well, is *Monarda didyma*, also known as Oswego tea because plants were first collected around Oswego, New York, and used to brew a tea-like concoction. Many cultivars may be purchased, or more likely you will find a gardener who will welcome the opportunity to share some with you. Cultivars vary from each other in color and height, and in their susceptibility to powdery mildew. All breeders claim to have found the cleanest introduction, but until you actually try them in the garden, no one truly knows for sure.

I find that all *Monarda* hybrids grow well, in colors ranging from pink and red to blue and lilac. 'Blue Stocking' has violet-blue flowers and grows like a blue streak; it is reliably mildew resistant. Both 'Cambridge Scarlet' and 'Talud' provide bright red-scarlet flowers. 'Croftway Pink' and 'Beauty of Cobham' are a couple of older cultivars but are still popular, presumably because their flowers blend so well with other garden plants. 'Squaw' is a large plant with flowers of a rosy scarlet; 'Donnerwolke' has handsome lilac flowers; and white blooms can be found in 'Snow White'. I have grown many of them, and all have their moments, all are invasive, and none are absolutely resistant to mildew, no matter what is claimed. Most are about 3' tall, but a breakthrough in beebalm hybridizing, 'Petite Delight', offers pink flowers on an 18" tall frame—with little mildew, at least in my trials. All prefer full sun, hardy in zones 3 to 7.

Monarda 'Beauty of Cobham'

Monarda 'Donnerwolke'

Monarda 'Snow White'

Narcissus

DAFFODIL

I can't think of an easier way to obtain color in the spring garden than to plant bulbs in the fall, and narcissus are almost foolproof. Nature—and the Dutch—have already done the hard work, providing us with a self-contained flowering unit that allows us to expend a minimum of effort to reap the maximum benefit. The perenniality of daffodils is outstanding: from the deep South to the frozen North, they come back year after year.

So much hybridization has been accomplished with the major bulbs—and daffodils are certainly one—that they have been classified into different groups. For hybrid daffodils, twelve divisions have been identified, based on the size of the perianth (petals) and the corona (cup), resulting in daffodil terms like trumpet, large-cupped, small-cupped, and double. The single-flowered trumpet and large-cupped daffodils are probably the most popular harbingers of spring, but let us not ignore the many colorful cultivars that produce flowers in clusters. *Narcissus bulbocodium*, the hoop petticoat daffodil, and *N. cyclamineus*, cyclamen daffodil, are small but interesting species daffodils (a thirteenth division) useful for naturalizing and rock garden work. These species, less vigorous than the hybrids, are seen more on the West Coast than in the rest of the country. Full sun, zones 3 to 8.

Narcissus bulbocodium 'Primrose' (bulbocodium group)

Narcissus cyclamineus

Narcissus 'Biscayne' (large-cupped group)

Narcissus 'February Gold' (cyclamineus group)

MORE →

Narcissus 'Foresight' (trumpet group)

Narcissus 'Unsurpassable' (trumpet group)

Narcissus 'Ice Follies' (large-cupped group)

Narcissus 'Carlton' (large-cupped group)

Narcissus 'Barrett Browning' (small-cupped group)

Narcissus 'Bridal Gown' (double group)

Narcissus 'Flower Drift' (double group)

Narcissus 'Stint' (triandrus group)

Narcissus 'Susy' (jonquilla group)

Narcissus 'Hillstar' (jonquilla group)

Narcissus 'Pipit' (jonquilla group)

Narcissus 'Jenny' (cyclamineus group)

Narcissus 'Garden Princess' (cyclamineus group)

Narcissus 'Baby Moon' (misc. group, miniatures)

Narcissus 'Tuesday's Child' (triandrus group)

Narcissus 'Hawara' (misc. group, miniatures)

Narcissus 'Actaea' (poeticus group)

MORE →

Narcissus 'Avalanche' (tazetta group)

Narcissus 'Geranium' (tazetta group)

Narcissus 'Belcato' (split-corona group)

Narcissus 'Tête-à-Tête' (misc. group, miniatures)

Narcissus 'Cum Laude' (split-corona group)

Nepeta

CATNIP

Nepeta is one of those genera that gardeners learn to appreciate but find difficult to define. That it consists of more than 250 species suggests a genus with a good deal of diversity; for most gardeners, however, it is difficult to get past the fact that it is some kind of catnip. *Nepeta* is in the mint family, whose members may be recognized by their square stems, opposite leaves, and whorled flowers. One helpful way to discriminate between *Nepeta*, *Salvia*, and other minty plants is by using your nose. Nepeta, in general, smells like—well, smells like nepeta! Pick a leaf of nepeta, one of salvia, and one of mint, and let your nose do the walking. Of course, when I do this, my nose does more running than walking, as well as sneezing. All species of *Nepeta* are excellent for the edge of garden beds or even along a pathway, where their fragrance is released when one touches the leaves in passing.

The main species in the trade is Faassen's hybrid, *Nepeta ×faassenii*,

Nepeta ×faassenii

Nepeta ×faassenii

with numerous short cultivars such as 'Blue Dwarf' and 'Blue Wonder'. The highly popular *N. ×faassenii* 'Six Hills Giant', sometimes referred to as *Nepeta gigantea* because of its large leaves and 3' height, is a terrific plant for cooler climates but tends to be weedy in warm summers.

A wonderful low grower (1–2' tall) with the boldest flowers of the genus is the veined nepeta, *Nepeta nervosa*. The veins on the leaves are easily visible, thus the common name. A tall species, with only the faintest catnipy odor, is the very cold hardy (to zone 3) Siberian nepeta, *N. sibirica*. This is a beautiful plant, not as floppy as *N.*

Nepeta ×faassenii 'Six Hills Giant'

Nepeta nervosa

Nepeta sibirica

Nepeta ×faassenii 'Six Hills Giant'

MORE →

×*faassenii* and others and much more classic in habit. Probably the most un-nepeta-like species is the light yellow-flowered *N. govaniana* (zones 4 to 7). Growing 2–4' tall with mild catnip odor, it is more curious than useful. All require full sun, although after-noon shade is useful in the South. Most are hardy in zones 5 to 7, often to zone 4.

Nepeta sibirica

Nepeta govaniana

Oenothera

EVENING PRIMROSE, SUNDROPS

Many plants go under the name of evening primrose (those that open during the evening) or sundrops (those that show their colors during the day). With the introduction of new species and hybridization among spe-cies, the distinction has become blurred, and the common names are used interchangeably. The flowers of *Oenothera* have four petals; the sepals are pink to purple, particularly in bud; and the distinctive pistil is in four parts. A good number of species are weeds, but half a dozen better ones are offered in the trade. All enjoy full sun and require good drainage.

Oenothera fruticosa, common sun-drops, is the species most often of-fered. The bright yellow flowers are held well above the 15–18" tall plants. The flowers are 1–2" wide and open most of the day, even if the sun is not shining. The sepals are red, and often the foliage is spotted red as well. Dif-ferences are not always obvious among available cultivars. I like 'Sonnen-wende', for its pink flower buds and large bright yellow flowers; 'Lady Brookborough', with dozens of smaller flowers; and 'Yellow River', which

Oenothera fruticosa 'Lady Brookborough'

stands about 18" tall and is covered with yellow blooms. I would be hard-pressed, however, to tell the difference between the three without a correct label. Full sun, hardy in zones 4 to 8.

Oenothera missouriensis, Ozark sun-drops, has the largest flowers relative to the size of the plant in the genus. The yellow flowers are up to 5" across (although 3" is more common) and are held on 6–12" tall plants. Sepals are also tinged pink, and leaves are long, narrow, and entire. They are excellent plants for the rock garden, enjoying the extra drainage found there, but do not cope particularly well with heat and humidity. Few cultivars have war-ranted naming; one, 'Greencourt Le-mon', has pale yellow flowers and slightly grayer leaves. Full sun, hardy in zones 4 to 7.

Oenothera fruticosa 'Sonnenwende'

Oenothera fruticosa 'Yellow River'

Another large-flowered yellow species is known as beach evening primrose, *Oenothera drummondii*. Large (3–4" wide) flowers on long stems mark this plant. It will grow in sand and prefers well-drained soils. Full sun, hardy in zones 7 to 10.

Easily discernible from most other species is the southcentral native, *Oenothera speciosa* (showy evening primrose), which bears pink rather than yellow flowers. The flowers are about 2" across, and the linear leaves are about 2–3" long. Plants can easily become weeds, taking over entire counties in a single growing season.

A dream plant at first glance, a bit of a nightmare after a few years. The white-flowered 'Alba' is equally aggressive; 'Ballerina Hot Pink' is a brighter selection but is difficult to locate. Full sun, zones 5 to 8.

A similar species is Mexican evening primrose, *Oenothera berlandieri*, na-

Oenothera missouriensis

Oenothera speciosa

Oenothera speciosa 'Alba'

Oenothera missouriensis 'Greencourt Lemon'

Oenothera speciosa 'Ballerina Hot Pink'

Oenothera berlandieri 'Woodside White'

Oenothera drummondii

Oenothera speciosa

MORE →

tive to the Southwest and the Pacific Coast. Differing only slightly in appearance from *O. speciosa*, it is a bit less aggressive. Available in several cultivars; 'Siskiyou', with 2" wide pink flowers, and 'Woodside White', the white entry, are worth looking for. Full sun, zones 6 to 8.

Oenothera berlandieri 'Siskiyou'

Osmunda cinnamomea fiddleheads coming up through *Epimedium*

Osmunda

FLOWERING FERN

"Flowering fern" is a misnomer for sure: *Osmunda* has no flowers at all, much less pretty flowers. Rather, its common name is a reference to the conspicuous spore cases and fertile fronds of some of the species. These are some of the largest and most vigorous ferns, and coarser than many others. After all, the genus was named for Osmunder, the Saxon god of war, and what self-respecting Saxon would choose anything but a gung-ho fern. Although obvious differences distinguish the species, all prefer moist conditions and shade.

The cinnamon fern, *Osmunda cinnamomea*, is the most versatile species in the genus, easy to grow from North to South while still providing the classic fern habit. The fiddleheads are most beautiful when they unfold in the spring, whether by themselves on the woodland floor or coming through shade tolerant ornamentals like mayapples or epimediums. The base of each frond bears scattered tufts of

cinnamon-colored hairs, hence the common name. The spores are found in the handsome cinnamon-colored fertile leaves. Too much heat and humidity yields stunted plants; shade and consistent moisture is required. An excellent fern for the beginning gardener, useful in zones 3 to 7, zone 8 on the West Coast.

Osmunda claytoniana is known as the interrupted fern, a perfect fit for the plant. The arrangement of the spore cases in the middle of many of the fronds is unique to this species, and I have yet to meet anyone who isn't fascinated with this interrupted arrangement. Plants are large (up to 3' tall and equally wide), and they eat up significant portions of woodland floor where they are established. The green fronds, apart from their being interrupted, are like those of most other ferns. Once the spores are shed in early summer, the interrupted area becomes bare. It is the most common fern in the Berkshires of western Massachusetts and easily established in areas of cool temperatures and moist soils. Best for woodland gardens; does poorly in the South, as lots of shade and moisture

Osmunda cinnamomea

are necessary for best growth. Too aggressive for formal borders. Good for zones 3 to 6, zone 8 on the West Coast.

Osmunda regalis, the royal fern, is the most classic of this classic group of ferns. Where happy, they are some of the largest, most robust plants in the fern family. The light green fronds are compound, unlike the simple fronds of *O. claytoniana*. The fertile spores of the plant are borne on the ends of the fronds, rather than separately as in the cinnamon ferns. Plants can be up to 6' tall and 4' across, eventually producing a huge tussock of roots, the source of osmunda fiber, long used as an amend-

ment for growing orchids. Absolutely stunning in areas of partial shade and heavy moisture. Needs copious or-

ganic matter and cool nights to look its best. Zones 3 to 7, zone 8 on the West Coast.

Osmunda claytoniana

Osmunda claytoniana

Osmunda cinnamomea

Osmunda regalis

Osmunda regalis

Osmunda regalis reflected

Paeonia 'Balliol' (single bush form)

Paeonia

PEONY

"The colder the winter, the better the blooms." Thus was I taught the First Law of Peonies by my grandmother as a young boy in Montreal, and sure enough, every now and then, winters would be milder than usual, and the peonies would produce half the number of usual flowers. The scraggly old plants in that Montreal yard were as ugly as could be—except for a two-week period when they put on their springtime flowers. One does not have to be a zone 3 Montrealer to enjoy peonies: they are excellent south to zone 5, satisfactory to zone 6, but only marginal in zone 7. Since peony performance also declines with high heat in the summer, southern gardeners are

Paeonia 'Nadin' (single bush form)

Paeonia 'Zu Zu' (semi-double bush form)

Paeonia 'Rose Garland' (single bush form)

Paeonia 'White Cockade' (semi-double bush form)

Paeonia 'First Lady' (double bush form)

always on the cusp as they cheer their peonies on. West Coast-ers benefit from moderate summers and usually enjoy excellent flowering.

Peonies come in two shapes, the bush form and the tree form. Most of my preceding comments refer to the incredibly popular and highly bred bush peonies, which are classified as early-, mid-, and late-flowering, with single, semi-double, and double blooms. As a general rule of thumb, the further south one gardens with bush peonies, the more early, single to semi-double forms should be selected. The tree peony, although much more expensive, is increasing in popularity and availability. Most are hybrids of *Paeonia suffruticosa*. They can grow 6–7' tall and are more handsome when not in flower than the bush peonies. The massive blooms are usually double, although singles are occasionally found. Flowers grow to 5" across and

Paeonia 'Red Imp' (double bush form)

Paeonia 'Argosy' (semi-double tree form)

Paeonia 'Honey Gold' (double bush form)

Paeonia 'Banquet' (semi-double tree form)

Paeonia 'Golden Hind' (semi-double tree form)

Paeonia 'Souvenir de Maxime Cornu' (double tree form)

Paeonia 'Daffodil' (double tree form)

Paeonia 'Red Moon' (double tree form)

MORE →

are so heavy, they have to be lifted to be admired. Hardiness zones of 4 to 7 are most appropriate. Full sun in the North; afternoon shade is tolerated in the South.

All the clinical information just offered belies the lure and emotion associated with this fine flowering plant. Everybody loves peonies. They are hugely popular as cut flowers, and displaced Northerners struggle to find at least one cultivar for their new homes in Tucson, Atlanta, or New Orleans. Hundreds of cultivars are available through specialty growers, better garden centers, and mail-order catalogs, and collecting peonies can quickly become an expensive obsession.

Papaver rhoeas

Papaver

POPPY

From Flanders Field to the Wizard of Oz, from fresh rolls and bagels to blighted city streets, poppies have been woven into our poetry, literature, and social structure for many years. That they have been memorialized and cursed with equal vigor underscores the longevity and the beauty of some of the species. Both the Flanders poppy, *Papaver rhoeas*, and the opium poppy, *P. somniferum*, are considered annuals in most American gardens but will occasionally reseed to produce a "perennial" show. The Flanders poppy is easy and colorful, and to see a European field in full finery can bring tears of joy or sadness to the eyes, depending on how quickly John McCrae's poem comes to mind. ("In Flanders fields the poppies blow / Between the crosses, row on row.") It is definitely an age thing. The opium poppy is so handsome that it cannot be ignored as a garden plant, drugheads be damned. The scarlet flowers of the species are beautiful on their own, but 'Album' (a white selection) and the peony-flowered variety *paeoniflorum* are happy to

A field of *Papaver rhoeas*

make the choosing more difficult. Add to that handsome blue-green foliage and the everlasting seed capsules, and we have a plant that can be enjoyed both in the garden and in the vase. What a shame that poeple have messed up such a great plant.

All poppies love cool climates, as their common names make pretty obvious. For example, the Iceland poppy, *Papaver nudicaule*, does not suggest sunny beaches and outdoor picnics, but its colorful crepe paper flowers make it worthwhile no matter where you garden. The best thing is that it can be used as a fall-planted complement to the trillions of pansies that are set out in southern and western American landscapes each autumn. Numerous cultivars are offered, usually in mixed colors and nearly always grown from seed. 'Champagne Bubbles' and

'Party Fun' can be found in both single colors and as a mix; occasionally double-flowered cultivars ('Flore Pleno') are available, but they do not have the

simple classic beauty of the singles. The Iceland poppy will not make it through summers in about seventy percent of the country, but so what?

Papaver somniferum

Papaver somniferum

Papaver somniferum seed heads

Papaver somniferum 'Album'

Papaver somniferum var. *paeoniflorum*

Papaver nudicaule 'Champagne Bubbles'

Papaver nudicaule with pansies

MORE →

As long as you know what to expect, plant and enjoy.

By far the most popular perennial species is the Oriental poppy, *Papaver orientale*, whose bold, colorful flowers enliven late spring. The dark green, coarse leaves appear prickly (they are not), but as tough as they look, they are wimpy, going dormant as temperatures warm up in the summer. The most common color is red, but cultivars are offered in salmon-pink ('Cedric Morris'), pink ('Lighthouse'), crimson ('Avebury Crimson', 'Goliath'), and bicolors ('Picotee'). From the extraordinarily garish singles of 'Suleika' to the warped double flowers of 'Fireball' to the dainty colorful blooms of 'Ladybird', nobody ever accused an Oriental poppy of being subtle.

Oriental poppies do poorly in the heat and should be avoided south of

Papaver nudicaule 'Party Fun'

Papaver orientale

Papaver orientale 'Cedric Morris'

Papaver nudicaule 'Flore Pleno'

Papaver orientale 'Avebury Crimson'

Papaver orientale 'Fireball'

Papaver orientale 'Ladybird'

Papaver orientale 'Lighthouse'

Papaver orientale 'Goliath'

Papaver orientale 'Picotee'

Papaver orientale 'Suleika'

zone 6, although some zone 7 gardeners will be successful for a few seasons. Where they do well, however, they are spectacular. All poppies are most comfortable in zones 3 to 5 (occasionally zone 6 for the Oriental poppy), zone 8 on the West Coast. Full sun, good drainage.

Patrinia

This plant emerged like a lightning bolt when first introduced and continues to be popular for its ability to shrug off inclement weather. Hot or cool, dry or wet, one patrinia or another continues to do its thing. Of the approximately fifteen species, only three are real choices for the garden and landscape, the differences among them attributable more to height and

Patrinia villosa

Patrinia triloba

stature than overall appearance. The shortest of the available taxa is *Patrinia triloba*, which is the least showy of the group but useful where small garden spaces don't lend themselves to the larger members of the clan. Partial shade, morning sun. Hardy in zones 5 to 7 (maybe 8). I also enjoy the foliage of another relatively small member, the white patrinia, *P. villosa*. The foliage can act as a bright ground cover and to me is prettier than the flowers. Full sun, zones 5 to 8.

The most common species is also the tallest. The scabious patrinia, *Patrinia scabiosifolia*, bears large leaves of deep green and hundreds of bright yellow flowers. Plants will grow 3–6'

Patrinia scabiosifolia

Patrinia scabiosifolia

MORE →

Patrinia scabiosifolia 'Nagoya'

Penstemon cardwellii

tall and should not require staking if placed in full sun. Initially, when in flower, this species looks like an over-grown mustard, but as you learn to appreciate its resiliency and lack of maintenance requirements, it grows on you. Plants will reseed, but if that is not in the garden plan, simply whack them down before the fruit forms. If cut when flowers are about half open, however, the blooming stems may be brought inside as a wonderful filler for other cut flowers. The most popular of the smaller introductions is 'Nagoya', whose full-blown stature is usually around 3'. Full sun, zones 5 (4 with protection) to 8.

Penstemon

BEARDTONGUE

The genus *Penstemon* is one of the more interesting groups of plants to use in the garden, not only for its diversity of form and color but also for the botanizing you can enjoy on your own. The name "penstemon" refers to the five stamens in the flower; however, if one looks inside, only four stamens are obvious. The fifth one is there, but looks quite different from the other four; it is properly referred to as a staminode, in case anybody really wants to know such things. In

Penstemon barbatus 'Skylight'

Penstemon barbatus 'Hyacinth'

many species and cultivars, this thin, narrow tongue-like structure is hairy, accounting for the common name. I guess you have to be there . . .

Penstemons create blocks of colorful flowers and/or foliage, and nearly all are native to the United States. They are among the most versatile of plants, ranging from short ground-covering species hardly known at all (*Penstemon cardwellii*) to a handful of well-known upright selections (*P. digitalis* 'Husker Red') to the dozens of garden hybrids. Flowers are mostly in the white, red, purple, and pink range; however a few species, such as *P. confertus*, also bear quite dramatic yellow flowers.

The most cold tolerant species is common beardtongue, *Penstemon barbatus*, whose large wide-lipped flowers are slightly bearded on the lower lip. They are easy to grow, provide numerous colors, and persist for many years. Many cultivars have been selected, including 'Hyacinth', with large rosy pink flowers, and 'Skylight', which produces handsome rose-and-white bicolor blooms. The species has also been included as a parent to many hybrids, passing on its larger flowers and additional cold tolerance. Full sun, zones 2 to 8.

Three native species have proven their worth: *Penstemon digitalis*, *P. pinifolius*, and *P. smallii*, native to the Southwest, Southeast, and East, respectively. Smooth white penstemon, *P. digitalis*, is probably the best known, mainly due to the breeding efforts of

Penstemon confertus

Penstemon digitalis 'Husker Red'

Penstemon digitalis 'Husker Red'

Penstemon barbatus 'Hyacinth'

Penstemon digitalis

MORE →

Penstemon pinifolius

Dale Lindgren at the University of Nebraska, where the purple-leaved cultivar 'Husker Red' was developed. The species itself is terrific, with large deep green leaves and wonderful white flowers held well above the foliage. The leaves of 'Husker Red' are the reddest during cool weather, but when temperatures remain over 85°F for a period of time, they tend to lose much of their red pigment. Still and all, a great plant in much of the country. Full sun, zones 4 to 8.

The pineleaf penstemon, *Penstemon pinifolius*, with thin green leaves and wonderful tubular, rosy salmon blooms, comes alive with flower power in the late spring and summer. It welcomes full sun but does not appreciate areas of high humidity and summer rain. Hardy in zones 7 to 9. On the other hand, heat, humidity, and rainfall do not bother Small's penstemon, *P. smallii*, nearly as much. Its flowers are pink-purple on the outside and white on the inside. This species also tolerates shade better than most penstemons, although some direct sun

Penstemon pinifolius

Penstemon smallii

Penstemon smallii

Penstemon 'Port Wine'

Penstemon 'Schönholzeri' ('Firebird')

builds stem strength. Partial shade, zones 6 to 8.

The numerous species of *Penstemon* are quite lovely, but it is the hybrids that are stealing the show in American gardens. Although the parentage of most of them may be traced to North American species, they had to go to Europe, especially the British Isles, for gentrification. They are finally returning home and have been strutting their stuff in many locations. Most are hardy in zones 4 to 7 (8 on the West Coast) and prefer full sun, but in the South they appreciate a little afternoon shade if possible. Some of the red- to wine-colored cultivars I enjoy are 'Port Wine', 'Ruby', and 'Schönholzeri' ('Firebird'). They differ in flower size and vigor, but all are eye-catching. Purples and blues include 'Sour Grapes' and 'Stapleford Gem'; white flowers can be found in 'White Bedder' and 'Snowstorm'. 'Hidcote Pink' is a wonderful pink, while the bicolors

Penstemon 'Sour Grapes'

Penstemon 'Hidcote Pink'

Penstemon 'Stapleford Gem'

Penstemon 'Snowstorm'

Penstemon 'Ruby'

Penstemon 'White Bedder'

MORE →

are represented by the outstanding 'Thorn' and 'Mother of Pearl'. The list goes on and on, and a good deal of money will be spent before your short list of favorites can be determined. Full sun to a little afternoon shade, zones 5 (sometimes 4) to 8.

Penstemon 'Mother of Pearl'

Perovskia atriplicifolia

RUSSIAN SAGE

I used to enjoy telling the story of how *Perovskia atriplicifolia*, Russian sage, got its common name—that the foliage was so pungent it was said to smell like the feet of marching Russian soldiers. But with the Cold War over and political correctness rampant, I apologize to all the Russian soldiers whose feet I maligned. (The foliage actually smells like my son's feet, on a good day, but enough of that.) The genus was in fact named for Russian general V. A. Perovsky, and this species is tough and reliable throughout the country. In northern gardens, the flowers are an intense blue and remain that way all summer; in southern gardens, the intense blue tends to fade as summer temperatures increase. Plants grow tall, up to 5' in height, and tend to flop over no matter the intensity of sun or summer temperatures. A good haircut in late spring encourages branching and reduces height. Regardless of the problems, the silver foliage is handsome, and its fragrance is an additional bonus for those with sinus problems.

A few cultivars are listed, but I don't see a great deal of difference from one to the other. 'Longin' does have darker blue flowers, and 'Filagran', with its deeper cut foliage, provides a more lacy appearance. Full sun, zones 5 to 9.

Penstemon 'Thorn'

Perovskia atriplicifolia

Perovskia atriplicifolia 'Longin'

Phlomis

JERUSALEM SAGE

I am sure that all gardeners go through various stages of plant fixations in their gardening years, and people have embraced trilliums, campanulas, saxifrages, and salvias with the zeal of philatelists and numismatists. I have gone through my "salvia stage of life" but am presently enamored of another sage, *Phlomis*. Fortunately, Jerusalem sages are not nearly as numerous as salvias, and I can't find that many for sale anyway, so my present affliction is much easier to control. Jerusalem sages occur in two main flower colors, yellows and lavender-pinks. All have hairy foliage, with some silvering to it, and the flower buds are almost as beautiful as the flowers themselves. *Phlomis* is a useful companion to almost all plants in the garden, regardless of season or stage of flowering.

The yellow forms are bigger but also more compact in habit. They are best represented by *Phlomis fruticosa*, the most popular species, and *P. russeliana*, both known as Jerusalem sage. *Phlomis fruticosa* has 2–4" long silvery green leaves and is handsome throughout the season in the North, throughout the year in the South. The green flower buds occur in whorls up the stem, then give way to bright yellow flowers, like lights on a candelabra. Outstanding in leaf, terrific in bud and flower, and as a bonus, wonderful in fruit. The fruit remains on the plants for many weeks, adding yet another ornamental charm to an already interesting plant. Plants get woody at the base; a hard prune in the spring every two to three years rejuvenates them. Full sun, hardy in zones 4 to 8. Plants tend to reseed, so get ready to share them with others.

Phlomis russeliana is bigger in every way, with larger leaves and habit, but

Phlomis russeliana in bud

Phlomis fruticosa in winter

Phlomis fruticosa

Phlomis fruticosa

MORE →

Phlomis russeliana

Phlomis russeliana

the leaves are much more dull green than silver green, and the flowers are a softer yellow. Not quite as hardy, nor as compact of habit. Full sun, zones 5 to 8.

The lavender-pinks are well represented by *Phlomis bovei*, the Moroccan sage, and *P. italica*, the Italian sage. In general, the plants and leaves are smaller than the yellow-flowered species just described, but the flower color is equally arresting. Plants stand about 2–4' and appear rather lanky. It is more difficult to find nurseries selling lavender-pink *Phlomis*, likely because they are cold hardy only to zone 8 (7 with protection). Provide full sun and well-drained soils.

Phlomis bovei

Phlomis italica

Phlomis russeliana

Phlomis fruticosa (left) and P. russeliana

Phlox

In 1745 the American botanist John Bartram sent a specimen of *Phlox* to England, billing it as "a fine creeping Spring Lychnis." No sooner did it land than it became a hit in that land of gardens, and the English embraced it as their own. The genus enjoyed such popularity there that in 1919 Reginald Farrar enthusiastically wrote of it, "The day that saw the introduction, more than a century since . . . ought indeed to be kept as a horticultural festival." So many good garden plants are now available that Messrs. Bartram and Farrar would probably have no trouble at all drumming up support for a phlox festival.

I enjoy all the low growers, but I think some of the finest garden plants have to belong to the woodland phlox, *Phlox divaricata*, with its handsome coat of lavender flowers and thin dark green leaves, 1½–2" in length. The species is a denizen of woodland edges, allowing the gardener to fill in many partially shaded areas in a rock garden or shaded spot. Woodland phlox are more substantial than many other low-growing phlox, growing 12–15" tall and harmonizing well with other low growers; it also combines beautifully with plants with colorful foliage, like golden spirea. If the plants reseed, various shades of blue, lavender, and light purple are sure to appear. Some wonderful cultivars are available. Try the clean white of 'Fuller's White', the outstanding icy cold blue of 'Dirigo Ice', and the regal

Phlox divaricata with golden spirea

Phlox divaricata

Phlox divaricata 'Dirigo Ice'

Phlox divaricata 'Fuller's White'

Phlox divaricata 'Louisiana Blue'

MORE →

Phlox divaricata 'Clouds of Perfume'

Mildew damage on *Phlox paniculata*

Phlox paniculata 'David'

purple of 'Louisiana Blue'. I also enjoy the pale blue blossoms of 'Clouds of Perfume', which is neither like a cloud nor particularly fragrant, but I like the name. Place in partial shade, hardy in zones 5 to 8.

Phlox paniculata is a tough perennial, tolerating late freezes, droughts, and hot summers for five to eight years; dozens of flowers, averaging about an inch across, are held at the top of each plant in 8" wide clusters. Their classic habit and reliability make them the choice for the gardens of many houses, from my daughter's fixer-upper to those of Frank Lloyd Wright. These are plants that turn the summer gar-

den into a veritable rainbow, flowering in June through August. Unfortunately, in many cultivars, one of those veritable colors is the white of powdery mildew. This disease starts on the bottom leaves and can rapidly disfigure the entire plant. I have seen much worse cases of mildew in Montreal than in Athens; however, on highly susceptible cultivars, it matters very little where the plants reside. Providing good circulation and thinning the emerging plants to four or five strong stems in the spring can help.

With hundreds of *Phlox paniculata* cultivars from which to choose, gardeners can afford to be picky: color

Mixed display of *Phlox paniculata*

Phlox paniculata 'Robert Poore'

Phlox paniculata 'Bright Eyes'

of flower, vigor of plant, and susceptibility to mildew are all characteristics to be considered. Two vigorous selections that have enjoyed immense popularity are the white-flowered 'David' and 'Robert Poore', with large trusses of iridescent purple flowers on 5' tall plants. I have seen very little mildew on either. Other handsome cultivars include the beautiful 'Prospero', whose white flowers with blushes of pink stand out in the summer garden. I also enjoy the popular 'Bright Eyes', with pale pink flowers and a crimson eye, and 'Franz Schubert', with light pink flowers on 3' tall plants. 'Red Indian' is a rosy pink; 'Starfire' is a brilliant scarlet; 'Red Eyes' provides exactly that in the middle of light pink flowers; and 'Fairest One' has many trusses of rose-colored flowers with

a darker red eye. For lavender hues, 'Blue Boy' is a useful addition. Those after variegated foliage will find 'Norah Leigh' striking, if not particularly easy to grow, with her green-and-white leaves and pink to lavender flowers. Place in full sun; plants grow 3–5' tall. Hardy in zones 4 to 8.

The neat thing about the genus *Phlox* is the number of low growers that justify Reginald Farrar's obsession. One is creeping phlox, *Phlox stolonifera* (6–12" tall), which creeps around rapidly and is an excellent ground cover to boot. The leaves are about 2" long, and plants bear 1–1$\frac{1}{2}$"

Phlox paniculata 'Fairest One'

Phlox paniculata 'Norah Leigh'

Phlox paniculata 'Prospero'

Phlox paniculata 'Red Indian'

Phlox paniculata 'Franz Schubert'

Phlox paniculata 'Starfire'

Phlox paniculata 'Red Eyes'

MORE →

Phlox stolonifera 'Bruce's White'

Phlox stolonifera 'Sherwood Purple'

Phlox stolonifera 'Variegata'

Phlox stolonifera 'Homefires'

wide flowers. They do well in light shade and should not be planted in full sun, except in the far North. Creeping phlox gets around in various colors: 'Bruce's White' is the best white of the group, and one of the better darker selections is 'Sherwood Purple'. If I must have a pink-flowering creeping phlox in the Armitage garden, I would choose 'Homefires'. Last but not least is 'Variegata', a slow grower whose variegated foliage makes a lovely contrast to the other green-leaved cultivars in this fine group of plants. Partial shade, zones 2 to 8.

All species of *Phlox* arc native to the United States. Bartram could have sent any one of them, so why was such a commotion made over *Phlox subulata*, a plant we call the gas station plant, the outhouse plant, and other ghastly names—properly known as moss phlox? Let there be no doubt: scorned as it is, this is a great plant. It covers grand hillsides, sneaks under picket fences, grows beside driveways, and makes festive gas stations and trailer parks everywhere. It may be faulted for its short bloom time, but how extraordinary that time is. Dense carpets of pink appear in early spring, obscuring the leaves; when the blooms have faded, carpets of green leaves, each an inch long and an eighth of an inch

A drift of *Phlox subulata*

Phlox subulata on a smaller scale

wide, simply blend into the landscape. These 4–6" tall mats come in an astonishing range of colors. Some of my favorites include 'Oakington Blue', with flowers of light blue, and 'Candy Stripe', an outstanding white-and-pink bicolor. I think I stopped maligning moss phlox when I stumbled across the indescribable pastel flowers of 'Coral Eye' and the starry white flowers of 'Snowflake', which is so white in flower that the foliage all but disappears. I also can't help but single out 'Scarlet Flame', whose names describes its effect, and 'Maiden's Blush', with the lightest of pinks on its dozens of flowers. Great plants, easy to grow in full sun and well-drained soils. Full sun, hardy in zones 2 to 8.

Phlox subulata 'Candy Stripe'

Phlox subulata 'Coral Eye'

Phlox subulata 'Scarlet Flame'

Phlox subulata 'Maiden's Blush'

Phlox subulata 'Oakington Blue'

Phlox subulata 'Snowflake'

Physostegia virginiana 'Bouquet Rose' ('Pink Bouquet')

Physostegia virginiana

OBEDIENT PLANT

If gardeners were ever to compile a list of misnomers in common names, obedient plant would be near the very top. *Physostegia virginiana*, a native of the eastern United States, is many things, but obedient is not one of them. It is an elegant plant, with opposite leaves, square stems, and handsome pink flowers on a spiky flower head, but its beauty and elegance belie its land-grabbing proclivity. If you don't have sufficient space to allow for a little roaming, don't plant obedient plant. If room is available, however, the 12–18" plants are excellent companions for yellow evening primroses and blue asters. Dozens of one-inch-long lipped flowers open from the bottom to the top, and when about a third of the flowers are open, they are perfect for picking and bringing in the house. As a cut flower, they persist for at least a week in tap water, longer if a flower preservative is used.

Some excellent selections of *Physostegia virginiana* can be found in nurseries and mail-order catalogs. The pink-flowered 'Bouquet Rose' ('Pink Bouquet') grows 3–4' tall and is an excellent choice, differing only slightly from the species. 'Vivid', with darker flowers, grows only 2–3' tall and may be the best choice for the smaller garden. The white-flowered cultivars are probably the prettiest; they are a little more dwarf than the pink-flowered

Physostegia virginiana 'Vivid'

Physostegia virginiana 'Alba'

Physostegia virginiana 'Alba'

Physostegia virginiana 'Summer Snow'

Physostegia virginiana 'Variegata'

selections and flower a few weeks earlier. 'Alba' and 'Summer Snow' are similar in flower color, but 'Alba' is a little shorter. The most interesting selection is 'Variegata', which sports pink flowers and outstanding white-and-green variegated foliage. The plant is probably more handsome when flowers are absent. Plant in full sun in well-drained soils, hardy in zones 2 to 9.

Pinellia

The genus *Pinellia* will never enjoy a large following, partly because so few gardeners and growers know about it. The requirements of these plants are similar to others in the Jack-in-the-pulpit family (Araceae), that is, shade and consistent moisture. Also similar to other members of the family, they are appreciated for their deep green foliage and the long lazy tongues (Jacks) that protrude from the small purple pulpits.

Two useful species are *Pinellia pedatisecta*, with its four to five compound leaves, and *P. tripartita*, with only three leaves. Both have long tongues and are similar in flower. Plants can reseed with abandon, particularly if the shade is airy (as under tall pines), not dense (as under oaks or maples). These are plants for plant lovers who enjoy a quiet stroll through the garden to admire the less obvious. Hardy in zones 6 to 8.

Pinellia pedatisecta

Pinellia tripartita

Physostegia virginiana 'Variegata'

Pinellia pedatisecta

Pinellia tripartita

Platycodon grandiflorus in bud

Platycodon grandiflorus

Platycodon grandiflorus 'Shell Pink'

Platycodon grandiflorus 'Mariesii' with *Hemerocallis*

Platycodon grandiflorus

BALLOONFLOWER

Although *Platycodon grandiflorus* is native to the Far East, these plants have become American favorites, thanks mostly to their curious swollen buds and chalice-shaped blue to purple flowers, which open wide in mid to

Platycodon grandiflorus 'Albus'

Platycodon grandiflorus 'Plenus'

Platycodon grandiflorus 'Sentimental Blue'

late summer. Slow to emerge, even given up for dead by rookie ballooners, they grow rapidly into sizeable 3' plants. The flower buds swell and swell, just like a balloon, finally popping open to reveal beautiful five-petaled flowers with dark blue veins. They are particularly useful growing with lilies or other summer-flowering white or yellow plants.

The diversity in the genus is seen in cultivars with white ('Albus'), pink ('Shell Pink'), double ('Plenus'), and occasionally even spotted ('Florovariegatus') flowers. One of the problems with balloonflower is that stems are weak, and staking is often required, particularly in inclement weather. Because of this, two shorter selections have been bred: 'Mariesii' is 1–2' tall and 'Sentimental Blue' is only 6–9" tall. Both require less maintenance but are not as classy as the real thing. Plants require full sun, or they will flop over. Hardy in zones 3 to 7.

Platycodon grandiflorus 'Florovariegatus'

Platycodon grandiflorus 'Sentimental Blue'

Polemonium

JACOB'S LADDER

The genus *Polemonium* is diverse, ranging from 3' tall plants to dwarf runners, and all are happier in cool rather than warm summers. The blue, white, or pink flowers generally present themselves in early to mid summer. Of the twenty-five or so species, one or two are quite endearing, if not enduring, and a few others are well worth trying.

Polemonium caeruleum and *P. folio-sissimum*, common upright species, have about twenty leaves climbing the stem, each leaf representing a rung of the Jacob's ladder we are climbing. They stand 2–3' tall and produce masses of lavender-blue flowers in the spring and early summer. I have seen excellent stands in Franklin Park, Columbus, Ohio, and in Trois Rivières, Quebec, where they grow like weeds. The two species are fine plants in their own right; however, several excellent cultivars of *P. caeruleum* have been developed.

The white-flowered *Polemonium caeruleum* 'Album' is also upright, and the white flowers make a nice contrast to the dark green leaves. Subspecies *himalayanum* ('Himalayanum') is a little taller and probably more cold tolerant. Lower growers, such as 'Dawn Light', have emerged; their shorter stature is their main claim to fame. The newest and most unique is the variegated 'Brise d'Anjou', with clean green-and-white leaves and blue flowers. The foliage is the best part of this plant, as the open flowers tend to be lost in the leaves. All cultivars are cold hardy to at least zone 4, and heat tolerant to

Polemonium caeruleum

Polemonium caeruleum 'Album'

Polemonium caeruleum subsp. himalayanum ('Himalayanum')

Polemonium foliosissimum

Polemonium caeruleum 'Brise d'Anjou'

MORE →

about zone 6 east of the Rocky Mountains, zone 8 west of the Rockies. Full sun, well-drained soils.

Polemonium caeruleum 'Dawn Light'

Polemonium carneum

Both *Polemonium carneum*, salmon Jacob's ladder, and *P. reptans*, creeping Jacob's ladder, are much lower growing than *P. caeruleum* and *P. foliosissimum* and therefore are perfect for the front of the garden bed. The salmon-flowered *P. carneum*, native to the western United States, is beautiful but less adaptable than the blue-flowered species. Plants are also more difficult to obtain, but if your local nursery carries the plant, give it a try. It is only about 18–24" tall, with pink to salmon flowers. *Polemonium reptans* is native to the eastern United States and—although it does not run fast—can be a pest in gardens it takes a liking to; its selection 'Blue Pearl' grows about 8–10" tall, with bright blue flowers. The type provides excellent greenery and numerous flowers throughout the season; it is easy to grow and makes a nice filler in partially shaded to sunny areas. Neither species does well in hot summer climates, and zone 6 is about as far south as they want to be. *Polemonium carneum* is only cold tolerant to zone 6 (perhaps 5), but *P. reptans* can tolerate temperatures in zone 2. Well-drained soils, partial shade to sun.

Polygonatum

SOLOMON'S SEAL

The genus *Polygonatum* provides a wonderful store of shade tolerant plants for the woodland, many of them among our finest natives. The common name has many a good yarn associated with it; one is that, during the times of the great kings, the roots acted as a glue to heal broken bones, and it was this sealing property that begat the name Solomon's seal. (I don't believe it either.) Of the many closely related species, three have a definite place in the woodland or garden.

Both *Polygonatum commutatum*, great Solomon's seal, and *P. odoratum*, fragrant Solomon's seal, are upright species (at least 2' tall) and bear lovely dangling white flowers at the leaf nodes. I love the way the stems of *P. commutatum* burst through the spring ground, the leaves tucked in and the entire stem resembling a fat green shish-kabob skewer. As the leaves unfurl, the small floating flower buds break open to reveal clean white flowers dangling from each node. Plants look good even

Polemonium reptans 'Blue Pearl'

Emerging stems of *Polygonatum commutatum*

after the season is finished, the amber leaves and old flowers a study in nature's beauty. So common in the Northeast and Midwest that it is hardly even noticed, this plant richly deserves a place in the shaded woodland.

The fragrant Solomon's seal, *Polygonatum odoratum*, is the European version of the great one but is a pretender compared to it. Similar in habit, with green leaves and white flowers, the stature of the species itself is less imposing and its performance not as good. Hope is offered, however, by the main offering in the garden catalogs, the excellent selection 'Variegatum'. Now this is a marvelous plant, its white flowers adding to the beauty of the variegated leaves, which turn an outstanding bronze by autumn. It is obvious, at least to me, why this is a

favorite Armitage plant in the oak forest I call a garden.

Both *Polygonatum commutatum* and *P. odoratum* require partial shade with two to three hours of bright light to be their best. Hardy in zones 3 to 8.

As robust and grand as the previous two species are, *Polygonatum humile*, dwarf Solomon's seal, is refined and charming. Plants grow only 6–9" tall, still with the characteristic small white flowers formed at the nodes. A rich full planting can be obtained in two to three years, and a better ground cover

Polygonatum commutatum

Polygonatum commutatum in fall

Polygonatum odoratum 'Variegatum'

Polygonatum commutatum

Polygonatum odoratum 'Variegatum'

Polygonatum odoratum 'Variegatum' in fall

215

MORE →

for a small area is hard to imagine. Plants prefer partial shade, but not as much as the upright Solomons. One of the problems with its size is that other plants quickly overgrow it, resulting in too much shade and moisture and a subsequent loss of plants. While I admire and use the upright species, I lust after this one. Partial shade, hardy in zones 5 to 7.

Polygonatum humile

Polygonatum humile

Polygonum affine 'Hartford'

Polygonum

KNOTWEED, SMARTWEED, FLEECEFLOWER

The knotweeds are probably more cursed than loved, bringing a mixture of beauty and downright belligerence. That the best-known plants are weeds like Pennsylvania smartweed, lady's thumb, and common knotweed tells us that the genus *Polygonum* is indeed adaptable. Several species are widely planted and don't share the overly aggressive behavior of their impolite cousins. All polygonums have red to pink flowers on thin inflorescences, and the petioles of their leaves clasp the stem, a telltale characteristic of the genus. Some taxonomists insist that the genus *Polygonum* should be changed to *Persicaria*, but some do not. Until consensus is reached, I will continue to talk about polygonums and the quite wonderful common names associated with them.

When conditions suit it, the low-growing *Polygonum affine* (*Persicaria affinis*; Himalayan fleeceflower) can be considered a ground cover. The small leaves emerge purple-green in the spring. As the plants mature, spikes of rosy red flowers appear, covering the planting by early summer. They do well in cool summers; I have had no success in north Georgia but have seen terrific stands in the Northeast, Midwest, and Northwest. Available cultivars include 'Hartford' and the more aggressive 'Superbum'. Excellent drainage is essential. Plants perform better in full sun to partial shade; too much shade results in sparse plantings. Hardy in zones 3 to 7.

Probably the best known and most planted of the garden species, *Polygonum bistorta* (*Persicaria bistorta*;

snakeweed) can be found doing well everywhere but in the deep South. The plants consist of wavy green leaves, each with a white midrib, and above them, looking something like pink bottlebrushes, are 4–5" spikes of pink flowers. They look particularly good combined with purple flowers, such as ornamental onions. Plants do very well where moisture accumulates, although they are not bog plants. The flowers are highly prized as cut flowers and persist for about a week in a bouquet. Excellent plantings may be found from Pennsylvania to Chicago to Den-

Polygonum affine 'Superbum'

Polygonum bistorta with *Allium*

Polygonum affine

MORE →

ver. Subspecies *carneum* has cherry-red flowers; variety *regelianum* bears creamy white flowers. All pink-flowering offerings are likely 'Superbum'. Full sun is appropriate if consistent moisture can be provided, otherwise some afternoon shade is useful. Hardy in zones 3 to 7.

Polygonum bistorta 'Superbum'

Polygonum bistorta 'Superbum'

Polygonum bistorta subsp. *carneum*

Primula

PRIMROSE

Oh, to live in primrose country! When I visit my gardening friends on the West Coast or overseas, I revel in the magic of spring primroses. Not that the Armitage garden is entirely bereft of this wonderful genus, but the primrose path is easier trodden in climates where extremes of cold and heat are uncommon. Of the four hundred or so species, we in the States are lucky to find two or three different kinds for sale, even in quality garden centers, and must instead peruse the mail-order seed and plant sources for any satisfaction. Seed is generally not difficult to germinate, and many species may be obtained through specialist

Primula denticulata

Polygonum bistorta var. *regelianum*

seed sources. Essentially all primroses perform better with mild winters, mild summers, partially shaded areas, and consistent moisture in the soil. Some require boggy soils to do well and wimp out at the first hint of drought or heat, while others are much tougher than they look.

Both *Primula denticulata*, the drumstick primrose, and *P. veris*, cowslip, require similar growing conditions—that is, shady, moist, and not too cold—but cowslips tolerate heat much better. Looking at the flower of *P. denticulata* reaffirms its common name; these drumsticks occur in shades of lavender, rose-blue ('Rosea'), and white ('Alba'). They flower early, in February or March, then succumb to the rigors of heat in much of the country. They are beautiful when in flower, and their foliage simply disappears into the plants that grow up around it. Hardy in zones 5 (4 with protection) to 7.

The common cowslip, *Primula veris*, is a terrific, adaptable, and functional primrose that works well in American gardens. The dark green leaves are in perfect contrast to the deep yellow flowers, which continue to open for four to six weeks in the spring. One of the best primroses for southern gardeners—heat is not a problem, assuming water is available, and plants reseed easily. A primrose path is almost possible. Hardy in zones 5 (4 with protection) to 8.

Some of the most beautiful and architectural primroses of all fall into the candelabra group. The flowers of these several species are arranged on long flower stems, like lights on an exquisite candelabra. They all require copious amounts of water and in fact are best suited for water gardens, sides of streams, or boggy soils. If such conditions are provided, then plants can tolerate full sun, but afternoon shade is usually appreciated. The best known of the candelabras, the Japanese primrose, *Primula japonica*, is usually seen in a mixture of flower colors. Some monochromatic selections can also be found occasionally, such as 'Postford White' and the rosy pink 'Splendens'.

Primula denticulata 'Rosea'

Primula denticulata 'Alba'

Primula veris

Primula japonica

Primula japonica 'Postford White'

MORE →

The American gardener doesn't have access to as many of the candelabras as their European colleagues; however, if you are successful with Japanese primrose, then all sorts of primrose doors open. I would be like a kid in a candy store and try some that look impossible, such as Bulley's primrose, *Primula bulleyana*, with its vibrant orange flowers. Even the name is terrific. For a more refined effect, I would plant some florinda primroses, *P. florindae*, by the side of my pond. With its dangling yellow flowers and classic habit, it is a plant well worth trying. My candelabra collection would be incomplete without a few plants of the butter-yellow *P. heladoxa*, the rosy flowers of *P. pulverulenta* 'Bartley's Strain', or my all-time favorite from Ireland, *P.* 'Rowallane Rose'. These may not take you, your garden, and your neighborhood miles along that primrose path—still, half the fun is in the trying. All are probably hardy in zones 5 to 7, prefer the Northwest, and

Primula japonica 'Splendens'

Primula bulleyana

Primula florindae

Primula heladoxa

Primula heladoxa

need lots of water and partial shade.

Almost everyone who sees Vial's primrose, *Primula vialii*, has to look twice to even recognize it as a primrose, but once the synapses click, the next thoughts are "I must have it" and "Where do I get it?" The purple flowers extend nearly 2' into the air and are only vaguely primrose-like. A good deal of interest in establishing this plant in American gardens is underway, and they soon may be more readily available. Success requires mild summers and winters, moisture, and a protected area. Partial shade, hardy in zones 5 to 7.

Primula 'Rowallane Rose'

Primula pulverulenta 'Bartley's Strain'

Primula vialii

Primula pulverulenta 'Bartley's Strain'

Primula vialii

MORE →

The common English primrose, *Primula vulgaris*, is not all that common in the United States but very common in Europe, where many selections have been made. Short in stature but frost and heat tolerant, they are usually available in yellows and whites. 'Alba' has creamy white flowers with yellow centers; 'Atlantia' has the cleanest white blooms I have seen. The most common variations on the theme are 'Gigha White' and subspecies *sibthorpii*, which are white or off-white and pink, respectively. The English primrose is also known for the old-fashioned highly bred double-flowerers, such as 'Double Burgundy' and 'Double Yellow', which were mostly grown for exhibition and not the garden. Still available, but not nearly as popular as in Queen Victoria's time. Partial shade, hardy in zones 5 to 8.

Primula vulgaris 'Gigha White'

Primula vulgaris subsp. *sibthorpii*

Pulmonaria

LUNGWORT

A favored shade plant, lungwort can be counted on to produce a blend of handsome foliage and wonderful blue, lavender, red, or white flowers. I love the earliness of leaves and flowers, the beauty of the foliage, and the flowers. They are tougher than they look, asking only for some shade and well-drained soils. Lungworts occur in different guises: those with plain green leaves and flowers in the blue to lavender range (*Pulmonaria angustifolia*); those with plain green leaves and flowers of pink to red (*P. rubra*); those with spotted leaves that are long and narrow (*P. longifolia*); and those with spotted leaves that are relatively short and wide (*P. saccharata*). Noting the differences in leaf shape and spotting is the easiest way to sort out the spe-

Primula vulgaris 'Alba'

Primula vulgaris 'Double Burgundy'

Leaves of *Pulmonaria saccharata* (left), *P. longifolia* (middle), and *P. angustifolia*

Primula vulgaris 'Atlantia'

Primula vulgaris 'Double Yellow'

Pulmonaria angustifolia

cies. A good deal of breeding and selection occurred in the 1990s, and the number of cultivar choices has risen exponentially.

There is little to choose between *Pulmonaria angustifolia*, common lungwort, and *P. rubra*, red-flowered lungwort, as far as leaf shape and leaf color are concerned. They both have hairy unspotted green leaves that poke out of the soil early in the spring,

Pulmonaria angustifolia 'Mawson's Variety'

either at the same time as the flowers or a little after. The plainness of the foliage makes these lungworts less popular among gardeners; however, they offer some of the finest flowers in the genus. Some of the biggest and bluest flowers can be found in selections of *P. angustifolia*, such as 'Mawson's Variety' and 'Munstead Blue', respectively. They also possess good heat tolerance, performing well in our trials at the University of Georgia. Happy and hardy in zones 3 to 7 in the East, to zone 8 in the West.

The selections of *Pulmonaria rubra* are a bit more complex than others. The nonspotted leaves are similar to those of *P. angustifolia*, although they may be a little larger. The pink to red flowers open as the new leaves emerge. Plants are not as vigorous or as tough

as others, and we had more losses in this group of lungworts than in any other. Still, their color guarantees them popularity, and some of the selections are interesting, including 'Bowles' Red', the toughest of the group we tested, and 'David Ward', by far the most ornamental but least robust, with its red flowers and variegated foliage. Perform well in zones 3 to 6 in the East, to zone 8 in the West.

The species *Pulmonaria longifolia* makes up many of the lungworts in American gardens, probably because the spotted foliage is handsome long after the flowers have come and gone. The common name, long-leaved lungwort, describes the long, narrow leaves, which are quite distinct from all other lungworts. The flowers are usually lavender to blue. The best-

Pulmonaria angustifolia 'Munstead Blue'

Pulmonaria rubra 'Bowles' Red'

Pulmonaria rubra 'Bowles' Red'

Pulmonaria rubra 'David Ward'

Pulmonaria rubra 'David Ward'

MORE →

Pulmonaria 'Roy Davidson'

Pulmonaria saccharata 'Berries and Cream'

Pulmonaria saccharata 'Berries and Cream'

known selection is 'Bertram Anderson', with its long narrow leaves and striking blue flowers. Several others have shown excellent promise. The selection sold both as subspecies *cevennensis* and 'Little Blue' has some of the most ornamental foliage in the entire genus, while the hybrid between *P. longifolia* and *P. saccharata*, *P.* 'Roy Davidson', possesses some of the leaf characteristics of *P. longifolia* but bears light blue flowers. All the long-leaved selections and hybrids are excellent performers, tolerating hot, humid summers better than other lungworts and providing excellent foliage and habit in most of the country. Hardy in zones 3 to 7.

Selections of spotted lungwort, *Pulmonaria saccharata*, are by far the most easily available and popular. The

foliage is wider than those of *P. longifolia*, and spotting patterns are highly variable. In fact, they are like fingerprints, no leaf being exactly the same as another. Flowers range from pink to lavender to deep blue. So many fine selections have been produced that you should have no problem finding one for the shade. Try 'Benediction', with its fine light blue flowers, or 'Berries and Cream', a favorite in the Armitage garden for its pink flowers and beautiful spotted pattern. 'Excalibur' is almost white; 'Spilled Milk' is an apt description; and the lightly spotted 'Highdown' is among the best of them all, providing excellent ornamental value, good flowering, and a tough disposition. 'Mrs. Kittle' has clean spots and feels at home in the shade of small shrubs like golden spirea, and the light

Pulmonaria longifolia 'Bertram Anderson'

Pulmonaria saccharata 'Benediction'

Pulmonaria longifolia 'Bertram Anderson'

Pulmonaria longifolia subsp. *cevennensis* ('Little Blue')

blue flowers and good leaves of 'Mrs. Moon' have made her a longtime favorite. Finally, the white flowers of 'Sissinghurst White' are always a welcome addition in the spring. Given the depth and range of offerings, describing lungworts is becoming as difficult as describing coral bells, daylilies, or hostas. All the better for us gardeners! Hardy in zones 3 to 7 in the East, to zone 8 in the West.

Pulmonaria saccharata 'Excalibur'

Pulmonaria saccharata 'Mrs. Kittle'

225

Pulmonaria saccharata 'Highdown'

Pulmonaria saccharata 'Spilled Milk'

Pulmonaria saccharata 'Sissinghurst White'

Pulmonaria saccharata 'Mrs. Moon'

Pulsatilla pratensis

Pulsatilla vulgaris

Pulsatilla

PASQUEFLOWER

Except to the hard-core alpine and rock garden enthusiasts, the diversity of the genus *Pulsatilla* is largely unknown. Those in the know grow pasqueflowers for the beauty of their dissected foliage and their handsome purple to white flowers in early spring. Flowers emerge before the foliage in most cases, followed by the leaves, but the waving seed heads are the most striking part of the plants, persisting for many weeks after the ephemeral flowers have disappeared. Because they flower in late winter and early spring when snow may still be on the ground, the flowers and seed heads persist for as long as the cool weather

holds up. I have seen absolutely stunning plantings in the Denver Botanic Gardens (there the pasqueflowers are seeding everywhere) and have grown them in north Georgia with reasonable success. If one lives in an area where alpines do well, then it is worth chasing down plants of *Pulsatilla halleri* or *P. pratensis*, both of which flower early and often. But most gardeners don't have the time or money to find such gems and will usually be limited to the common pasqueflower, *P. vulgaris*. That certainly is not all bad: the plant provides excellent foliage and dozens of deep purple flowers. And the seed heads persist for many weeks, giving another dimension to the plant. A few cultivars have been selected, but I have been most impressed with the white-flowered 'Alba', which forms similar

Pulsatilla halleri

Pulsatilla vulgaris

Pulsatilla vulgaris seed heads

Pulsatilla vulgaris 'Alba'

seed heads and whose white flowers contrast well with the foliage. Provide full sun, excellent drainage. Hardy in zones 4 (3 with protection) to 7.

Ranunculus

BUTTERCUP

Buttercups are a study in diversity, for sure. Plants may develop from a tuber, like a potato, or from fibrous roots, like most other perennials. Although most people think of buttercups as yellow, their flowers appear in a full spectrum of hues, including white. Some species turn over and die at the first feel of frost; others are tough as nails through all kinds of inclement weather, elbowing-out any other plant in their proximity.

The most colorful and the most persnickety is the tuberous-rooted Persian buttercup, *Ranunculus asiaticus*. Usually seen as a pot plant from the

greenhouse or as a cut flower grown in cool summer areas, it produces some of the prettiest flowers in the genus. They are favorites among bulb aficionados, but they seldom act as a perennial, being frost tolerant only to about 28°F. Tubers should be soaked in water and put in the garden in the fall in mild areas, and in the spring in areas of cold winters and cool summers.

Coolness is necessary for best performance, and plants will produce many double flowers in the spring, then go dormant in the summer. Selections may be purchased as single ('Bloomingdale Yellow') or mixed ('Sunningdale Mix') colors. Full sun and excellent drainage are necessary. Hardy in zones 7 to 9.

Another little tuberous species is

Ranunculus asiaticus 'Sunningdale Mix' with dusty miller

Ranunculus ficaria

MORE →

Ranunculus asiaticus 'Bloomingdale Yellow'

Ranunculus ficaria, which if conditions are to its liking can become terribly invasive. One selection of the plant that is not at all invasive (I continue to hope it will grow faster) is 'Brazen Hussy', who lives up to her name in March when the shamelessly brash yellow flowers sit atop the small deep purple leaves. Plants are only about 6" tall, but they shine like brass in an otherwise drab garden. They flower for weeks on end, and the foliage remains richly bronze until plants go dormant in midsummer. They will reseed; the little hussies that appear the following spring will produce flowers in a couple of years. A wonderful plant, hardy in zones 6 to 8.

Ranunculus aconitifolius is a lovely white-flowered double, whose leaves resemble those of wolfsbane (*Aconitum*). Seldom seen, but worth a try; it is not as aggressive as some of the yellows. Hardy in zones 5 to 8.

The common yellow buttercups are represented by numerous species. The

Ranunculus ficaria

Ranunculus ficaria 'Brazen Hussy'

Ranunculus aconitifolius

Ranunculus bulbosus 'Flore Pleno'

Ranunculus bulbosus 'Flore Pleno'

Ranunculus repens 'Susan's Song' ('Buttered Popcorn')

double yellow flower of the invasive *Ranunculus bulbosus* 'Flore Pleno' is quite lovely, but note the thuggery in its eyes. Creeping buttercup, *R. repens*, is equally invasive. If one is going to use these plants as a ground cover, then being invasive is a good quality. One of the prettiest selections of *R. repens* is the white-and-green variegated 'Susan's Song' ('Buttered Popcorn'). In mild winters, the foliage is as pretty in the winter as in the summer. It looks terrific with bronze foliage of *Ajuga* and *Oxalis*. My favorite, but be warned—she gallops!

Ranunculus repens 'Susan's Song' ('Buttered Popcorn') with *Ajuga*

Rehmannia angulata

Rehmannia

CHINESE FOXGLOVE

Rehmannia elata and *R. angulata* (Chinese foxglove) are marvelous plants that never fail to elicit all sorts of favorable comments, as well as the all-too-common "What are they?" and "Where did you find them?" They belong to the same family (Gesneriaceae) as African violets and gloxinias and are also characterized by hairy stems and alternate leaves, which in the case of both species are light green and deeply lobed or toothed, like an oak leaf. *Rehmannia angulata* is smaller (about 2' tall) than *R. elata* (2–4' tall) and not as hairy. The flowers of *R. angulata* bear orange dots inside the lower lip; the flowers of *R. elata* have yellow throats and red dots. It is hard to tell the two apart unless they are

growing side by side. Although plants stand only about 2' tall, they present a handsome look in late spring and midsummer, when the large flower buds open. Indeed, the plants are grown for their beautiful flowers, usually of a bright rose-purple. The flowers are bunched together in terminal clusters, and when in flower, the plants are similar to foxglove, only shorter. They spread rapidly by seed and even in the same season, seedlings will grow and flower, quickly resulting in a reasonably large colony. Although they are native to China, these two species are not cold hardy north of zone 7, and even there, cold winters can take them out. They should be planted in partial shade in a protected area sheltered from the worst of the winter winds. Winter wetness can be a serious problem, therefore a raised bed is best for longer lasting stands.

Rehmannia elata

230

Rodgersia aesculifolia

Rodgersia

People are forever looking for foliar character in their gardens, wanting large bold plants with flowers secondary to the foliage. It is not easy to find such plants, and in fact, the desire for foliage accounts for much of the recent turn to ornamental grasses. *Rodgersia* is such a plant: its foliage provides wonderful contrast to all sorts of flow-

ering plants. That the foliage is outstanding is only part of the appeal; the flowers, like giant astilbes, are also enchanting in midsummer. The leaves of most of the species are bronze or become so later in the season. The flowers are borne in large panicles well above the foliage and are found mainly in whites, pinks, and reds.

Alas, the tale is not fully told. Beautiful as they are, rodgersias have serious intimate needs. They are not at all

Rodgersia aesculifolia

Rodgersia sambucifolia

Rodgersia pinnata 'Rubra' (left) and 'Superba Alba'

Rodgersia pinnata 'Superba'

comfortable when temperatures are warm, and once temperatures consistently reach 80°F or more, their foliage looks a little tatty. Furthermore, they are plants best suited for a bog or streamside condition: placing these plants in dry soils is like potting up primroses in Miami. They prefer shady conditions, and a combination of moist soils, cool summers, and partial shade will ensure your chance for success with them. They do well on the West Coast but with proper attention to moisture and shade, they can be wonderful additions to gardens in zones 5 and 6, even though they will be a challenge. Additional mulching is necessary in zone 5; keep out of the worst winter winds.

Four species are occasionally offered, all bearing many similarities.

Rodgersia aesculifolia and *R. sambucifolia* have leaves that look surprisingly like those of horsechestnut (palmate) and elderberry (pinnate), respectively, and lovely pink flowers to boot. The flowers of *R. pinnata* can be white ('Alba'), tall and white ('Superba Alba'), red ('Rubra'), or the best of all, tall, brassy, and rose-red ('Superba'); its leaves are pinnate and bronze through most of the growing season. The most commonly offered species is *R. podophylla*, with wonderful bronze palmate leaves and creamy white flowers.

I am not sure if any one species is easier than the others, but given the dearth of architectural plants, any one is worth a try. What else do you know that is big, bold, and beautiful and wants to be planted in a bog?

Rudbeckia

CONEFLOWER, BLACK-EYED SUSAN

Of all the genera in the daisy family, *Rudbeckia* is one of the best known and popular. Gardeners who couldn't tell an astilbe from an aster have no trouble confidently inquiring after your rudbeckias. For a long visual show with a minimum of upkeep and maintenance, the coneflowers fit just about everybody's idea of a good perennial.

By far the most popular of the coneflowers, *Rudbeckia fulgida*, an orange species, has smothered summer and fall gardens in the selection *R. fulgida* var. *sullivantii* 'Goldsturm'. In every garden from Dallas to Duluth, from every spit of land, wherever the sun shines, 'Goldsturm' is there. The species itself, which does not differ greatly from this ubiquitous representative, is only to be found occasionally in botanical gardens and herbaria specimens. 'Goldsturm' originated in 1937 at Foerster's Nursery in Germany, described as a late summer- to fall-flowering perennial with persistent orange ray flowers surrounding a rounded black disk. Plants grow 2–3' tall and large colonies form rapidly, complementing everything from ornamental grasses

Rodgersia pinnata 'Alba'

Rodgersia podophylla

Rodgersia podophylla

Rudbeckia fulgida var. *sullivantii* 'Goldsturm'

MORE →

to white lilies. Although they are over-planted, it is with good reason. I admit I am tired of seeing this thing in every garden and gas station in the country, but I am equally pleased that a plant with this much beauty can please so many people who would otherwise have planted five geraniums and watched them die. Full sun, heavy feeder, adequate moisture. Plants hate shade and don't do well in drought. Hardy in zones 3 to 8.

Both *Rudbeckia laciniata* and *R. nitida*, cutleaf coneflowers, are tall (4–7') and have pinnately compound or pinnately cut leaves and yellow flowers with a greenish disk. The species are quite dramatic, especially when one comes across a sole specimen, standing like a sentinel. A few excellent cultivars are so large that one plant is sufficient for a good show; they make good eye-popping fall-flowering specimens. They may be listed as selections of one species or another, but similarities to both species may be found upon close observation.

One of the finest is the double-flowered *Rudbeckia laciniata* 'Goldquelle', which is only 3–4' tall and forms significant clumps in a year or two. The double yellow flowers are terrific when they first open, and for a few days thereafter, but can look scruffy when they start to decline. This is a more serious problem in hot, humid climates than in those with cool nights. I really

Rudbeckia laciniata

Rudbeckia laciniata 'Goldquelle'

Rudbeckia fulgida var. *sullivantii* 'Goldsturm'

like the tall (up to 7') *R. nitida* 'Herbsonne' ('Autumn Sun'). Dozens of long drooping sulfur-yellow petals surround a cylindrical green disk, making a glorious show from September through November, dwarfing red dahlias or red cannas. Both require full sun, good drainage, and protection from winds. Too much shade or exposure to high winds results in the need for staking. Zones 3 to 8 for 'Goldquelle', zones 5 (perhaps 4) to 8 for 'Herbsonne'.

Rudbeckia triloba, the three-lobed coneflower, is another native of the Great Plains. This prairie species provides plants absolutely covered with small (1½" across) flowers on 3–5' tall plants. The bottom leaves are trilobed, thus accounting for the common name. Plants are not as perennial as other species, generally flowering themselves to oblivion after two or three years; but they reseed and reappear with abandon, never going away entirely. The yellow to orange ray flowers surround a black to purple disk. A great plant, even when not in flower. Full sun, good drainage, zones 3 to 10.

Rudbeckia nitida 'Herbsonne' ('Autumn Sun')

Rudbeckia triloba

Rudbeckia triloba

Rudbeckia triloba

234

Salvia guaranitica

Salvia guaranitica 'Argentina Skies'

Salvia guaranitica 'Purple Knight'

Salvia

SAGE

I went through my "salvia stage of life" a few years ago, and fortunately I emerged reasonably unscathed. Going through the SSOL is like going through the teenage years: out of control and out of money. Salvias are perfect for the plant collector, but putting the first new salvia in newly prepared ground is like putting the first tropical fish in a newly purchased aquarium. It is impossible to stop at one. It is such a large genus, replete with species, selections, and hybrids, that just when you think you have seen the end of them, someone comes along with another. For the beginner, common sage, *Salvia officinalis*, with its numerous variations, is enough to get one hooked; it is then a simple matter to move on to more beautiful and more robust specimens. Many species of *Salvia* are native to South America, southern United States, and Mexico, so cold tolerance is not one of their better attributes. Cold tolerance only to zone 5 is not uncommon; zone 7 is typical for many species and cultivars.

Want a big, bold salvia in blooming color for at least twelve weeks, from early summer on? The 4–6" long dark

Salvia guaranitica

Salvia guaranitica 'Black and Blue'

Salvia guaranitica 'Purple Splendour'

green opposite leaves of *Salvia guaranitica*, blue anise sage, provide a subtle contrast to the deep blue flowers, which open all over the 4–6' tall plants. At the University of Georgia Horticulture Gardens, this has been such an outstanding and long-lived plant that it was designated a "Georgia Gold" winner, a plant that is almost foolproof. This no-brainer also has a few selections of its own. Probably the most popular is the light blue–flowered 'Argentina Skies', which is as beautiful as the species but not as floriferous. Several old-fashioned cultivars are out there, but few have found common acceptance. 'Black and Blue', 'Purple Knight', and 'Purple Splendour' are big (up to 7' tall) and possess large flowers, but they are somewhat weedy. Full sun, good drainage, zones 7 (sometimes 6) to 10.

Salvia involucrata, bulbous pink

sage, and *S. koyamae*, yellow sage, are about as different as plants can be in the same genus, but both are coveted for the qualities they deliver to the gardener. The bulbous pink sage is actually cherry pink, and the flowers terminate in a swollen knob—not exactly useful for a common name. Plants are large (4–5' tall stems) and are very lax and open. In most gardens they'll need at least one pinch, but since they don't flower until late summer and fall, two pinches may be required. A more compact selection of *S. involucrata*, although still large, is 'Bethellii', a much better choice for the gardener than the species. Weedy, lanky, and lax it may be, but people love the color and the weird-looking flowers. Useful in the vase as a cut flower as well as in the

garden. Full sun, zones 8 (perhaps 7) to 10.

Salvia koyamae has much less exciting flowers but fits in many gardens. Plants can spread rapidly and the 6–8" long green leaves make an outstanding show throughout the season. Plants are only about 2' tall, therefore no staking or pinching is required. The short light yellow flower stems may not be as eye-catching as others, but I think they are wonderful. The other wonderful characteristic of this species is its tolerance to shade—in the Armitage garden, it grows and flowers well with only about three hours of sunlight a day. Partial shade, good drainage, zones 6 to 8.

While its virtues are well known to lovers of spice and good food, sage

Salvia koyamae

Salvia koyamae

Salvia involucrata

Salvia involucrata 'Bethellii'

Salvia involucrata

MORE →

(along with the others in the Simon and Garfunkle line-up of "parsley, sage, rosemary, and thyme") is now recognized as a fine ornamental, one of the more vigorous and robust of the culinary herbs. *Salvia officinalis*, common sage, historically sat in the herb garden, waiting for an alchemist, monk, or Victorian lady to wander by and pull off its leaves for some medicinal or culinary use, like kids pulling wings from butterflies. In these more enlightened times, however, it doubles as a fine garden plant, by itself or interplanted among roses and other ornamentals. The beautiful whorled light purple flowers are the highlight of the species.

White flowers make *Salvia officinalis* 'Albiflora' come to life, and the foliar selections of the species hardly qualify the plant as "common" anything. They produce few blooms, but their lack of flower color is more than compensated for by their diversity of foliage. 'Icterina' has light and darker green splashed on the leaves; 'Purpurescens' bears purple leaves and looks terrific on its own but really shines when placed with brighter colors. 'Tricolor' looks like my son was painting nearby and spilled a mixed palette of paint on the leaves. Full sun, excellent moisture required. Hardy in zones 4 to 7 in the East, but plants do well in West Coast zone 8 as well.

Hybrid purple sage goes under numerous botanical names, including *Salvia nemerosa*, *S. ×superba*, and *S. ×sylvestris*. Given cool nights and good

Salvia officinalis 'Purpurescens'

Salvia officinalis 'Purpurescens'

Salvia officinalis

Salvia officinalis 'Albiflora'

Salvia officinalis 'Icterina' with *Felicia*

moisture, hybrid purple sage can make an outstanding display. Plants grow about 2–2½' tall and flower throughout the summer. They do poorly in hot summers and high humidity, but elsewhere they are wonderfully eye-catching. Common hybrid cultivars in the American nursery trade are confused in nomenclature, offered variously as selections of *S. nemerosa* and *S. ×sylvestris*. 'East Friesland' ('Ostfriesland') and 'Lubecca' are marvelous hybrids, with their deep purple to blue, compact full flowers. 'Tanzerin', 'Blue Hill', and 'Blue Queen' ('Blaukönigin') are probably hybrids, with *S. nemerosa* as the dominant par-

ent, but regardless of parentage are just as useful as *S. ×sylvestris* hybrids, if not quite as vigorous. Full sun, good drainage, zones 4 to 7.

Salvia 'Indigo Spires' grows 4–5' tall but flowers all season long. Outstandingly tough in heat and humidity, it is often one of the few plants flowering

Salvia nemerosa 'Blue Queen' ('Blaukönigin')

Salvia nemerosa 'Blue Hill'

Salvia officinalis 'Tricolor'

Salvia ×sylvestris 'East Friesland' ('Ostfriesland')

Salvia nemerosa 'Tanzerin'

Salvia ×sylvestris 'Lubecca'

MORE →

even when summer heat approaches the unbearable. Its drawback is its gangly growth, and a spring pinch is a good idea. Also beautiful in the fall.

Salvia 'Indigo Spires' with *Phlomis*

Salvia 'Indigo Spires'

Santolina

The plants themselves cannot take credit for the popularity of *Santolina*; rather it is what the gray-green foliage does for their neighbors that makes them so desirable. Not particularly tolerant of hot summers and high humidity, and absolutely intolerant of poor drainage, *Santolina* is not for everybody. But if you are designing a garden stroll through fragrant foliage, be sure to include this herb. The fragrance is not soon to be forgotten—not awful, but very pungent, a great identification feature.

Santolina chamaecyparissus

Santolina chamaecyparissus, lavender cotton, is the most common of the species encountered in gardens. Its many finely divided leaflets are a soothing gray-green with a white sheen beneath, a very effective softener of the intense greens and bright flower colors of summer. When well grown, they make loose leafy balls in the landscape and later in the summer produce rather forgettable yellow daisy flowers. They are often sheared and used as an edging, which is cruel and unusual punishment for any plant. They become woody at the base after a year or so in the garden and may require a hard pruning of old wood for

Santolina pinnata

Santolina pinnata 'Edward Bowles'

rejuvenation. Full sun, excellent drainage, zones 6 to 8.

A closely related species is *Santolina pinnata*, also with gray-green to silver foliage but with lovely off-white flowers. 'Edward Bowles', with large primrose flowers, is its excellent selection. Plants are winter hardy only to zones 7 or 8.

Santolina virens, green lavender cotton, is grown as much for its yellow flowers as its bright green foliage, which resembles that of rosemary (the plant is also known as *S. rosmarinifolia*). The leaflets are quite small (less than half an inch), resulting in more stick-like foliage. Plants do not have the powerful smell of the common species, but rather a sanitized aroma. Not nearly as much fun or exercise for the nose. Full sun, excellent drainage, hardy in zones 7 to 9.

Santolina virens

Saponaria ocymoides

Saponaria

SOAPWORT

Plants of *Saponaria ocymoides*, rock soapwort, are far better falling off rocks or running through a sunny rock garden than they are planted in the "common" garden ground. In the spring, flowers cover the plants like pink lava. The one-inch-long leaves are flat and olive green. Great plants, but they do roam. Once established, they reseed vigorously and stay around for years. They are less heat tolerant than *S. officinalis*, and don't do well in areas of hot summers and high

Saponaria officinalis

Saponaria ocymoides

humidities. Full sun to partial shade, good drainage, zones 2 to 7.

The leaves of *Saponaria officinalis*, soapwort, "yeelde out of themselves a certain juice when they are bruised, which scoureth almost as well as soap." This was written in 1597, when real soap was quite expensive and used only sparingly (perfumes and washing in lavender water were far more common). But there was a drawback to boiling the leaves of *S. officinalis* and lathering up with the result—the itchy problem of dermatitis, which occurred quite regularly. Otherwise this weak challenger to Irish Spring makes a wonderful, rambunctious garden

Saponaria officinalis 'Alba'

MORE →

plant. "Rambunctious" is a nice word; "aggressive," "weedy," and "invasive" are apt descriptions as well, especially in the West. It is a plant usually found in cottage gardens, where its romping and bouncing around are appreciated. Plants are effective setting off a white picket fence or roaming by a streambank. The opposite leaves occur on 2–3' tall plants, topped with pink flowers all summer. Single white-flowered cultivars, such as 'Alba', are also available, but double-flowerers, such as 'Rosea Plena' (pink), are probably the most common of all soapworts. Full sun, moderate drainage, zones 2 to 8.

Scabiosa

SCABIOUS, PINCUSHION FLOWER

Not many people have pin cushions in their sewing drawers anymore (most people don't have sewing drawers anymore), but as one looks at the flower head of scabious, one appreciates immediately how apt the common name is. (The genus name, on the other hand, is Latin for "scabies," the disease the plant was incorrectly thought to cure.) Three species of scabious are found in gardens: the mostly cool-toned *Scabiosa caucasica* and *S. columbaria* and the less frequently encountered yellow-flowering *S. ochroleuca*.

Both *Scabiosa caucasica*, common scabious, and *S. columbaria*, pincushion flower, grow 2–3' tall and are similar in their garden look, environmental response, and availability. Historically, *S. caucasica* has been a mainstay for lilac to purple flowers for the summer garden. The plants consist of pinnately lobed opposite leaves and form large mounds with light blue to purple flowers. Many variations of the species occur, from larger lavender ('Denise', 'Perfecta'), deeper blue ('Moerheim Blue'), and taller cut flower selections ('Fama') to plants with handsome white flowers ('Bressingham White', 'Miss Willmott'). We anxiously await the flowers, but let us not ignore the

Scabiosa caucasica 'Fama'

Scabiosa caucasica 'Denise'

Scabiosa caucasica 'Moerheim Blue'

Scabiosa caucasica 'Perfecta'

Scabiosa Scabiosa caucasica 'Miss Willmott'

wonderful clean-looking pinwheel fruit. Like an architect's model of a futuristic domed restaurant revolving on a giant leg, such is the fruit of scabious.

Shorter, more compact, and more floriferous plants are the claims to fame for selections of *Scabiosa columbaria*. For the most part, the two culti-vars that took the gardening world by storm were worthy of the hype. 'Butterfly Blue' provides persistent flowering on 2' tall plants nearly all summer and is the best scabious to hit the market in many years. Its companion, 'Pink Mist', is not as colorful as 'Butterfly Blue' but is a good plant nevertheless.

Both *Scabiosa columbaria* and *S. caucasica* require full sun and good drainage and are hardy in zones 3 to 7.

Most gardeners believe that blue, lavender, and purple are the only colors available in the genus *Scabiosa*. While those hues are common, the wonderful primrose-yellow flowers of *Scabiosa ochroleuca*, cream scabious, should not be overlooked. Plants are much taller (3–4') than *S. caucasica*, and although its flowers are similar in

Scabiosa caucasica 'Bressingham White'

Fruit of *Scabiosa caucasica*

Scabiosa columbaria 'Butterfly Blue'

Scabiosa columbaria 'Butterfly Blue' with *Knautia*

Scabiosa columbaria 'Pink Mist'

Scabiosa ochroleuca

Scabiosa ochroleuca

MORE →

form and size (1–2" wide) to *S. caucasica*, they provide a much more muted color in the summer garden. The pinnate leaves are divided into eleven to thirteen lobes and blend well with other garden plants. It is not as tolerant of heat and humidity as the blue pincushions but is effective in the Midwest, Northeast, and Northwest. Plants are often mistaken for the closely related *Cephalaria gigantea*, which is larger in every way, including height, leaves, and flowers. Full sun to partial shade, good drainage, zones 5 to 7.

Sedum

STONECROP

I love the sedums for their amazing diversity of foliage, flower, and plant habit. Many of the more than three hundred species are succulent and may be upright or low growing, as useful for rock gardens as they are for borders. All sedums perform best in full sun and have moderate water requirements and persistent flowers. Hardiness differs from species to species, but in general plants do well in zones 4 to 7.

Botanically the low-growing sedums (*Sedum acre, S. kamtschaticum, S. spathulifolium, S. spurium, S. reflexum, S. ternatum*) differ from each other in many ways, including their flower form, rootstock development, and foliar characteristics. From the gardener's point of view, however, they are used in the same manner. They are all best for rock gardens, ground covers, or simply as low-growing border or edging plants. While they broadly prefer similar conditions, the choice of low growers may be further narrowed when performance, flower color, aggressiveness, or disease tolerance are taken into consideration.

Goldmoss stonecrop, *Sedum acre*, is one of the most aggressive and best-known species in American gardens. "Goldmoss" is descriptive indeed: when the plants are in flower, the golden yellow flowers entirely cover the mossy foliage. The small quarter-inch-long leaves overlap like shingles, and the leaves appear scaly. Only 2–3" tall, plants will move in and around anything in their path, and a wonderful soft green ground cover often results. Over time, if Lady Luck is smiling, one finds themselves digging out rather than planting *S. acre*, and the Lady may not be quite as welcome anymore. Hardy in zones 3 to 8.

Another popular ground cover is

Sedum acre

Sedum acre

Sedum spurium 'Green Mantle'

Sedum spurium 'Fuldaglut'

two-row stonecrop, *Sedum spurium*, whose foliage can look awful much of the time. Luckily, many cultivars sport arresting bronze foliage or flowers, as well as a few good green-leaved sedums that can occasionally be discovered. One such green selection is 'Green Mantle', which looks unusually good in leaf. I also enjoy the bronze 'Fuldaglut', which combines earthy leaves and flowers and reaches a height of 2–6". Hardy in zones 3 to 7.

The choice of aggressive low growers also extends to stone orpine, *Sedum reflexum*, which looks like a tiny evergreen with bluish green needle-like leaves. Plants spread like stoloniferous junipers, filling in areas with blinding speed—at least for a sedum. One of the finest choices is 'Blue Spruce', outstanding but aggressive, with plants about 6–10" tall. Hardy in zones 5 to 8.

For some of the most beautiful foliage and handsome flowers to boot, particularly for gardeners in the West, try *Sedum spathulifolium*. Plants have blue-green spatulate (shaped like a spatula) leaves and short trailing stems. I love the silvery leaves of 'Cape Blanco' and its dozens of yellow flowers, each three-quarters of an inch wide. Plants are up to 6" tall. Hardy in zones 6 to 8.

Yet one more low grower is the whorled stonecrop, *Sedum ternatum*. The light green leaves are whorled around the stems, and plants grow about 6" tall. Above the foliage, many small starry white flowers are produced in spring. A bonus for these plants is their higher tolerance of shade compared to other ground-covering species. Partial shade, zones 4 to 8.

Finally, to round out the low growers, from the Kamchatka peninsula comes *Sedum kamtschaticum*, a diminutive clumper rather than an aggressive ground cover. The 1½" long leaves and purple buds and yellow flowers provide an outstanding display in spring and early summer. With its large number of bicolored buds and flowers, 'Diffusum' is even more eye-catching. The most popular cultivar, from the Weihenstephan Test Gardens near Tubingen, Germany, is the unpronounceable 'Weihenstephaner Gold', with golden yellow flowers over a ground-hugging plant. Full sun, good drainage, zones 3 to 8.

The upright *Sedum* species and cultivars grow 1–3' tall, with the many branches growing up instead of out.

243

Sedum reflexum 'Blue Spruce'

Sedum spathulifolium 'Cape Blanco'

Sedum ternatum

Sedum kamtschaticum

Sedum kamtschaticum 'Diffusum'

Sedum kamtschaticum 'Weihenstephaner Gold'

MORE →

The best-known example of this group by far is *Sedum* 'Autumn Joy' ('Herbst-freude'), one of the toughest and best-known perennials in American gardens. Other sedums can easily challenge 'Autumn Joy' for beauty if not

Sedum aizoon var. *aurantiacum*

for persistence. The 12–15" tall aizoon stonecrop, *Sedum aizoon*, has flat 2" long leaves and dozens of yellow flowers in early summer. Variety *auranti-acum*, with its red stems and deep yellow to orange flowers, is even showier. Full sun, zones 4 to 8.

Many fine upright hybrids have recently been selected with various parents in the progeny, including the showy stonecrop, *Sedum spectabile* (*Hylotelephium spectabile*), and *S. tele-phium*, among others. *Sedum* 'Autumn Joy' seems to be grown in every garden in the entire universe, but how can one complain about such success? Large succulent leaves, pink flower buds that

darken as they age, and bronze-red flowers in late summer and fall have made this sun-loving plant a desirable addition. Some people even find its spent flowers ornamental in the winter. I don't. *Sedum spectabile* 'Meteor' is equally beautiful, but I for one cannot find a great deal of difference between it and 'Autumn Joy'. Other close relatives of 'Autumn Joy' are *S. specta-bile* 'Carmen', with large rosy pink flowers; *S.* 'Ruby Glow', with ruby red flowers; *S.* 'Sunset Cloud', which bears dozens of rosy red flowers; and the fabulous *S.* 'Strawberries and Cream'. I enjoy all these colored hybrids, but none is as foolproof, throughout the

Sedum 'Autumn Joy' ('Herbstfreude') in winter

Sedum 'Autumn Joy' ('Herbstfreude') in flower

Sedum 'Autumn Joy' ('Herbstfreude') in bud

Sedum 'Autumn Joy' ('Herbstfreude')

country, as 'Autumn Joy'. They all flower in mid to late summer and early fall. Full sun, zones 3 to 8.

For darker foliage, *Sedum* 'Atropurpureum' has outstanding bronze-red foliage on a 2–3' upright plant; *S.* 'Vera Jameson', similar but with better flowers, is probably more readily available than 'Atropurpureum' and is frequently mixed-up with it at nurseries. *Sedum* 'Mohrchen' came to us from Germany. Its large glossy purple leaves are gaudy, and the plant performance has been a disappointment to me. To each his own—some people simply gush over the plant. The upright cultivars, green- or purple-leaved, are highly useful garden plants and combine well with a wide assortment of other perennials, annuals, and shrubs. Full sun, zones 4 to 8.

Sedum spectabile 'Meteor'

Sedum spectabile 'Carmen'

Sedum 'Ruby Glow'

Sedum 'Sunset Cloud'

Sedum 'Strawberries and Cream'

Sedum 'Atropurpureum'

Sedum 'Vera Jameson'

Sedum 'Mohrchen'

Silene virginica

Silene regia

Silene polypetala

Silene

CAMPION

The campions provide low-growing species for containers, rock gardens—any place where colorful spots of color are welcome. Leaves are entire; the flowers may be notched or fringed, often with an inflated calyx that looks like a small bladder. Some of the most brilliant red colors can be seen in our native fire pink, *Silene virginica*, whose flowers dare you to pass them by without comment. The 10–20" tall plants do well in cool climates and are occasionally offered to the gardener who must have native plants in the garden, but truth be told, enjoying them in their native habitat makes far more sense. The western relative of the eastern fire pink is called wild pink, *S. regia*. Plants are taller (2–3') but bear the same stunning scarlet flowers. Both species require partial shade and good drainage, and do well in zones 4 to 7.

A wonderful eastern native is fringed campion, *Silene polypetala*. Plants are only 4–6" tall, with light green leaves, but the fringed pink flowers are unlike any others in the eastern woodland. They are not easy to grow: even when it appears that a population has been established, the colony may disappear the next year. If nursery-grown plants are available, however, they are worth a try because of their unique beauty. They are on some state endangered lists and absolutely must not be shorn for the wild. An interesting hybrid between *S. polypetala* and *S. virginica* is 'Longwood', bearing

Silene 'Longwood'

Silene caroliniana 'Millstream Select'

Silene uniflora

Silene fimbriata

deeper pink flowers with the same fringed look (partial shade, zones 6 to 8). Unfortunately, plants don't appear to be any longer lived than either of the parents when domesticated.

Silene caroliniana, Carolina campion, is another low-growing species, with slightly notched pink flowers on 4–8" tall plants. 'Millstream Select' (full sun to partial shade, zones 5 to 8) is an example of one of the selections from the garden at Millstream House, the home of the much-missed H. Lincoln Foster. In our haste, let us not ignore the Mutt and Jeff of the whites: the 6" seaside campion, *S. uniflora*, with swollen calyces and off-white flowers, and the little-known 2–3' tall white fimbriated campion, *S. fimbriata*. *Silene fimbriata* has panicles of few, large, white fringed flowers, but since it is seldom grown in American gardens, it is difficult to know where it will thrive (I'd hazard full sun to partial shade, probably zones 5 to 8).

Sisyrinchium

BLUE-EYED GRASS

It is only recently that American gardeners noticed these All-American plants. Perhaps because the genus name has so many syllables, people would just as soon not have to tell anybody about it. The common name is simple enough, however, and quite descriptive of the native species.

In the spirit of horticultural nomenclature, it should be noted that blue-eyed grass is not a grass at all but actually belongs to the iris family. In spring the tufted grassy leaves of southeastern native *Sisyrinchium angustifolium* are interspersed with small (half-inch-wide) rounded blue flowers, arising from the base. The white flowers of 'Album' are similar in shape and size and are easier to see in the dark green leaves. From the eastern United States comes *S. atlanticum*, quite similar to *S. angustifolium* but with larger, darker flowers, often with a yellow center. They are lovely plants, quite popular among gardeners who enjoy something a little different, but I have trouble getting excited about them—perhaps because in the Armitage garden they become overgrown with weeds every year. Both species are quite prostrate, occasionally rising up to 12–18" tall. Partial shade; *S. angustifolium* is hardy in zones 3 to 8, and *S. atlanticum* in zones 5 to 9.

The outstanding large-flowered species of the western United States can take your breath away. My favorite is *Sisyrinchium idahoense*, which is a stand-alone plant when properly grown. Plants have 2' tall linear leaves and marvelous 1–1½" dark blue flowers with a yellow eye. 'California Skies' is outstanding, and for a fine white, try 'Album'. Plants are not vigorous in heat and humidity and are not often successful in the eastern part of the country. Full sun to partial shade, excellent drainage, zones 4 to 7.

Sisyrinchium angustifolium

Sisyrinchium angustifolium 'Album'

Sisyrinchium idahoense 'California Skies'

Sisyrinchium idahoense 'Album'

MORE →

Sisyrinchium striatum 'Aunt May'

Sisyrinchium striatum

Sisyrinchium striatum, yellow blue-eyed grass, is native to Argentina and Chile. This fine upright grower is well known to gardeners on the West Coast but, like many of the more ornamental forms, struggles in the East. The one-inch-wide leaves grow 1–3' tall, but without the flowers, the plant is rather nondescript, like an iris without flowers. The creamy yellow flowers, on the other hand, are quite distinctive, much different from our native species. They are up to an inch wide and striped with purple on the backsides, thus the term *striatum*. Plants will reseed if grown in suitable conditions and can be a bit of nuisance for lucky gardeners. I am not among the lucky ones, having killed this and its variegated cousin at least half a dozen times. I am nothing if not persistent! This variegated cousin is 'Aunt May', whose combination of handsome green-and-white leaves and yellow flowers won me over immediately. I bought this wonderful plant at a small nursery in England, washed its roots in the hotel toilet (not a good idea), and waited in line to present my treasure to the fine inspectors of the U.S. Department of Agriculture. After much head-scratching, book-searching, and root-prob-ing, Aunt May and I were off to the Armitage garden. Alas, it wasn't to be, and Aunt May and I parted company for the last time two years later. Plants are now available in the United States, and such efforts are no longer necessary for me to kill the plant. I can do it all locally. Full sun to partial shade, good drainage, zones 5 to 8.

With the plethora of *Sisyrinchium* species and cultivars, it is not surprising that hybrids, man-made or natural, would be promoted to American gardeners. A few have such outrageous names that curious gardeners simply must have them. The best name is probably 'Quaint and Queer'; it simply demands attention. 'Biscutella' isn't far behind. 'Quaint and Queer' is small and has dull purple flowers with yellow centers. The biscuit one is quite similar, with dusky purple flowers and yellow centers, but is taller and more vigorous, except in my garden, where they both perish with equal vigor. Another lovely hybrid that has escaped the Armitage survival test is 'E. K. Balls', with dark mauve flowers and gray-green foliage. All hybrids perform well in the North and West. Full sun to partial shade, good drainage, zones 5 to 7, zone 8 on the West Coast.

Sisyrinchium 'Biscutella'

Sisyrinchium 'Quaint and Queer'

Sisyrinchium 'E. K. Balls'

Smilacina racemosa

FALSE SOLOMON'S SEAL

False Solomon's seal is a common native plant in almost any eastern woodland, and although it cavorts well with *Mertensia*, *Polygonatum*, and all sorts of other natives, this species is lovely in its own right when spied in the shade of oaks or poplars. While making your way through the woods, look for creamy white flowers, alternate leaves, and fruit changing from dull green to mature red. Such woodland walks are indeed good for the soul, but that does not mean *Smilacina race-mosa* will not positively shine when placed under garden conditions. Flowers open in early spring, and foliage remains handsome until late fall. Shade, cool nights, and well-drained soils are needed for best performance. Buy two or three nursery-grown plants, place them side by side, and bring a little woodland home. Zones 3 to 7.

Fruit of *Smilacina racemosa*

Smilacina racemosa

Smilacina racemosa

Stachys byzantina

Stachys byzantina

Stachys byzantina 'Countess Helene von Stein'

Stachys

BETONY

The last time most of us felt the ear of a lamb was probably the last time most of us milked a cow. But if I can't on short notice feel the ear of a lamb, I can at least caress the sheepskin we bought in New Zealand. (You know New Zealand: the country that has a population of ten million, three million of them people.) When I caress that skin, then run outside and caress the leaves of lamb's ears (*Stachys byzantina*), they both feel wonderful. Nothing alike, but wonderful nevertheless. The handsome gray foliage of *S. byzantina* looks good from a distance and is used effectively both to soften harsh colors and edge brick walkways. But get up close and you will see that the lamby feel comes from soft hairs, easily visible on the upper and lower sides of the leaves. The purple flowers shoot up in late spring to early summer, but I think they detract from the foliage. Plants look great anywhere in the spring, but leaves can melt out in areas of high heat and humidity.

'Countess Helene von Stein' is the best selection of *Stachys byzantina* for most of the country; she has significantly larger leaves and fewer flowers than the species, but she is also more tolerant of heat and humidity, her true raison d'être. 'Sheila Macqueen' is more compact; the leaves are less hairy than the type, and the flowers are sterile. The most colorful cultivar is 'Primrose Heron', whose primrose-yellow leaves are most beautiful in the spring even though they revert to the normal gray color in the summer. My favorite, at least in the spring. Excellent drainage necessary, partial shade, zones 4 to 7.

Stachys byzantina 'Sheila Macqueen'

Stachys byzantina

Most weekend gardeners know about lamb's ears, but the numbers fall way off when you ask the same group to name another species of *Stachys*. Actually there are about three hundred of them, but let's not get too picky. *Stachys macrantha*, big betony, has 1½–2" long dark green leaves with scalloped edges; the foliage is roughly hairy, not soft like that of its gray cousin. But whatever the leaves lack is more than made up for by the dozens of violet-pink flowers in late spring and early summer. Plants grow up to 2' tall and when in flower can be seen a football field away. Big betony is seen much more in European gardens than in this country, which may be attributed to its dislike of temperature extremes. The only cultivar ever seen is 'Robusta', which is a bit more robust than the species. Both selection and species prefer full sun and good drainage, and do well in zones 2 to 7.

Stachys byzantina 'Primrose Heron'

Stachys macrantha

Stachys macrantha 'Robusta'

Stachys macrantha 'Robusta'

Stokesia laevis

STOKES'S ASTER

Stokesia laevis, Stokes's aster, is a native of the eastern United States, with small one-inch-wide lavender flowers; but the original native has undergone a significant transformation through selection and breeding. Native plant lovers enthusiastically embrace this meadow dweller, while mainstream gardeners use the new and improved models with equal enthusiasm. The 6–8" long entire leaves have a pronounced white midrib and are evergreen in milder locations. The flowers open in early to mid summer and consist of two rows of ray flowers up to 4" across, although 2–2½" is normal. Plants are 1–2' tall and equally wide. They are tough, do well in full sun to partial shade, and persist for many years as long as winter drainage is good.

The selections of *Stokesia laevis* for the garden are many, the most common being 'Blue Danube', with compact habit and 2–2½" wide lavender flowers. Others in the blue to lavender range include 'Klaus Jelitto', with even larger flowers; 'Wyoming', with its deeper blue flowers; and the perfectly named upright form of 'Omega Sky-

Stokesia laevis 'Blue Danube'

MORE →

rocket', whose strong flower stems head straight into the air, giving it a unique appearance, interesting as a garden plant and highly useful as a cut flower. Last but not least, an off-white flowerer, 'Alba', is also available. Full sun, good drainage, zones 5 to 9.

Stokesia laevis 'Blue Danube'

Stokesia laevis 'Klaus Jelitto'

Stokesia laevis 'Wyoming'

Stokesia laevis 'Alba'

Stokesia laevis 'Omega Skyrocket'

Stylophorum diphyllum

WOOD POPPY, CELANDINE POPPY

Native from Tennessee to Missouri, *Stylophorum diphyllum* is simply a terrific species for the woodland garden, providing bright yellow spring flowers even in heavy shade. It comports well with Virginia bluebells and other early spring woodland plants: the blue and yellow flowers go together like apples and strudel. Early in the spring, as the poppies emerge from their winter rest, light green deeply cut basal leaves and $1^{1}/_{2}$–2" wide flowers unfold. A yellow sap exudes from cut parts of the plant, providing great fun for any face- and fingerpainters who happen by. Keep it out of your eyes. Plants reseed, which means that two or three plants can become a significant colony in three to five years. No cultivars are available; the Chinese native *Stylophorum lasiocarpum* bears a similar flower and has larger coarser foliage. Partial to heavy shade, zones 4 to 8.

Stylophorum diphyllum with *Mertensia*

Stylophorum diphyllum

Stylophorum lasiocarpum

Symphytum

COMFREY

Plants of the genus *Symphytum* were once used as a poultice, believed, among other things, to speed the setting of broken bones. With such an important healing property, boneset (as it was also known) became a staple of monastic and herb gardens. About thirty-five species are counted in the genus, and that is about thirty-three too many for most gardeners. Essentially, they have the same look, fill the same shady spaces, and bear similar pendulous bell-shaped flowers on long one-sided inflorescences. But they are loved by many. Whether one goes with the 5–6' tall prickly comfrey, *Symphy-*

tum asperum; the low-growing blue-flowered *S. caucasicum* or light blue *S. grandiflorum*; or the variable *S. officinale*, the differences in plant habit and flower color are only slight.

Symphytum offers some highly ornamental variegated plants. Most sought after are the variegated cultivars of the hybrid between *Symphytum asperum* and *S. officinale*, known as *S. ×uplandicum*. They include 'Variegatum' and 'Axeminster', an extraordinarily vigorous introduction from Canada. Another excellent variegated cultivar is *S. officinale* 'Variegatum'. *Symphytum* 'Goldsmith' has yellow-and-white foliage and has become quite popular but does not seem as vigorous or as tough as the others. The variegated plants are eye-catching and

Symphytum caucasicum

Symphytum asperum

Symphytum grandiflorum

MORE →

must-have plants for many gardeners. Unfortunately, they are very difficult to propagate and thus difficult to locate and quite expensive.

All comfreys require good drainage. They do best in partial shade and burn up in full sun in many areas of the country. Hardy in zones 4 to 7 in the East, to zone 8 on the West Coast.

Symphytum officinale

Symphytum officinale

Symphytum officinale 'Variegatum'

Symphytum ×*uplandicum* 'Variegatum'

Symphytum ×*uplandicum* 'Variegatum'

Symphytum 'Goldsmith'

Symphytum ×*uplandicum* 'Axeminster'

Tanacetum

TANSY

Several plants that long resided under the *Chrysanthemum* umbrella have been repositioned under cover of *Tanacetum*. These interesting garden plants are all fetid of foliage; they are also fairly temperamental, not much liking cold winters, hot or humid summers, wet feet, or drought. Other than that, they are good garden plants.

Tanacetum vulgare has to be one of the most aromatic herbs available to the gardener. To touch it is to be tansied for an hour or more. I avoid planting herbs in the Armitage garden as I have determined that I am not an herb kind of a guy. Tansy is my exception, however, and I enjoy the deeply cut dark green foliage, its smell, and its sturdy stature. Plants may grow up to 4' tall (although 2–3' is more common), but seldom need support. The yellow flowers are small, buttonlike, and entirely forgettable. Though it is smaller in height, the best selection by far is 'Crispum', with its fabulous finely cut foliage. Plants seldom flower, also a plus. The species is considered invasive in parts of the West. Full sun, excellent drainage, hardy in zones 5 to 7.

Thalictrum

MEADOW RUE

Thalictrum species are natural inhabitants of damp, shady areas, flowering in early summer, with lacy foliage that presents a fernlike appearance. In general, the ornamental parts of the flowers consist of colorful stamens and sepals. About 130 species of meadow rue have been identified, and the gardener may choose, with difficulty, from upright clumpers to 6–9" ground covers.

Prostrate meadow rues, most suitable to rock gardens and alpine environments, can sometimes be found in specialty nurseries. The maidenhair fern–like appearance of *Thalictrum minus* 'Adiantifolium' is the best part of the plant and can be enjoyed even if flowering is sparse. Plants grow in 1–2' tall clumps and perform well in zones 3 to 7. The deeper green foliage and numerous lavender flowers of China meadow rue, *T. ichangense*, are outstanding in late spring and early summer. Plants are only 6–9" tall and fill in rocky outcrops or other well-drained areas in zones 5 to 7. Neither of these low growers does well in areas of hot summers and high humidity.

Thalictrum ichangense

Tanacetum vulgare

Tanacetum vulgare 'Crispum'

MORE →

The most common of the upright meadow rues is the columbine meadow rue, *Thalictrum aquilegiifolium*. The foliage is blue-tinted and similar to that of columbine, thus the common and botanical names. Plants are generally 2–3' tall, but well-satisfied plants can grow 5' tall and 3' wide. The normal flower color, provided by

Thalictrum minus 'Adiantifolium'

Thalictrum aquilegiifolium

sepals and long stamens in the spring, is lavender; but the species itself is generally seed-propagated and flower color can be quite variable, deeper or lighter lavender. Unfortunately, flowers are not persistent and tend to shatter after a week or so. Sometimes the flowers are dioecious (male or female only); however, the fruit is especially handsome on plants that have female, or perfect, flowers. Cultivars include the white-flowered 'Album' (sometimes sold as 'White Cloud'), which discolors to creamy white over time; the darker 'Atropurpureum'; the pink

Thalictrum aquilegiifolium 'Album' ('White Cloud')

'Roseum'; and the rose-purple 'Thundercloud' ('Purple Cloud'). Partial shade, good drainage, zones 5 to 7.

Another upright species is *Thalictrum flavum*, yellow meadow rue, a robust grower that bursts out of the ground like John Glenn's Discovery rocket, with smooth divided foliage and thick stems. Plants grow tall and thin and are best planted in clumps of three or four. Single plants grow too tall for their width and easily outgrow the space provided. Clumps form rapidly, and panicles of small yellow flowers appear in late spring. Flowers consist mainly of long stamens, which fall like yellow confetti within a few days of opening. Height is generally 4–6', and plants are used to great advantage as a backdrop to shorter plants. 'Glaucum', the most popular selection of this plant, presents a winning combination of blue-green foliage and yellow flowers that is even better than the species. Full sun, good drainage, zones 5 to 8.

Thalictrum lucidum is another tall (5–7') grower with light yellow flowers and fine green divided foliage. The leaves do not have the blueness of 'Glaucum', but these outstanding plants grow rapidly and quickly fill in a large area. Full sun, zones 4 to 7.

Thalictrum rochebrunianum, lavender mist, is my favorite upright meadow

Thalictrum aquilegiifolium 'Atropurpureum'

Thalictrum aquilegiifolium 'Roseum'

rue, tall and thin, producing dozens of small lavender-purple flowers atop 4–6' tall stems. Although many small compound leaves are formed, the plant can be considered a see-through plant: one that reduces but does not block vistas behind it. As with *T. flavum*, plants look better in groups than they do a plant at a time. Plants are a little better in the North than the South, but they look terrific anywhere. Little diversity occurs within the species—the common name is also used for the cultivar 'Lavender Mist'. Partial shade, good drainage, zones 4 to 7.

Thalictrum flavum

Thalictrum flavum

Thalictrum flavum

Thalictrum flavum 'Glaucum' with *Delphinium*

Thalictrum rochebrunianum 'Lavender Mist'

Thalictrum flavum 'Glaucum'

Thalictrum lucidum

Thalictrum rochebrunianum 'Lavender Mist'

Thermopsis montana

Thermopsis

FALSE LUPINE

The native false lupines are well named because both the leaves and the flowers resemble the much more appreciated European lupines. In general, the foliage of *Thermopsis* is palmately compound, and the early spring flowers are yellow. Few differences occur from species to species; the eastern and western natives, *Thermopsis caroliniana* (*T. villosa*) and *T. montana*, respectively, are particularly similar. They flower in very early spring, providing bright color often before other plants have even started to expand. White selections ('Alba') of both species have also been offered, but they are much less common than those with yellow flowers. The foliage can remain handsome for a long time, but eventually the garden is better served by hiding plants with late-flowering perennials or annuals. *Thermopsis fabacea*, native to Kamchatka and the Kurile Islands, bears larger leaves, flowers in summer, and tends to be more vigorous. Full sun, good drainage, zones 3 to 8 (sometimes 9).

Thermopsis montana 'Alba'

Thermopsis caroliniana

Thermopsis fabacea

Thermopsis montana

Thymus

THYME

Thymus is an immense genus of more than 350 species, best known for their culinary and ornamental properties. All thymes available to gardeners are low-growing spreading plants and, without a label, are incredibly difficult to tell apart. The best way to distinguish thyme from other herbs is to sniff the fragrance of its opposite leaves; remember, however, that thyme not only smells like thyme but also, in some selections, like caraway or lemon. Most taxa are native to the Mediterranean, and therefore excellent drainage and full sun are necessary. Plants lend themselves well to rock, trough, and alpine gardens.

One of the most handsome species is woolly thyme, *Thymus pseudolanuginosus*, whose common name comes from the long hairs on the prostrate stems. Although pink flowers are produced, the plant's fuzziness is its best attribute in dry climates. In warm areas that receive a good deal of summer rain, however, it is a detriment, because water does not evaporate easily from the leaves and plants may melt out badly. Full sun, zones 5 to 8.

A couple of common species with lavender-purple flowers are *Thymus praecox*, creeping thyme, and *T. serpyllum*, wild thyme. They both form thick mats under conditions of cool nights and good drainage. *Thymus vulgaris*, common thyme, is the culinary thyme of the grocery aisle; it forms purple or white flowers on 12–15" tall plants. Several selections of these species are available, including the variegated *T. vulgaris* 'Silver Posie'. All cultivars do poorly in rainy and humid summers and must be planted where drainage is excellent. Full sun, zones 5 to 8.

Thymus vulgaris

Thymus pseudolanuginosus

Thymus praecox

Thymus serpyllum

Thymus vulgaris 'Silver Posie'

Tiarella cordifolia

Tiarella cordifolia 'Oakleaf'

Tiarella cordifolia var. *collina*

Tiarella

FOAMFLOWER

Many excellent selections and hybrids of *Tiarella cordifolia*, an outstanding native plant, have been developed recently, attracting keen interest in the entire genus. Particularly useful for shady gardens, these plants are generally 6–12" tall, forming slow-growing colonies that bear white or pink flowers in the spring. One of the earlier introductions, *T. cordifolia* 'Oakleaf', with dark green leaves and pink flower buds and flowers, is still a favorite. Variety *collina* is similar to the species but is more of a clumper than a colonizer. The leaves of both the type and the variety are heart-shaped and are evergreen in most climates.

Flowers are similar in most foamflowers, and the newer hybrids of *Tiarella* have been mainly selected for their foliage characteristics, giving the gardener greater choices than ever before. 'Dunvegan' has marvelous foliage, each leaf consisting of five lobes with the central one long and narrow; excellent flowering in the spring as well. 'Skeleton Key' is equally fresh-looking in the spring, with dozens of white flowers and light green lobed leaves. Other hybrid entries are 'Brandywine' and 'Snowflake', each with vigorous shiny green leaves and creamy white flowers. Interest in leaf coloration and leaf mottling resulted

Tiarella 'Dunvegan'

Tiarella 'Brandywine'

Tiarella 'Skeleton Key'

Tiarella 'Snowflake'

in cultivars such as 'Ink Blot', 'Dark Star', and 'Tiger Stripe', to name but a few. The genus provides outstanding characteristics for the garden and has been unfairly stuck in the "shady native" category for too long. It should be a mainstream plant. Partial shade, good drainage, zones 3 to 8.

Tiarella 'Ink Blot'

Tiarella 'Dark Star'

Tiarella 'Tiger Stripe'

Tradescantia

SPIDERWORT

The genus *Tradescantia* commemorates the family Tradescant, in particular the father and son, known as Tradescant the Elder and Tradescant the Younger. As gardeners to Charles I of England in the early 1600s, they received many plants from the colonies. The Younger also traveled to America, bringing back to the Empire such treasures as Virginia creeper and Michaelmas daisies.

Although our native species *Tradescantia virginiana* has gone through significant changes, it remains a staple in American gardening. The light green straplike foliage is common to all the selections, and all produce dozens of flowers, each opening for a single day. Breeding has concentrated

Tradescantia virginiana 'Bilberry Ice'

Tradescantia virginiana 'Bluestone'

on flower colors, and many are available. Flower color, flower persistence, and compact habit make many of the newer cultivars interesting. 'Bilberry Ice' has a cool lavender look; 'Bluestone', 'Zwanenburg Blue', and 'Purple Dome' have good blue-lavender flowers; 'Concord Grape', 'Purewell Giant',

Tradescantia virginiana 'Zwanenburg Blue'

Tradescantia virginiana 'Purple Dome'

Tradescantia virginiana 'Concord Grape'

MORE →

Tradescantia virginiana 'Purewell Giant'

Tradescantia virginiana 'Joy'

Tradescantia virginiana 'Pauline'

Tradescantia virginiana 'Innocence'

and 'Joy' provide deeper rose-purple flowers; 'Pauline' has the best pink flowers in the group; and white flowers can be found in 'Innocence'. Afternoon shade and moisture is essential for good performance, but spiderworts don't do well in boggy soils. Hardy in zones 4 to 8.

Tricyrtis

TOAD LILY

It's obvious that the common name for the genus *Tricyrtis* was not chosen with commercial sales in mind. Just try to talk someone into buying a toad lily—not an easy task. That the flowers tend to be spotted and brownish maroon like a toad is simple bad luck, because no matter how shamelessly one promotes the plant and flower, it is not until you see it in its glory that it can be appreciated. A good deal of effort in breeding has brought toad lilies out of obscurity, and although they all still look "kind of the same" to my students, the world of toad lilies is just unfolding. Gardeners know they have

reached the highest possible gardening plateau when they ask for cow manure for their birthday and peruse catalogs in search of toad lilies. No turning back then. Spouses beware!

Tricyrtis formosana, Formosa toad lily, is one of the easiest toad lilies to grow for much of the United States and is reasonably easy to obtain. The leaves are softly hairy and ascend the 2–4' tall stem like those of a real lily. The green leaves sort of fade into the garden for most of the season, then flower buds begin to form in late summer and early fall. Even in flower, nothing about it will knock your socks off, as the maroon color of the flowers is not one the eye locks on. But the flowers, with their spotted petals and sepals, are a study in subtlety and complexity, and will reward notice—once one takes the time to look (turn the flower over and note the warts). Plants are both clump formers and stoloniferous, meaning that they move around the garden and increase in number over

Tricyrtis formosana

Tricyrtis formosana

Tricyrtis formosana 'Alba'

the years, but they are certainly not invasive. 'Alba', a white variant, occasionally appears from a population, and the few I have seen are even more handsome than the species.

Tricyrtis formosana differs from common toad lily, *T. hirta*, by being more upright and having most of its flowers on the upper third of the stem. It is an excellent plant for late summer and fall flowering. The species is not without problems, however, the most serious being the tendency of the leaf tips to turn brown under stress, such as drought or excessive heat. This results in terrible-looking plants that even the weird flowers cannot overcome. Some years they are almost perfect, others perfectly awful. Partial shade, moist soils, zones 4 to 9.

Tricyrtis hirta, the most common species of toad lily, is a plant of classic beauty—leaf tip burn notwithstanding. The flowers and foliage are similar to those of *T. formosana*, but plants differ by being pendulous rather than upright, and the flowers tend to be a little larger and occur along at least half of the 2–3' long stem. The spotted flowers are maroon to purple (occasionally lighter) and occur in late summer and fall. I love seeing them arching gracefully over rocks by a pond or other water feature. 'Miyazaki' is a popular selection of the species.

Numerous toad lily cultivars have been offered to the gardening public, and while response among the general populace has not been overwhelming, veteran gardeners cannot get enough.

Most are hybrids between *Tricyrtis hirta* and *T. formosana*; the differences between them are often subtle, but that should not be surprising in this subtle genus. The hybrids, despite their sometimes unpronounceable names, are generally vigorous growers and somewhat pendulous in form, with lighter, often larger flowers. 'Kohaku' is large and popular, while the

Flowers of *Tricyrtis hirta* (left) and *T. formosana*

Tricyrtis formosana 'Alba' with *Salvia*

Tricyrtis hirta

Tricyrtis hirta 'Miyazaki'

Tricyrtis 'Kohaku'

Tricyrtis 'Lemon Glow'

MORE →

chartreuse leaves distinguish 'Lemon Glow' from the others. I also really enjoy the shrubby habit and the dozens of spotted flowers of 'Shirohotogisu', which is neither pendulous nor upright but somewhere in between. Partial shade, moist soils, zones 4 to 8.

Tricyrtis 'Shirohotogisu'

Trillium

Rose trillium, nodding trillium, great white trillium, wake-robin, showy trillium, snow trillium, wood lily, stinking Benjamin, sessile trillium, toad trillium, yellow trillium—these are but a few of the names describing members of this great genus. That trilliums prefer woodland conditions, that their flowers appear in early spring and are gone soon thereafter, that plants disappear entirely in the summer—all this doesn't make the trillium sound particularly enchanting. But don't tell a trillium fan that. It is a truth universally acknowledged that if trilliums were native to England, the War of the Roses would have been known as the War of the Trilliums. Trillium lovers are passionate.

All reason seems to have left them, and heaven forgive the unsuspecting novice who digs a trillium from the wild. The game of "what trillium is that?" can still get violent among trillites. I must admit to such tendencies, but I am now reformed, I think.

Passions aside, trilliums have a place in the shade garden, and like any other genus, some species are more adaptable than others in a given environment. The easiest way to describe members of this large genus is by describing how the flower is held: either by a short flower stem called the pedicel (pediceled), or attached directly to the top of the plant (sessile), like a king perched on his throne. Each has its own special beauty and charm, but making definite identification is best left to the taxonomists. Exacting propagation techniques make wide distri-

Trillium cuneatum

Trillium sessile

Trillium cuneatum 'Eco Silver'

Trillium sessile 'Eco Strain'

Trillium stamineum

bution of many trilliums difficult, although tissue culture should soon help to overcome some of the problems. Meanwhiile, if you can't find trilliums in the nursery, take a walk in the woods and enjoy nature's treasures. Take a photo, not a plant.

The sessile species include *Trillium cuneatum*, *T. sessile*, *T. decipiens*, *T. stamineum*, *T. luteum*, and *T. discolor*. The first three species are similar to the non-trillium eye. Regardless of their exact identity, all are equally ornamental, bearing maroon-brown flowers on top of the three leaves, which vary immensely in their degree of mottling. The flowers of *T. cuneatum* (toad trillium; zones 5 to 9) are usually longer and more narrow than those of *T. sessile* (sessile trillium; zones 4 to 7). The leaves of *T. cuneatum* are also narrower than those of *T. sessile*, which tend to be rhomboidal in shape. *Trillium cuneatum* and *T. decipiens* (zones 6 to 9) are more southern in habitat than *T. sessile*. The nice thing about many of the sessile trilliums is that the foliage is actually more handsome than the flowers, although if they don't flower, gardeners are a little disappointed. Every now and then, selections of some of the sessile trilliums will be offered, and differ from the various species by having a different leaf or flower color. For instance, the mottled leaves of *T. sessile* 'Eco Strain' and the dull silvery leaves of *T. cuneatum* 'Eco Silver' are interesting and subjectively showy.

After so many remarkably similar trilliums, *Trillium stamineum* (twisted trillium) is easily recognized by the twisted purple petals which lie flat, showing off the large conspicuous stamens. Quite lovely, certainly different.

Two sessile species sport yellow flowers. The long pointed petals of *Trillium luteum* (yellow trillium; zones 5 to 7) vary from deep butter-yellow to the more common light yellow. While the purple to maroon flowers of the others can sometimes get lost in the woodland canopy, no such problem with *T. luteum*. Outstanding. But for classical pale yellow flowers, I much prefer the look of the primrose trillium, *T. discolor* (zones 6 to 8). The petals are spatula-shaped, and even in bud, the plant is eye-catching.

Pediceled species include *Trillium catesbaei*, *T. cernuum*, *T. erectum*, *T. grandiflorum*, and *T. vaseyi*. The flowers of *T. catesbaei* (rose trillium; zones 6 to 9) and *T. cernuum* (nodding trillium; zones 3 to 7) have a similar characteristic, that is, they nod. They nod below the leaves, and it is easy to pass them by without ever glimpsing the flower. That would be a shame because the light to deep rose flowers of *T. catesbaei* and the white blooms of *T. cernuum* are really quite lovely. Another

Trillium decipiens

Trillium luteum

Trillium discolor

Trillium discolor in bud

MORE →

characteristic the two species share is their flared-back petals; when you are bending down and looking up, the stamens and pistil can be appreciated, even as you slip a disc.

The flowers of *Trillium erectum* (stinking Benjamin; zones 4 to 7) have a subtle mangy smell to them, but their beauty cannot be denied. The flower is held on a long pedicel and points slightly downward. The petals are usually red to maroon, but a good deal of diversity occurs in the wild, where whites and pale yellows may occasionally be seen. The leaves are about as wide as they are long and seldom mottled.

Trillium vaseyi (Vasey's trillium; zones 5 to 7) has the same purple flower color as *T. erectum* but that is about as similar as it gets. The flower is among the largest in the genus. They are carried on a pedicel but are held beside rather than above the leaves. An absolutely stunning plant, although not particularly easy to find commercially or to establish.

The granddaddy, aunt, and uncle of all North American trilliums is *Trillium grandiflorum* (great white trillium; zones 4 to 7). Carpeting open woods and regaling all those who view it, whether en masse or one at time, the white trillium is the epitome of native woodland plants. As the flowers decline, they often turn a rosy red color, yet another charm to this quite marvelous plant. Plants are so revered in Canada that it was adopted as the provincial flower of Ontario. With its successful carpeting of the northern woodland and its stunning beauty, this species has probably been subjected to more abuse from picking, gathering, and digging than any other trillium. It puts up with humans anyway, making our springtimes even brighter. Garden cultivars have been developed such as the double-flowered 'Flore Pleno' and the rosy-flowered 'Roseum'.

Trillium catesbaei

Trillium cernuum

Trillium catesbaei

Trillium erectum

Trillium cernuum

Trillium erectum

Trillium vaseyi

Trillium vaseyi

Trillium grandiflorum

Aging flowers of *Trillium grandiflorum*

Trillium grandiflorum 'Flore Pleno'

Trillium grandiflorum 'Roseum'

Uvularia grandiflora 'Sunbonnet'

Uvularia perfoliata

Uvularia perfoliata

Uvularia

BELLWORT, MERRY BELLS

Subtlety is the hallmark of this genus of woodland plants. Not particularly showy, but admired by those who do not equate beauty with showmanship. Five species are known, all shade tolerant and moisture loving and all native to eastern North America. The bellworts are remarkably similar in makeup and garden performance, bearing small pale yellow flowers, which hang from the nodes of the upper leaves. It is the leaves that differ among the species, and although not particularly striking, the differences are notable. In *Uvularia grandiflora* (large-flowered bellwort) and *U. perfoliata* (perfoliate bellwort), the stem appears to pierce and pass through the leaves—a unique arrangement described by the term "perfoliate." The flowers of *U. grandiflora* are significantly larger than those of *U. perfoliata*, and on the whole it is a more visual plant. *Uvularia perfoliata* appears to spread throughout the garden more rapidly, which is either good or bad, depending if you like the thing. A few cultivars are occasionally offered by mail-order specialists, such as 'Sunbonnet', a bigger, brighter selection of *U. grandiflora*.

The leaves are sessile (that is, no leaf

Uvularia grandiflora

Uvularia sessilifolia

Uvularia sessilifolia

stem or petiole) in the third common species, *Uvularia sessilifolia*. An even more vigorous plant under shady, moist conditions, plants can quickly colonize an area. The flowers are similar to those of *U. perfoliata*. All require shade and moisture and are hardy in zones 4 (3 with protection) to 9.

Veratrum

FALSE HELLEBORE

Veratrum was the ancient name of *Helleborus*, thus accounting for this genus's common name. From a stout black rhizome emerges a plant grown for the wonderful pleated leaves and unique branched flower heads. I love *Veratrum viride* (American false hellebore) but have a difficult time finding it for the Armitage garden. That all parts of the plant are poisonous may tend to limit its use somewhat, but only mad dogs and Englishmen would ever think of putting that fact to the test. The flowers rise from within the plant to form otherworldly branched green panicles. Plants grow 3–6' tall and when in flower, are guaranteed to elicit all sorts of oohs and aahs and a concluding "what is it?" from any and all passers-by. Plants go dormant in the heat of the summer. Partial shade and moisture are needed. Hardy in zones 3 to 7.

Two species from Europe and Asia are equally outstanding. The European false hellebore, *Veratrum album*, differs from *V. viride* only in its native setting and flower color, being whitish on the inside and greenish yellow outside. The other difference is that it is even more difficult to locate than its American counterpart. Plants are only about 2–4' tall but, like their American cousins, are knockouts. The black false hellebore, *V. nigrum*, is similar in habit and foliage but the black-purple flowers, which occur in dense racemes, are incredible. Plants are about 4' tall. To locate any of these fine plants is to willingly go into debt, no questions asked! Partial shade, moisture, zones 4 to 7.

Veratrum viride

Veratrum nigrum

Veratrum album

Veratrum viride

Verbena peruviana

Verbena tenuisecta

Verbena tenuisecta 'Imagination'

Verbena

VERVAIN

Verbenas have been a mainstay of perennial gardens since great grandmother's time and will continue to be one of those plants that comes and goes from the horticultural stage. Colorful annual bedding verbenas are offered every spring, vying with the many perennial offerings for attention. Perennial verbenas are extremely diverse, varying in height from upright-growing *Verbena bonariensis* and its dwarfer twin, *V. rigida*, to low growers like *V. peruviana* and hybrids of *V. ca-* *nadensis* and *V. tenuisecta*. All require full sun and exceptionally good drainage.

Verbena peruviana, *V. tenuisecta*, and *V. canadensis* are low-growing species. From hugging the ground to romping over large areas of terrain, these species are outstanding for gardens, containers, and patio planters. *Verbena peruviana*, Peruvian verbena, is the most compact of the three, bearing deep red flowers on spreading mats of green, 2–4" tall. Full sun, zones 7 to 9.

The most handsome leaves are to be found in the fernlike foliage of cutleaf verbena, *Verbena tenuisecta* (zones 7

Verbena tenuisecta

Verbena 'Tapien Blue'

Verbena 'Tapien Pink'

to 10). Dozens of small lavender-blue flowers cover the foliage in midsummer and throughout the season. This species is probably the most heat tolerant of the three low growers. 'Imagination' is a seed-propagated selection of the type and variety *alba* is equally floriferous. Recent breeding using *V. tenuisecta* resulted in 'Tapien Blue' and 'Tapien Pink', both highly recommended cultivars. Full sun, hardy to zone 7.

Verbena canadensis, rose verbena, is native to North America and occurs naturally in the form of rose flowers. The most common verbena offered commercially, it is hardy to zone 7,

perhaps zone 6 if snow cover is sufficient. Hybrids between it and other species have exploded. 'Homestead Purple' is an excellent vigorous early flowerer that paved the way for many others. 'Taylortown Red' is a good red-flowered hybrid, while 'Sissinghurst' and 'Abbeville' provide handsome rosy

pink and lavender flowers, respectively. 'Carrousel' provides bicolor flowers, and 'Silver Anne' is always a popular, tempering color. All require full sun and excellent drainage and can occasionally be cut back if the plants grow too vigorous or the stems become spindly. Hardy in zones 7 (perhaps 6) to 10.

Upright species of verbena include

Verbena 'Carrousel'

Verbena 'Taylortown Red'

Verbena 'Sissinghurst'

Verbena 'Abbeville'

Verbena tenuisecta var. *alba*

Verbena 'Tapien Pink'

Verbena 'Homestead Purple'

Verbena bonariensis, tall verbena, and *V. rigida*, rigid verbena. Being upright is not the only characteristic these South American natives share. Both are square-stemmed, bristly hairy, and bear small rosy purple flowers for a long period of time. *Verbena bonariensis* is 3–6' high and flowers from early

Verbena bonariensis

Verbena 'Silver Anne'

Verbena rigida 'Polaris'

Verbena rigida 'Lilacina'

Verbena bonariensis

Verbena rigida

summer throughout the season. Like *Thalictrum*, it is a see-through plant, which even when densely planted remains open enough to allow one to see what is on the other side. Mildew is a serious problem if plants are in wet conditions or too much shade. Few cultivars of *V. bonariensis* have been developed, although since many are raised from seed, various shades of flower color occur. Full sun, zones 6 to 9.

Verbena rigida is similar in texture and color but only about 2' tall. The leaves are opposite, also bristly, and likewise susceptible to powdery mildew. Its selection 'Lilacina' has blue-purple flowers; 'Polaris' is vigorous and lavender-flowered. Both *V. rigida* and *V. bonariensis* reseed prolifically, but the resulting plants seldom flower as well as the parents. Full sun, zones 7 to 9.

Veronica

SPEEDWELL

The genus *Veronica* provides a wide range of height, color, and texture. The low growers work well in rock gardens and raised beds, and benefit from cool nights and good drainage; taller species are used in perennial borders, and some enjoy a well-deserved reputation as cut flowers. Many prostrate low growers have been made available to gardeners, even though the scientific names keep changing. It is likely that nobody has a clue what species gardeners are using anyway, and telling them that the names have been changed is not only confusing but more often than not, absolutely useless information. I figure if a plant is named after a saint

(in this case, Saint Veronica), it can't be all bad.

One of the ways to tell the low growers from the upright speedwells (other than height) is that the flowers on the low growers are always produced in the lateral leaf nodes. That is, they arise from the leaf nodes near the top of the stem, instead of being terminal as in the case of tall species like *Veronica spicata* or *V. longifolia*. The low growers are often bright blue, and the carpets of foliage may be totally hidden by the many flowers in late spring and early summer. Some of the more floriferous of the low growers are selections of *V. austriaca* subsp. *teucrium* ('Blue Fountain', 'Shirley Blue'), but plants with golden leaves ('Aurea') are also available to those who enjoy chartreuse foliage. Full sun, zones 4 to 7.

Veronica austriaca

Veronica austriaca subsp. *teucrium* 'Shirley Blue'

Veronica incana

Veronica austriaca subsp. *teucrium* 'Blue Fountain'

Veronica austriaca subsp. *teucrium* 'Aurea'

MORE →

Veronica prostrata 'Trehane'

Veronica longifolia 'Blauriesen'

Veronica incana, another prostrate species, generally has blue flowers and gray foliage, a contrast that works well in the Armitage garden. 'Silver Carpet' is a good representation of the species. I also enjoy the bright yellow-green foliage of *V. prostrata* 'Trehane', which makes an excellent ground cover even when not in flower. When plants start flowering in spring, the blue and gold are outstanding together. Both species need excellent drainage and full sun. Hardy in zones 3 to 7.

While many veronicas are useful for the front of the garden, the upright *Veronica longifolia*, long-leaved speedwell, is generally sufficiently tall to be viewed when placed in the middle or even in the back of a garden. Plants bear upright spikes of flowers on 3–4' long stems, each terminal spike consisting of dozens of small quarter- to half-inch-wide flowers. Plants are strong enough and tall enough to be used as a cut flower and are grown as such throughout the world. Mainte-

Veronica longifolia 'Blauriesen'

Veronica longifolia 'Schneeriesen'

nance is minimal in full sun, but plants require staking if placed in too much shade. Evidence of good breeding can be found in blue cultivars such as 'Blauriesen'—one of the most popular cut flower speedwells in the world—while white and rosy flowers, respectively, have been raised in 'Schneeriesen' and 'Rosalinde'. All selections of *V. longifolia* perform best in full sun in normal soils. Hardy in zones 4 to 8.

The best-known species of the entire genus is the upright *Veronica spicata*, spiked speedwell. It comes in many colors (blue and lavender are the main colors) and heights, the normal height range being 1–3'. The 2" glossy green leaves are usually serrated in the middle. The terminal upright flowers begin to open in early summer and often continue for two months or more, especially if spent flowers are deadheaded. The dozens of cultivars of *V. spicata* perform well in full sun and well-drained soils. Blue-flowered selections are most common, including the glossy-leaved 'Blue Bouquet' and the compact 'Blue Spires'. While I enjoy the blue flowers, the palette is expanded by selections such as 'Lili Corinna', which is about 2' tall with handsome lavender flowers. 'Barcarolle' and 'Erika' have upright pink flowers, and 'Heidekind' bears deep rosy red flowers in spring and summer. Hardy in zones 3 to 7.

Veronica spicata 'Barcarolle'

Veronica spicata 'Erika'

Veronica longifolia 'Rosalinde'

Veronica spicata 'Blue Spires'

Veronica spicata 'Heidekind'

Veronica spicata 'Blue Bouquet'

Veronica spicata 'Lili Corinna'

276

Veronicastrum virginicum 'Roseum'

Veronicastrum virginicum

Veronicastrum virginicum

CULVER'S ROOT

This native species is a fairly recent darling of American gardeners. Plants grow up to 5' tall and can be 3–4' wide. Whorls of three to six leaves occur along the stems, and it is this arrangement that is the easiest way to distinguish *Veronicastrum* from the closely related *Veronica*. The flowers of the two are similar, but the inflorescences are generally more narrow and longer in culver's root. There is some disagreement among eggheads as to whether the species is strictly lavender or both lavender and white. I prefer to agree with the lumpers rather than the splitters: white or lavender, I love this plant. The white-flowered variant is the most available color, and it not only makes an excellent garden plant but is highly prized as a cut flower. Put the flower stems together with yarrows and statice in a vase, and the effect is most dramatic. They are best when grown in full sun and provided with

Veronicastrum virginicum

Veronicastrum sibiricum

sufficient water and fertilizer. Occasionally the pink-flowered 'Roseum' may be found, and it too can be quite dramatic. The lavender variant of the type as well as *V. sibiricum* (zones 3 to 7), a European species, have blue to lavender flowers but are more difficult to locate. *Veronicastrum virginicum* requires full sun and is hardy in zones 4 to 8.

Viola

VIOLET

Over five hundred species of this old-fashioned plant have been documented—a genus sufficiently diverse to cause the same gardener to enthusiastically embrace some species while considering others obnoxious weeds. In fact, I find the latter to be more common than the former. In the Armitage garden, I yank and toss the fast-moving marsh violet, *Viola cucullata*, but carefully cultivate Labrador violet, *V. labradorica*, and birdsfoot violet, *V. pedata*. The genus *Viola* includes the fragrant sweet violet, *V. odorata*, sold as a cut flower since Roman times, as well as our modern pansies and violas. All species perform better in cooler climates than in hot weather: in the North, violets do well in the summer; in the South, in the winter. All ornamental violets are excellent in the spring in most locales.

Viola cornuta, the horned violet, is not as commonly seen in American as in European gardens, possibly the proliferation of bedding pansies and violas has smothered this species. A shame, because it offers wonderful diversity of color and form. The flowers, each 1–1½" across, are somewhat star-shaped and have a long slender spur, accounting for its common name. It is not as accommodating of weather extremes as other species, but plants generally flower well in the spring, and if cut back after flowering, may bloom again, at least in cooler summers. In the South, plants have a more difficult time surviving the summer and may have to be treated as winter annuals. Dozens of cultivars have been bred in Europe, some well worth seeking. I love the deep 'Jersey Gem' and the light 'Lilacina', both vigorous in growth and in flowering. The white flowers of 'Alba' brighten the garden, and the lavender-pink blossoms of 'Rosea' are also excellent. Full sun, good drainage, zones 6 to 9.

One of the best, easiest, and finest of the violets—the dark-leaved Labrador violet, *Viola labradorica*—can nevertheless be as aggressive as any other

Viola cornuta 'Lilacina'

Viola cornuta 'Jersey Gem'

Viola cornuta 'Alba'

MORE →

weed. Native to northern climates, plants are outstanding in the North and almost as good in the South. The mauve quarter-inch-wide flowers may be small but can almost cover up a plant in the spring. The plant essen-tially sits around in the summer but is outstanding in the fall, winter (in the South), and spring. The best part of this violet is the purple foliage: almost black in early spring, it lightens only slightly when the plant is in flower. Plants form nice clumps but also spread rapidly. No cultivars are avail-able, but since they reseed themselves, variations of leaf and flower color can sometimes be spotted. An Armitage favorite! Partial shade, zones 3 to 8.

Probably the best known, at least to native plant enthusiasts, of the native eastern violets, *Viola pedata*, birdsfoot violet, is also the easiest species to identify. The leaves are palmately compound (like the foot of a bird?), and bluish flowers with orange stamens are formed in the spring. As a garden member, birdsfoot violet is also one of the more difficult to establish, but that never stopped anyone from trying. Plants must be placed in partial shade, in extremely well-drained soil, or they will be difficult to establish. Several seed-raised colors occur naturally, and a few cultivars, such as 'Artist's Palette', have also been selected and propagated.

Viola cornuta 'Rosea'

Viola labradorica

Viola labradorica

Viola pedata

Waldsteinia

BARREN STRAWBERRY

Waldsteinia is a relatively unknown ground-covering genus, consisting of about five species, most of which are native to the United States. Plants are not vigorous growers, which limits the ability of these ground covers to cover ground. They do, however, produce strawberry-like foliage, consisting of

Viola pedata

Viola pedata 'Artist's Palette'

Waldsteinia fragarioides

three leaflets, often 1–2" long, which are rounded or wedge-shaped. In the summer, leaves are often glossy green, and in areas where little snow cover occurs, the foliage turns a handsome purple. They grow over each other to form a thick mat, and in the spring, light to deep yellow half-inch-wide flowers occur. The flowers are interesting if not dramatic. I have seen *Waldsteinia fragarioides* and *W. ternata* look good in the cooler climates, while *W. lobata* and *W. parviflora* handle warm summers well. Plants thrive in moist, shaded conditions. *Waldsteinia fragarioides* and *W. ternata* are hardy in zones 4 to 7, *W. lobata* and *W. parviflora* in zones 6 to 8.

Yucca

Yuccas are popular for their bold architectural form and strong upright, often spine-tipped leaves. The dense spikes of pendulous tulip-shaped blooms are also impressive. In long, warm summers, flowers occur in midsummer, and when summers are cool, flowers still occur but may be quite late. Yuccas have a reputation of being frost tender; however species such as *Yucca filamentosa*, Adam's needle, are cold hardy to about 5°F. Not exactly Winnipeg, but more hardy than most people think. The margins of the upright leaves vary dramatically in their amount of filaments, but some plants can be quite "filamentous" indeed.

Waldsteinia lobata

Waldsteinia parviflora

Waldsteinia ternata

Yucca filamentosa

Waldsteinia ternata in winter

Yucca filamentosa 'Gold Band'

MORE →

Selections of *Yucca filamentosa* with multicolored foliage have become popular in recent years, and the yellow-

Yucca filamentosa

Yucca filamentosa 'Golden Sword'

and white-variegated leaves have become part of town and garden landscape plantings. 'Gold Band', 'Golden Sword', and 'Bright Edge' are but three examples that have caught my eye. The diversity in the genus is incredible, and hybrids with *Y. filamentosa* are also becoming more numerous; I find myself admiring these much more living in the South than I ever did when I was gardening in the North. Full sun, good drainage, zones 5 to 9.

Yucca filamentosa 'Golden Sword'

Yucca filamentosa 'Bright Edge'

Zantedeschia

CALLA LILY

My fondest visual memory of the time I spent in New Zealand is the image of callas strewn like white lollipops over the green landscape. As a kid buying the occasional flower to assuage my guilt over some transgression, I thought these flowers were incredibly beautiful but rather artificial. Not to mention far more expensive than my guilt or transgressions dictated. Just as kids believe that milk comes from cartons, so did I think that callas came from florist shops. These flowers of the New Zealand fields changed all that.

The most common of these uncommon lilies is the white calla lily, *Zantedeschia aethiopica*. It is the embodiment of erotic cleanliness, with a large pure white spathe around an upright spadix. The wavy lustrous green leaves, which can be 8" wide and a foot long, are borne on plants which themselves can easily reach 3½' in height. In American gardens, the white calla is often planted in the spring, enjoyed

Zantedeschia aethiopica 'Green Goddess'

all summer, and dug up in the fall to be stored in a cool garage, like a dahlia. They usually grow about 3' tall and form three to five flowers in a year. They make exceptionally good cut flowers, persisting such a long time that the New Zealanders routinely ship the cut stems around the world. Plants are best suited for wet areas and naturalize well in moist grassy pockets or even in shallow ponds. In the Armitage garden, they are outstanding in the corners of the pond, where splashing water keeps them constantly moist.

A few cultivars of *Zantedeschia aethiopica* have been selected, the best known being 'Crowborough', which is hardier than the species and perhaps a little more refined. 'Green Goddess' has a spathe that can't decide to be white or green, so it is somewhere in between—a hideous thing. 'Little Gem' is one of my favorites, with many more flowers than the species and only about 2' tall.

Several colorful *Zantedeschia* hybrids have been developed in New Zealand, California, and Europe. Most have large colored spathes and spotted leaves. The best and most hardy is 'Black Magic', which easily grows 3–4' tall and produces myriad golden yellow flowers with black throats. Another favorite is 'Majestic Red', a tall

Zantedeschia 'Black Magic'

Zantedeschia aethiopica 'Little Gem'

Zantedeschia 'Majestic Red'

Zantedeschia aethiopica

Zantedeschia aethiopica 'Crowborough'

MORE →

hybrid suitable for cut flowers, as well as the more dwarf 'Pacific Pink', whose flowers differ only slightly in color but are smaller than the others. The hybrids are more shade tolerant and do not need or want the moist conditions required by the white callas. I like them all: it is difficult to beat a well-grown calla. Still, few gardeners want to dig them each year. Full sun to partial shade, moist conditions, zones 8 (7 in moisture) to 10.

Zantedeschia 'Pacific Pink'

Zauschneria

CALIFORNIA FUCHSIA

The genus *Zauschneria* has gardeners either very passionate or very frustrated. The scarlet to red flowers of *Zauschneria californica* (*Epilobium canum*; California fuchsia) are magnets to hummingbirds, thus accounting for its other common name, the hummingbird trumpet. They grow about 2' tall, making little shrublets that are rather woody at the base. The leaves are green and can be almost smothered by flowers in midsummer. To visit the garden of my friends Panayoti and Gwen Kelaidis in Denver, Colorado, is to immediately become a zauschneria convert. A beautiful sight. To visit my garden in Athens, Georgia, is to immediately understand the meaning of heat-stressed California fuchsias. A gruesome scene. Taxono-mists are arguing the nomenclature of *Zauschneria*. Many believe that the entire genus should be folded into the genus *Epilobium*, while others argue that it should remain where it is. Until the dust settles, I vote to leave it alone.

The most common cultivar came from the Irish National Botanical Garden at Glasnevin; it is properly called 'Dublin', although it is also distributed as 'Glasnevin'. Full sun, well-drained soils, zones 6 to 9.

Zauschneria californica

Zauschneria californica

Part Two
Selected Plants for Specific Characteristics or Purposes

Aggressive Plants

The following plants tend to grow more rapidly than "normal" perennials, often squeezing out their competitors in a year or two. Aggressiveness is often thought of as a negative trait, but when an area requires rapid filling, this tendency is much appreciated. Many of these plants could also be used as ground covers.

Ajuga genevensis
Ajuga reptans
Anemone sylvestris
Anemone tomentosa
Aster tataricus
Corydalis lutea
Eupatorium coelestinum
Helianthus angustifolius

Ipheion uniflorum
Lamium galeobdolon
Lamium maculatum
Lychnis coronaria
Lysimachia ciliata
Lysimachia clethroides
Lysimachia nummularia

Macleaya cordata
Monarda didyma
Oenothera berlandieri
Oenothera drummondii
Oenothera speciosa
Osmunda claytoniana
Physostegia virginiana

Ranunculus bulbosus
Ranunculus ficaria
Ranunculus repens
Salvia koyamae
Saponaria officinalis
Sedum acre
Stachys byzantina

Plants for Wet and Boggy Places

The following perennials perform better in consistently moist conditions.

Brunnera macrophylla
Canna hybrids
Geum rivale
Geum triflorum
Iris ensata
Iris fulva
Iris hexagona
Iris louisiana

Iris nelsonii
Ligularia dentata
Ligularia macrophylla
Ligularia sibirica
Ligularia stenocephala
Lobelia cardinalis
Lobelia tupa
Osmunda regalis

Polygonum bistorta
Primula bulleyana
Primula florindae
Primula heladoxa
Primula japonica
Primula pulverulenta
Ranunculus bulbosus

Ranunculus ficaria
Ranunculus repens
Rodgersia aesculifolia
Rodgersia pinnata
Rodgersia podophylla
Rodgersia sambucifolia
Zantedeschia hybrids

Cut Flowers

Everybody loves bouquets. It may be argued that every plant in the garden can be cut and brought indoors to enjoy, but the following plants are considered cut flowers because of their reasonably strong stems and good vase life. Always cut stems in the morning or evening, place immediately in water, and use a cut flower preservative in the vase.

Acanthus mollis
Acanthus spinosus
Achillea filipendulina
Achillea millefolium
Achillea ptarmica
Aconitum carmichaelii
Aconitum napellus
Allium christophii

Allium giganteum
Allium karataviense
Allium 'Beauregard'
Allium 'Globemaster'
Anemone coronaria
Artemisia ludoviciana
Aster novae-angliae
Aster novi-belgii

Aster tataricus
Astilbe ×arendsii
Astilbe chinensis var. taquetii
Astrantia major
Astrantia maxima
Baptisia alba
Baptisia australis
Baptisia sphaerocarpa

Baptisia viridis
Boltonia asteroides
Campanula lactiflora
Campanula latiloba
Centaurea macrocephala
Chrysanthemum coccineum
Chrysanthemum ×superbum
Crocosmia hybrids

Cut Flowers, continued
Dahlia hybrids
Delphinium elatum
Delphinium nudicaule
Dianthus barbatus
Dianthus caryophyllus
Digitalis purpurea
Dryopteris erythrosora (foliage)
Echinacea purpurea
Echinops ritro
Eremurus himalaicus
Eremurus stenophyllus
Eryngium alpinum
Eupatorium maculatum
Eupatorium purpureum

Gaillardia ×grandiflora
Geum triflorum
Helenium autumnale
Helianthus angustifolius
Helianthus ×multiflorus
Heliopsis helianthoides
Helleborus orientalis
Heuchera sanguinea
Hibiscus moscheutos
Hypericum androsaemum (fruit)
Iris ensata
Iris louisiana
Kniphofia hybrids
Liatris spicata
Lilium auratum

Lilium regale
Lupinus polyphyllus
Lycoris albiflora
Lycoris aurea
Lycoris radiata
Lycoris squamigera
Lysimachia clethroides
Macleaya cordata
Miscanthus sinensis
Monarda didyma
Nepeta ×faassenii
Nepeta sibirica
Paeonia hybrids
Papaver nudicaule
Papaver somniferum
Patrinia scabiosifolia

Penstemon barbatus
Penstemon digitalis
Phlox paniculata
Physostegia virginiana
Platycodon grandiflorus
Polemonium caeruleum
Polemonium foliosissimum
Polygonatum odoratum
Primula vialii
Scabiosa caucasica
Stokesia laevis
Thalictrum aquilegiifolium
Veronica longifolia
Veronica spicata
Veronicastrum sibiricum
Veronicastrum virginicum

Drought Tolerance

The following plants tolerate drought well, but remember: no plant "likes" to be grown under drought conditions, and performance is always better when some irrigation is provided.

Aster novae-angliae
Aster novi-belgii
Aster tataricus

Epimedium grandiflorum
Epimedium ×perralchium
Epimedium ×rubrum

Epimedium ×youngianum
Eryngium agavifolium
Eryngium yuccafolium

Yucca filamentosa
Zauschneria californica

Flower Color

The human eyeball is a mysterious thing, and the interpretation of a color is always somewhat subjective, so be warned: the following lists of plants of a particular flower color are guidelines only. For instance, "white," to me, is a range, including the creamy whites, perhaps with a hint of pink.

WHITE
Achillea ageratum 'W. B. Childs'
Achillea millefolium 'Nakuru'
Achillea ptarmica
Achillea ptarmica 'Ballerina'
Achillea ptarmica 'The Pearl' ('Boule de Neige')
Achillea sibirica
Aconitum septentrionale 'Ivorine'
Allium karataviense

Anemone blanda 'White Splendor'
Anemone coronaria
Anemone coronaria 'Mt. Everest'
Anemone coronaria St. Brigid series
Anemone ×hybrida 'Honorine Jobert'
Anemone sylvestris
Aquilegia flabellata 'Alba'
Arisaema candidissimum

Arisaema sikokianum
Arisaema sikokianum × A. takedae
Aruncus aethusifolius
Aruncus dioicus
Aruncus dioicus 'Kneiffii'
Aruncus dioicus 'Zweiweltenkind' ('Child of Two Worlds')
Aruncus 'Southern White'
Aster divaricatus
Astilbe ×arendsii 'Bridal Veil'

Astilbe ×arendsii 'Gladstone'
Astilbe ×arendsii 'Rheinland'
Astilbe biternata
Astilbe simplicifolia 'Dunkellanchs'
Astilbe simplicifolia 'Willy Buchanan'
Astrantia major 'Margery Fish' ('Shaggy')
Astrantia major 'Sunningdale Variegated'
Baptisia alba

Baptisia alba 'Pendula'

Boltonia asteroides

Boltonia asteroides 'Snow-bank'

Campanula lactiflora 'Alba'

Campanula latiloba 'Alba'

Centaurea montana 'Alba'

Cerastium buisseri

Cerastium tomentosum

Chrysanthemum ×superbum 'Aglaia'

Chrysanthemum ×superbum 'Becky'

Chrysanthemum ×superbum 'Polaris'

Chrysanthemum ×superbum 'Snow Cap'

Chrysanthemum ×superbum 'Snow Lady'

Chrysanthemum ×superbum 'White Knight'

Clematis integrifolia 'Alba'

Clematis terniflora

Clematis 'Huldine'

Clematis 'Miss Bateman'

Corydalis lutea 'Alba'

Crocus chrysanthus 'Cream Beauty'

Crocus vernus 'Jeanne d'Arc'

Dicentra spectabilis 'Alba'

Dicentra 'Langtrees'

Dicentra 'Snowflakes'

Digitalis purpurea 'Alba'

Disporum sessile 'Variegatum'

Echinacea purpurea 'White Lustre'

Echinacea purpurea 'White Swan'

Epimedium ×youngianum

Epimedium ×youngianum 'Milky Way'

Epimedium ×youngianum 'Niveum'

Eremurus aitchisonii

Eremurus himalaicus

Eryngium agavifolium

Eryngium yuccafolium

Eupatorium coelestinum 'Album'

Eupatorium rugosum

Eupatorium rugosum 'Chocolate'

Gaura lindheimeri

Gaura lindheimeri 'Corrie's Gold'

Geranium sanguineum 'Album'

Geum rivale 'Album'

Helleborus niger

Helleborus niger Blackthorn Group

Helleborus ×nigristern

Helleborus orientalis

Helleborus orientalis Party Dress series

Hemerocallis 'Gentle Shepherd'

Hemerocallis 'Ice Carnival'

Hemerocallis 'Luminous Jewel'

Heuchera villosa

Heuchera villosa 'Autumn Bride'

Heuchera villosa 'Purpurea'

Heuchera 'June Bride'

Heuchera 'White Cloud'

Hibiscus mutabilis

Hibiscus 'Disco White'

Hosta montana

Hosta montana 'Aureomarginata'

Hosta sieboldiana

Hosta sieboldiana 'Frances Williams'

Hosta 'Bright Lights'

Hosta 'Invincible'

Hosta 'Royal Standard'

Hosta 'Spritzer'

Hosta 'Sum and Substance'

Iris tectorum 'Album'

Iris xiphium 'White Wedgewood'

Iris 'Butter and Sugar'

Iris 'White Swirl'

Kalimeris pinnatifida

Kalimeris yomena

Kalimeris yomena 'Variegata'

Lamium maculatum 'White Nancy'

Liatris spicata 'Floristan White'

Lilium auratum

Lilium auratum 'Opala'

Lilium martagon 'Album'

Lilium regale

Lilium 'Apollo'

Lilium 'Casa Blanca'

Lilium 'Olivia'

Linum perenne 'Album'

Lunaria annua 'Alba'

Lunaria rediviva

Lupinus polyphyllus 'Albus'

Lychnis coronaria 'Alba'

Lychnis flos-cuculi 'Alba'

Lycoris albiflora

Lysimachia clethroides

Lysimachia ephemerum

Macleaya cordata

Mertensia virginica 'Alba'

Miscanthus sinensis

Miscanthus sinensis 'Adagio'

Miscanthus sinensis 'Arabesque'

Miscanthus sinensis 'Cabaret'

Miscanthus sinensis 'Malepartus'

Miscanthus sinensis 'Morning Light'

Miscanthus sinensis 'Silberfeder' ('Silver Feather')

Miscanthus sinensis 'Strictus'

Miscanthus sinensis 'Variegatus'

Miscanthus sinensis 'Yaku Jima'

Monarda 'Snow White'

Narcissus 'Actaea'

Narcissus 'Avalanche'

Narcissus 'Barrett Browning'

Narcissus 'Bridal Gown'

Narcissus 'Flower Drift'

Narcissus 'Geranium'

Narcissus 'Ice Follies'

Oenothera berlandieri 'Woodside White'

Oenothera speciosa 'Alba'

Paeonia 'White Cockade'

Papaver nudicaule 'Party Fun'

Papaver somniferum 'Album'

Penstemon digitalis

Penstemon digitalis 'Husker Red'

Penstemon 'Mother of Pearl'

Penstemon 'Snowstorm'

Penstemon 'White Bedder'

Phlox divaricata 'Dirigo Ice'

Phlox divaricata 'Fuller's White'

Phlox paniculata 'David'

Phlox stolonifera 'Bruce's White'

Phlox subulata 'Snowflake'

Physostegia virginiana 'Summer Snow'

Platycodon grandiflorus 'Albus'

Polemonium caeruleum 'Album'

Polygonatum commutatum

Polygonatum humile

Polygonatum odoratum

Polygonatum odoratum 'Variegatum'

Primula denticulata 'Alba'

Primula vulgaris 'Alba'

Primula vulgaris 'Atlantia'

Primula vulgaris 'Gigha White'

Pulmonaria saccharata 'Sissinghurst White'

Pulsatilla vulgaris 'Alba'

Ranunculus aconitifolius

Rodgersia pinnata 'Alba'

Rodgersia pinnata 'Superba Alba'

Rodgersia podophylla

Rodgersia sambucifolia

Salvia officinalis 'Albiflora'

White, continued

Saponaria officinalis 'Alba'
Sedum reflexum
Sedum reflexum 'Blue Spruce'
Sedum spurium
Sedum ternatum
Silene fimbriata
Silene uniflora
Sisyrinchium angustifolium 'Album'
Sisyrinchium idahoense 'Album'
Smilacina racemosa
Stokesia laevis 'Alba'
Thalictrum aquilegiifolium 'White Cloud'
Thermopsis montana 'Alba'
Tiarella cordifolia
Tiarella cordifolia var. *collina*
Tiarella cordifolia 'Oakleaf'
Tiarella 'Brandywine'
Tiarella 'Dunvegan'
Tiarella 'Ink Blot'
Tiarella 'Snowflake'
Tiarella 'Tiger Stripe'
Tradescantia virginiana 'Innocence'
Tricyrtis formosana 'Alba'
Trillium cernuum
Trillium grandiflorum
Trillium grandiflorum 'Flore Pleno'
Veratrum album
Verbena tenuisecta var. *alba*
Veronicastrum virginicum
Yucca filamentosa
Yucca filamentosa 'Bright Edge'
Yucca filamentosa 'Gold Band'
Yucca filamentosa 'Golden Sword'
Zantedeschia aethiopica

LAVENDER/BLUE

Acanthus mollis
Acanthus mollis 'Holland's Lemon'

Acanthus spinosus
Acanthus spinosus 'Spinosissimus'
Aconitum carmichaelii
Aconitum carmichaelii 'Arendsii'
Aconitum carmichaelii var. *wilsonii*
Aconitum napellus
Aconitum reclinatum
Ajuga reptans
Ajuga reptans 'Atropurpurea'
Ajuga reptans 'Bronze Beauty'
Ajuga reptans 'Burgundy Glow'
Ajuga reptans 'Catlin's Giant'
Ajuga reptans 'Silver Beauty'
Allium christophii
Allium giganteum
Allium 'Beauregard'
Allium 'Globemaster'
Anemone blanda
Anemone blanda 'Atrocaerulea'
Anemone blanda 'Blue Star'
Anemone coronaria
Anemone coronaria 'Mr. Fokker'
Anemone coronaria 'Sylphide'
Anemone coronaria St. Brigid series
Aquilegia alpina
Aquilegia caerulea
Aquilegia flabellata
Aquilegia flabellata 'Alba'
Aquilegia ×hybrida 'Blue Jay'
Aquilegia ×hybrida Biedermeier strain
Aquilegia vulgaris
Aquilegia vulgaris 'Blue Barlow'
Aster novae-angliae 'Hella Lacy'
Aster novae-angliae 'Purple Dome'
Aster novi-belgii 'Professor Kippenburg'

Aster tataricus
Baptisia australis
Baptisia minor
Baptisia 'Purple Smoke'
Brunnera macrophylla
Brunnera macrophylla 'Langtrees'
Brunnera macrophylla 'Variegata'
Campanula carpatica
Campanula carpatica 'Blue Clips'
Campanula carpatica 'Kobalt Bell'
Campanula carpatica var. *turbinata*
Campanula carpatica var. *turbinata* 'Isabel'
Campanula lactiflora 'Pritchard's Variety'
Campanula lactiflora 'Superba'
Campanula latiloba
Campanula latiloba 'Hidcote Amethyst'
Campanula latiloba 'Highcliffe'
Campanula portenschlagiana
Campanula portenschlagiana 'Bavarica'
Campanula portenschlagiana 'Resholt's Variety'
Campanula poscharskyana
Campanula poscharskyana 'Blue Gown'
Centaurea cyanus
Centaurea dealbata
Centaurea montana
Centaurea montana 'Grandiflora'
Ceratostigma plumbaginoides
Ceratostigma willmottianum
Ceratostigma willmottianum 'Forest Blue'
Clematis ×durandii
Clematis heracleifolia
Clematis heracleifolia 'Côte d'Azur'

Clematis heracleifolia 'Robert Briden'
Clematis heracleifolia 'Wyevale Blue'
Clematis integrifolia
Clematis ×jackmanii
Clematis 'Elsa Spath'
Clematis 'Madame Chalmondeley'
Corydalis flexuosa
Corydalis flexuosa 'Blue Panda'
Corydalis flexuosa 'China Blue'
Crocus chrysanthus 'Blue Pearl'
Crocus chrysanthus 'Lady Killer'
Crocus speciosus
Crocus speciosus 'Cassiope'
Crocus speciosus 'Conqueror'
Crocus speciosus 'Oxonian'
Crocus vernus 'Pickwick'
Crocus vernus 'Queen of the Blues'
Crocus vernus 'Remembrance'
Delphinium ×belladonna 'Volkerfrieden'
Delphinium grandiflorum 'Tom Thumb'
Delphinium 'Barba Blue'
Delphinium 'Blue Bird'
Delphinium 'Blue Dawn'
Delphinium 'Blue Jade'
Delphinium 'Molly Buchanan'
Delphinium 'Skyline'
Echinops ritro
Echinops ritro 'Blue Cloud'
Echinops ritro 'Taplow Blue'
Echinops ritro 'Taplow Purple'
Epimedium grandiflorum 'Lilafee'
Eryngium alpinum
Eryngium alpinum 'Blue Star'
Eryngium giganteum
Eupatorium coelestinum

Hepatica acutiloba
Hepatica americana
Hepatica nobilis
Hepatica nobilis 'Light Blue'
Hepatica transsilvanica
Hosta venusta
Hosta 'Antioch'
Hosta 'Blue Cadet'
Hosta 'Francee'
Hosta 'Gold Edger'
Hosta 'Red Neck Heaven'
Hosta 'Sun Power'
Ipheion uniflorum
Ipheion uniflorum 'Rolf Fiedler'
Ipheion uniflorum 'Wisley Blue'
Iris hexagona
Iris reticulata
Iris reticulata 'Cantab'
Iris reticulata 'Harmony'
Iris tectorum
Iris xiphium
Iris 'Ideal'
Iris 'Llewelyn'
Iris 'Lynn Hall'
Iris 'Regal'
Iris 'Sally Kerlin'
Linum perenne
Linum usitatissimum
Lobelia siphilitica
Lunaria annua
Lunaria annua 'Variegata'
Mertensia asiatica
Mertensia sibirica
Mertensia virginica
Monarda 'Blue Stocking'
Monarda 'Donnerwolke'
Nepeta ×*faassenii*
Nepeta ×*faassenii* 'Six Hills Giant'
Nepeta nervosa
Nepeta sibirica
Penstemon cardwellii
Perovskia atriplicifolia
Perovskia atriplicifolia 'Filagran'

Perovskia atriplicifolia 'Longin'
Phlox divaricata 'Clouds of Perfume'
Phlox divaricata 'Louisiana Blue'
Phlox paniculata 'Blue Boy'
Phlox stolonifera
Phlox stolonifera 'Sherwood Purple'
Phlox subulata 'Oakington Blue'
Physostegia virginiana 'Alba'
Platycodon grandiflorus
Platycodon grandiflorus 'Florovariegatus'
Platycodon grandiflorus 'Mariesii'
Platycodon grandiflorus 'Plenus'
Platycodon grandiflorus 'Sentimental Blue'
Polemonium caeruleum
Polemonium caeruleum 'Brise d'Anjou'
Polemonium caeruleum 'Dawn Light'
Polemonium caeruleum subsp. *himalayanum*
Polemonium foliosissimum
Polemonium reptans
Polemonium reptans 'Blue Pearl'
Primula denticulata
Pulmonaria angustifolia
Pulmonaria angustifolia 'Mawson's Variety'
Pulmonaria angustifolia 'Munstead Blue'
Pulmonaria longifolia
Pulmonaria longifolia 'Bertram Anderson'
Pulmonaria longifolia subsp. *cevennensis* ('Little Blue')
Pulmonaria saccharata
Pulmonaria saccharata 'Benediction'

Pulmonaria saccharata 'Excalibur'
Pulmonaria saccharata 'Highdown'
Pulmonaria saccharata 'Mrs. Moon'
Pulmonaria saccharata 'Spilled Milk'
Pulmonaria 'Roy Davidson'
Rodgersia aesculifolia
Rodgersia pinnata
Salvia guaranitica
Salvia guaranitica 'Argentina Skies'
Salvia guaranitica 'Black and Blue'
Salvia guaranitica 'Purple Knight'
Salvia guaranitica 'Purple Splendour'
Salvia nemerosa 'Blue Hill'
Salvia nemerosa 'Blue Queen' ('Blaukönigin')
Salvia nemerosa 'Tanzerin'
Salvia officinalis
Salvia officinalis 'Icterina'
Salvia officinalis 'Purpurescens'
Salvia officinalis 'Tricolor'
Salvia ×*sylvestris*
Salvia ×*sylvestris* 'East Friesland' ('Ostfriesland')
Salvia ×*sylvestris* 'Lubecca'
Salvia 'Indigo Spires'
Scabiosa caucasica
Scabiosa columbaria
Scabiosa columbaria 'Butterfly Blue'
Sisyrinchium angustifolium
Sisyrinchium atlanticum
Sisyrinchium idahoense
Sisyrinchium idahoense 'California Skies'
Sisyrinchium 'Biscutella'
Sisyrinchium 'E. K. Balls'
Sisyrinchium 'Quaint and Queer'
Stachys byzantina

Stachys byzantina 'Countess Helene von Stein'
Stachys macrantha
Stachys macrantha 'Robusta'
Stokesia laevis
Stokesia laevis 'Blue Danube'
Stokesia laevis 'Klaus Jelitto'
Stokesia laevis 'Omega Skyrocket'
Stokesia laevis 'Wyoming'
Symphytum asperum
Symphytum caucasicum
Symphytum grandiflorum
Symphytum officinale
Symphytum officinale 'Variegatum'
Symphytum ×*uplandicum*
Symphytum ×*uplandicum* 'Variegatum'
Symphytum 'Goldsmith'
Thalictrum aquilegiifolium
Thalictrum aquilegiifolium 'Atropurpureum'
Thalictrum ichangense
Thalictrum minus 'Adiantifolium'
Thymus praecox
Thymus pseudolanuginosus
Thymus serpyllum
Thymus vulgaris
Thymus vulgaris 'Silver Posie'
Tradescantia virginiana
Tradescantia virginiana 'Bilberry Ice'
Tradescantia virginiana 'Bluestone'
Tradescantia virginiana 'Concord Grape'
Tradescantia virginiana 'Purewell Giant'
Verbena bonariensis
Verbena rigida
Verbena rigida 'Lilacina'
Verbena rigida 'Polaris'
Verbena tenuisecta
Verbena tenuisecta 'Imagination'

Lavender/Blue, continued
Verbena 'Abbeville'
Verbena 'Homestead Purple'
Verbena 'Tapien Blue'
Veronica austriaca
Veronica austriaca subsp.
   teucrium
Veronica austriaca subsp.
   teucrium 'Aurea'
Veronica austriaca subsp.
   teucrium 'Blue Fountain'
Veronica austriaca subsp.
   teucrium 'Shirley Blue'
Veronica incana
Veronica longifolia
Veronica longifolia 'Blau-
   riesen'
Veronica prostrata
Veronica prostrata 'Trehane'
Veronica spicata
Veronica spicata 'Blue Bouquet'
Veronica spicata 'Blue Spires'
Veronica spicata 'Lili Corinna'
Veronicastrum sibiricum
Veronicastrum virginicum
Viola cornuta
Viola cornuta 'Jersey Gem'
Viola cornuta 'Lilacina'
Viola cucullata
Viola labradorica
Viola pedata
Viola pedata 'Artist's Palette'

YELLOW
Achillea filipendulina
Achillea millefolium 'Paprika'
Achillea 'Anthea'
Achillea 'Coronation Gold'
Achillea 'Martina'
Achillea 'Moonshine'
Aconitum lamarckii
Aquilegia canadensis
Aquilegia chrysantha
Aquilegia chrysantha var.
   hinckleyana
Aquilegia ×*hybrida* 'Music
   Yellow'

Artemisia ludoviciana
Artemisia ludoviciana 'Lati-
   loba'
Artemisia ludoviciana 'Silver
   King'
Artemisia ludoviciana 'Va-
   lerie Fennis'
Artemisia 'Huntington Gar-
   dens'
Baptisia sphaerocarpa
Baptisia tinctoria
Baptisia viridis
Canna 'Cleopatra'
Canna 'Richard Wallace'
Centaurea macrocephala
Centaurea montana
   'Ochroleuca'
Cephalaria gigantea
Chrysanthemum pacificum
Clematis cirrhosa
Coreopsis auriculata
Coreopsis auriculata 'Nana'
Coreopsis grandiflora
Coreopsis grandiflora 'Early
   Sunrise'
Coreopsis grandiflora 'Sunray'
Coreopsis lanceolata
Coreopsis lanceolata 'Brown
   Eyes'
Coreopsis verticillata
Coreopsis verticillata 'Golden
   Showers'
Coreopsis verticillata 'Moon-
   beam'
Coreopsis verticillata 'Zagreb'
Corydalis cheilanthifolia
Corydalis lutea
Crocosmia 'Citronella'
Crocosmia 'Rowallane Yellow'
Crocus chrysanthus 'Advance'
Crocus chrysanthus 'Moon-
   light'
Delphinium 'Butterball'
Delphinium 'Sun Gleam'
Dicentra scandens
Dicentra scandens 'Athens Yel-
   low'

Digitalis grandiflora
Digitalis lutea
Disporum sessile
Disporum sessile var. *flavum*
Echinacea paradoxa
Epimedium ×*perralchium*
Epimedium ×*perralchium*
   'Frohnleiten'
Epimedium ×*versicolor*
Epimedium ×*versicolor* 'Sul-
   phureum'
Eremurus stenophyllus
Euphorbia characias
Euphorbia characias 'Ember
   Queen'
Euphorbia characias 'John
   Tomelson'
Euphorbia characias 'Lam-
   brook Gold'
Euphorbia characias subsp.
   wulfenii
Euphorbia dulcis
Euphorbia dulcis 'Chameleon'
Euphorbia lathyris
Euphorbia myrsinites
Gaillardia ×*grandiflora*
Gaillardia ×*grandiflora* 'Gob-
   lin'
Gaillardia ×*grandiflora*
   'Golden Goblin'
Gaillardia ×*grandiflora* Lol-
   lipop series
Geum chiloense 'Lady
   Stratheden'
Helenium autumnale
Helenium 'Butterpat'
Helenium 'Riverton Beauty'
Helenium 'Wyndley'
Helianthus angustifolius
Helianthus giganteus
Helianthus giganteus 'Sheila's
   Sunshine'
Helianthus ×*multiflorus*
Helianthus ×*multiflorus*
   'Capenoch Star'
Helianthus ×*multiflorus*
   'Corona Dorica'

Helianthus ×*multiflorus* 'Lod-
   don Gold'
Helianthus ×*multiflorus*
   'Morning Sun'
Heliopsis helianthoides
Heliopsis helianthoides 'Balle-
   rina'
Heliopsis helianthoides
   'Golden Plume'
Heliopsis helianthoides 'Gold-
   greenheart'
Heliopsis helianthoides 'In-
   comparabilis'
Heliopsis helianthoides 'Mars'
Heliopsis helianthoides 'Sum-
   mer Sun'
Hemerocallis dumortieri
Hemerocallis fulva
Hemerocallis minor
Hemerocallis 'Atlanta Irish
   Heart'
Hemerocallis 'Eeenie Weenie'
Hemerocallis 'Golden Chimes'
Hemerocallis 'Heather Har-
   rington'
Hemerocallis 'Hyperion'
Hemerocallis 'Kindly Light'
Hemerocallis 'Mary Todd'
Hemerocallis 'Stella d'Oro'
Hypericum androsaemum
Hypericum androsaemum
   'Albury Purple'
Hypericum calycinum
Hypericum 'Hidcote'
Iris danfordiae
Iris 'All Aglow'
Iris 'Butter and Sugar'
Iris 'Moonlight'
Iris 'Sun Fury'
Kirengeshoma palmata
Kniphofia 'Sally's Comet'
Kniphofia 'Shining Scepter'
Kniphofia 'Sulphur Gem'
Kniphofia 'Sunningdale Yellow'
Lamium galeobdolon
Lamium galeobdolon 'Her-
   man's Pride'

Ligularia dentata
Ligularia dentata 'Desdemona'
Ligularia macrophylla
Ligularia sibirica
Ligularia stenocephala
Ligularia stenocephala 'The Rocket'
Lilium auratum var. *platyphyllum*
Lilium canadense
Lilium Blackhouse hybrid
Lilium 'Imperial Gold'
Lilium 'Soft Moonbeam'
Lilium 'Vivaldi'
Linum flavum
Lupinus arboreus
Lycoris aurea
Lysimachia ciliata
Lysimachia ciliata 'Purpurea'
Lysimachia japonica
Lysimachia japonica 'Minutissima'
Lysimachia nummularia
Lysimachia nummularia 'Aurea'
Narcissus bulbocodium
Narcissus bulbocodium 'Primrose'
Narcissus cyclamineus
Narcissus 'Baby Moon'
Narcissus 'Belcato'
Narcissus 'Biscayne'
Narcissus 'Carlton'
Narcissus 'Cum Laude'
Narcissus 'February Gold'
Narcissus 'Foresight'
Narcissus 'Garden Princess'
Narcissus 'Hawara'
Narcissus 'Hillstar'
Narcissus 'Jenny'
Narcissus 'Pipit'
Narcissus 'Stint'
Narcissus 'Susy'
Narcissus 'Tête-à-Tête'
Narcissus 'Tuesday's Child'
Narcissus 'Unsurpassable'

Nepeta govaniana
Oenothera drummondii
Oenothera fruticosa
Oenothera fruticosa 'Lady Brookborough'
Oenothera fruticosa 'Yellow River'
Oenothera missouriensis
Oenothera missouriensis 'Greencourt Lemon'
Paeonia 'Argosy'
Paeonia 'Daffodil'
Paeonia 'Golden Hind'
Paeonia 'Honey Gold'
Patrinia scabiosifolia
Patrinia scabiosifolia 'Nagoya'
Patrinia triloba
Patrinia villosa
Penstemon confertus
Phlomis fruticosa
Phlomis russeliana
Primula florindae
Primula heladoxa
Primula veris
Primula vulgaris
Primula vulgaris 'Double Yellow'
Ranunculus asiaticus 'Bloomingdale Yellow'
Ranunculus bulbosus
Ranunculus bulbosus 'Flore Pleno'
Ranunculus ficaria
Ranunculus ficaria 'Brazen Hussy'
Ranunculus repens
Ranunculus repens 'Susan's Song' ('Buttered Popcorn')
Rudbeckia fulgida
Rudbeckia fulgida var. *sullivantii* 'Goldsturm'
Rudbeckia laciniata
Rudbeckia laciniata 'Goldquelle'
Rudbeckia nitida
Rudbeckia nitida 'Herbsonne'
Rudbeckia triloba

Salvia koyamae
Santolina chamaecyparissus
Santolina pinnata
Santolina virens
Scabiosa ochroleuca
Sedum acre
Sedum aizoon
Sedum aizoon var. *aurantiacum*
Sedum kamtschaticum
Sedum kamtschaticum 'Diffusum'
Sedum kamtschaticum 'Weihenstephaner Gold'
Sedum spathulifolium
Sedum spathulifolium 'Cape Blanco'
Sisyrinchium striatum
Sisyrinchium striatum 'Aunt May'
Stachys byzantina 'Primrose Heron'
Stachys byzantina 'Sheila Macqueen'
Stokesia laevis 'Mary Gregory'
Stylophorum diphyllum
Stylophorum lasiocarpum
Tanacetum vulgare
Thalictrum flavum
Thalictrum flavum 'Glaucum'
Thalictrum minus 'Adiantifolium'
Thermopsis caroliniana
Thermopsis fabacea
Thermopsis montana
Trillium discolor
Trillium luteum
Uvularia grandiflora
Uvularia grandiflora 'Sunbonnet'
Uvularia perfoliata
Uvularia sessilifolia
Waldsteinia fragaroides
Waldsteinia lobata
Waldsteinia parviflora
Waldsteinia ternata

PINK/ROSE

Achillea millefolium
Achillea millefolium 'Nakuru'
Achillea millefolium 'Rose Beauty'
Achillea 'Appleblossom'
Aconitum napellus 'Carneum'
Ajuga genevensis 'Pink Beauty'
Anemone blanda 'Radar'
Anemone coronaria
Anemone coronaria St. Brigid series
Anemone hupehensis 'September Charm'
Anemone ×*hybrida* 'Kriemhilde'
Anemone ×*hybrida* 'Max Vogel'
Anemone tomentosa
Anemone tomentosa 'Robustissima'
Aquilegia vulgaris 'Nora Barlow'
Aquilegia vulgaris 'Pink Barlow'
Aquilegia vulgaris 'Treble Pink'
Aster carolinianus
Aster novae-angliae 'Alma Potschke'
Aster novae-angliae 'Harrington's Pink'
Aster novi-belgii 'Winston S. Churchill'
Astilbe ×*arendsii* 'Cattleya'
Astilbe ×*arendsii* 'Europa'
Astilbe ×*arendsii* 'Venus'
Astilbe simplicifolia
Astilbe simplicifolia 'Dunkellanchs'
Astilbe simplicifolia 'Hennie Graafland'
Astilbe simplicifolia 'Sprite'
Astilbe simplicifolia 'Willy Buchanan'
Astrantia major

Pink/Rose, continued

Astrantia major 'Margery Fish' ('Shaggy')
Astrantia major 'Sunningdale Variegated'
Astrantia maxima
Bergenia ciliata
Bergenia cordifolia
Bergenia purpurascens
Bergenia 'Abendglocken' ('Evening Bells')
Bergenia 'Ballawley'
Bergenia 'Bressingham Ruby'
Bergenia 'Distinction'
Bergenia 'Profusion'
Boltonia asteroides 'Pink Beauty'
Campanula lactiflora 'Loddon Anna'
Canna 'Cleopatra'
Canna 'Panache'
Canna 'Tropicana' ('Phaison')
Canna 'Pink Sunburst'
Canna 'Stuttgart'
Centaurea dealbata 'Steenbergii'
Centaurea hypoleuca
Centaurea hypoleuca 'John Coutts'
Chrysanthemum coccineum 'Eileen May Robinson'
Chrysanthemum coccineum 'Shirley Double'
Chrysanthemum 'Apricot Single'
Chrysanthemum 'Hillside Sheffield'
Chrysanthemum 'Ryan's Daisy'
Clematis integrifolia 'Rosea'
Clematis texensis
Clematis texensis 'Duchess of Albany'
Clematis 'Duchess of Edinburgh'
Clematis 'Pink Champagne'
Clematis 'Proteus'

Clematis 'Ville de Lyon'
Colchicum autumnale
Colchicum byzantinum
Colchicum speciosum
Colchicum 'Autumn Queen'
Colchicum 'Waterlily'
Coreopsis auriculata
Coreopsis rosea
Dahlia imperialis
Dahlia 'Good Interest'
Dahlia 'Gypsy Boy'
Dianthus barbatus
Dianthus barbatus 'Indian Carpet'
Dianthus deltoides
Dianthus gratianopolitanus
Dianthus gratianopolitanus 'Baby Blanket'
Dianthus gratianopolitanus 'Bath's Pink'
Dianthus gratianopolitanus 'Firewitch'
Dianthus gratianopolitanus 'Mountain Mist'
Dianthus gratianopolitanus 'Tiny Rubies'
Dicentra eximia
Dicentra formosa
Dicentra spectabilis
Dicentra 'Bacchanal'
Dicentra 'Boothman's Variety'
Dicentra 'Luxuriant'
Digitalis ×mertonensis
Digitalis purpurea
Echinacea purpurea 'Bright Star'
Epimedium grandiflorum
Epimedium grandiflorum subsp. *koreanum*
Epimedium grandiflorum 'Rose Queen'
Epimedium ×youngianum 'Roseum'
Gaillardia ×grandiflora
Gaillardia ×grandiflora 'Goblin'
Gaillardia ×grandiflora Lollipop series

Gaura lindheimeri 'Siskiyou Pink'
Geranium ×cantabrigiense
Geranium ×cantabrigiense 'Biokovo'
Geranium ×cantabrigiense 'Biokovo Karmina'
Geranium cinereum
Geranium cinereum 'Ballerina'
Geranium cinereum 'Lawerence Flatman'
Geranium cinereum 'Splendens'
Geranium endressii
Geranium endressii 'Wargrave Pink'
Geranium sanguineum 'Glenluce'
Geranium sanguineum 'Minutum'
Geranium sanguineum 'Striatum'
Helleborus orientalis Party Dress series
Hemerocallis 'Benchmark'
Hemerocallis 'China Bride'
Hemerocallis 'Pandora's Box'
Hemerocallis 'Tender Shepherd'
Heuchera sanguinea
Heuchera 'Canyon Pink'
Heuchera 'Fireglow'
Heuchera 'Huntsman'
Heuchera 'Oakington Jewel'
Heuchera 'Raspberry Regal'
Hibiscus mutabilis
Hibiscus mutabilis 'Flore Plena'
Hibiscus mutabilis 'Raspberry Rose'
Hibiscus 'Disco Belle'
Hibiscus 'Lord Baltimore'
Iris nelsonii
Iris 'Chensled'
Iris 'Glittering Amber'
Iris 'Pink Frost'

Lamium maculatum
Lamium maculatum 'Beacon Silver'
Lamium maculatum 'Chequers'
Lilium martagon
Lilium 'Acapulco'
Lilium 'Dandy'
Lilium 'Trance'
Lupinus polyphyllus 'Russell Hybrid Pink'
Lychnis chalcedonica 'Carnea'
Lychnis coronaria 'Abbotsford Rose'
Lychnis coronaria 'Angel Blush'
Lychnis flos-cuculi
Lycoris squamigera
Mertensia virginica 'Rosea'
Monarda 'Croftway Pink'
Monarda 'Petite Delight'
Oenothera berlandieri
Oenothera berlandieri 'Siskiyou'
Oenothera speciosa
Oenothera speciosa 'Ballerina Hot Pink'
Paeonia 'First Lady'
Paeonia 'Rose Garland'
Paeonia 'Souvenir de Maxime Cornu'
Papaver nudicaule 'Champagne Bubbles'
Papaver nudicaule 'Party Fun'
Papaver orientale 'Cedric Morris'
Papaver orientale 'Lighthouse'
Papaver orientale 'Picotee'
Penstemon barbatus
Penstemon barbatus 'Hyacinth'
Penstemon barbatus 'Skylight'
Penstemon smallii
Penstemon 'Hidcote Pink'
Penstemon 'Sour Grapes'
Penstemon 'Stapleford Gem'

Penstemon 'Thorn'
Phlomis italica
Phlox paniculata 'Bright Eyes'
Phlox paniculata 'Fairest One'
Phlox paniculata 'Franz Schubert'
Phlox paniculata 'Norah Leigh'
Phlox paniculata 'Robert Poore'
Phlox paniculata 'Starfire'
Phlox stolonifera 'Homefires'
Phlox stolonifera 'Variegata'
Phlox subulata 'Candy Stripe'
Phlox subulata 'Coral Eye'
Phlox subulata 'Maiden's Blush'
Physostegia virginiana
Physostegia virginiana 'Bouquet Rose' ('Pink Bouquet')
Physostegia virginiana 'Variegata'
Physostegia virginiana 'Vivid'
Platycodon grandiflorus 'Shell Pink'
Polemonium carneum
Polygonum affine
Polygonum affine 'Hartford'
Polygonum affine 'Superbum'
Polygonum bistorta
Polygonum bistorta subsp. *carneum*
Polygonum bistorta var. *regelianum*
Polygonum bistorta 'Superbum'
Primula denticulata 'Rosea'
Primula japonica
Primula japonica 'Splendens'
Primula pulverulenta 'Bartley's Strain'
Primula vialii
Primula vulgaris subsp. *sibthorpii*
Primula 'Rowallane Rose'
Pulmonaria rubra
Pulmonaria rubra 'Bowles' Red'

Pulmonaria rubra 'David Ward'
Pulmonaria saccharata 'Berries and Cream'
Pulmonaria saccharata 'Mrs. Kittle'
Ranunculus asiaticus
Rehmannia angulata
Rehmannia elata
Rodgersia pinnata 'Rubra'
Rodgersia pinnata 'Superba'
Salvia involucrata
Salvia involucrata 'Bethellii'
Saponaria ocymoides
Saponaria officinalis
Scabiosa columbaria 'Pink Mist'
Sedum spectabile 'Carmen'
Sedum spectabile 'Meteor'
Sedum spurium
Sedum spurium 'Fuldaglut'
Sedum spurium 'Green Mantle'
Sedum 'Atropurpureum'
Sedum 'Autumn Joy' ('Herbstfreude')
Sedum 'Mohrchen'
Sedum 'Ruby Glow'
Sedum 'Sunset Cloud'
Sedum 'Vera Jameson'
Silene caroliniana
Silene caroliniana 'Millstream Select'
Silene polypetala
Silene 'Longwood'
Thalictrum aquilegiifolium
Thalictrum aquilegiifolium 'Roseum'
Tradescantia virginiana 'Joy'
Tradescantia virginiana 'Pauline'
Tradescantia virginiana 'Purple Dome'
Trillium catesbaei
Trillium grandiflorum
Trillium grandiflorum 'Flore Pleno'

Trillium grandiflorum 'Roseum'
Verbena canadensis
Verbena peruviana
Verbena 'Carrousel'
Verbena 'Silver Anne'
Verbena 'Tapien Pink'
Veronica longifolia 'Rosalinde'
Veronica spicata 'Barcarolle'
Veronica spicata 'Heidekind'
Viola cornuta 'Rosea'
Zauschneria californica

ORANGE/RED
Achillea millefolium 'Colorado'
Achillea millefolium 'Paprika'
Achillea 'Terra Cotta'
Achillea 'The Beacon' ('Fanal')
Anemone coronaria
Anemone coronaria 'Mona Lisa Red'
Anemone coronaria St. Brigid series
Anemone hupehensis 'Prinz Heinrich' ('Prince Henry')
Aquilegia canadensis
Aquilegia ×*hybrida* 'Cardinal'
Astilbe ×*arendsii* 'Bonn'
Astilbe ×*arendsii* 'Montgomery'
Astrantia major 'Lars'
Astrantia major 'Ruby Wedding'
Bergenia 'Morning Red'
Canna 'Bengal Tiger' ('Pretoria')
Canna 'King Humpert'
Canna 'Wyoming'
Chrysanthemum coccineum
Chrysanthemum coccineum 'Brenda'
Chrysanthemum coccineum 'James Kelway'
Crocosmia 'Lucifer'
Crocosmia 'Spitfire'

Dahlia 'Pink Michigan'
Dahlia 'Royal Dahlietta Apricot'
Dahlia 'Scarlet Beauty'
Dahlia 'Single Salmon'
Delphinium nudicaule
Dianthus caryophyllus 'Red Sims'
Dianthus deltoides
Dianthus deltoides 'Brilliant'
Dianthus deltoides 'Red Maiden'
Dianthus deltoides 'Zing Rose'
Epimedium ×*rubrum*
Euphorbia griffithii
Euphorbia griffithii 'Dixter'
Euphorbia griffithii 'Fireglow'
Geum chiloense
Geum chiloense 'Fire Opal'
Geum chiloense 'Mrs. Bradshaw'
Geum rivale
Geum rivale 'Leonard's Variety'
Geum triflorum
Geum triflorum var. *campanulatum*
Helenium autumnale 'Rubrum'
Helenium 'Brilliant'
Helenium 'Coppelia'
Helenium 'Gartensonne'
Hemerocallis 'Red Joy'
Hemerocallis 'Red Rain'
Hemerocallis 'Scarlet Tanager'
Hepatica nobilis 'Rubra'
Hibiscus coccineus
Hibiscus moscheutos
Hibiscus 'Anne Arundel'
Iris fulva
Iris 'Wild Ginger'
Kniphofia 'Atlantia'
Lilium henryi
Lilium 'Amourette'
Lilium 'Campfire'
Lilium 'Enchantment'
Lobelia cardinalis

Orange/Red, continued

Lobelia ×speciosa
Lobelia ×speciosa 'Bee's Flame'
Lobelia ×speciosa 'Compliment Scarlet'
Lobelia tupa
Lupinus 'Gina Lombaert'
Lychnis ×arkwrightii
Lychnis chalcedonica
Lychnis chalcedonica 'Flore Plena'
Lycoris radiata
Monarda 'Cambridge Scarlet'
Paeonia 'Balliol'
Paeonia 'Banquet'
Paeonia 'Red Imp'
Paeonia 'Red Moon'
Paeonia 'Zu Zu'
Papaver nudicaule
Papaver nudicaule 'Party Fun'
Papaver orientale
Papaver orientale 'Avebury Crimson'
Papaver orientale 'Fireball'
Papaver orientale 'Goliath'
Papaver orientale 'Suleika'
Papaver rhoeas
Papaver somniferum
Papaver somniferum var. *paeoniflorum*
Penstemon pinifolius
Penstemon 'Ruby'
Penstemon 'Schönholzeri' ('Firebird')
Phlox paniculata 'Red Eyes'
Phlox subulata 'Scarlet Flame'
Primula bulleyana
Primula pulverulenta

Silene regia
Silene virginica
Trillium vaseyi
Verbena 'Sissinghurst'
Verbena 'Taylortown Red'

PURPLE

Arisaema consanguineum
Arisaema fargesii
Arisaema japonicum
Arisaema ringens
Arisaema sazensoo
Arisaema sikokianum
Arisaema sikokianum × A. takedae
Arisaema tortuosum
Arisaema triphyllum
Asarum arifolium
Asarum canadense
Asarum splendens
Asarum yakushimanum
Astilbe chinensis
Astilbe chinensis 'Finale'
Astilbe chinensis 'Pumila'
Astilbe chinensis var. *taquetii*
Astilbe chinensis var. *taquetii* 'Purple Lance'
Astilbe chinensis 'Visions'
Astilbe ×arendsii 'Rheinland'
Echinacea pallida
Echinacea purpurea
Echinacea purpurea 'Magnus'
Echinacea purpurea 'Robert Bloom'
Eupatorium maculatum
Eupatorium maculatum 'Gateway'
Eupatorium purpureum
Euphorbia dulcis 'Chameleon'

Geranium psilostemon
Geranium psilostemon 'Bressingham Flair'
Geranium sanguineum
Geranium sanguineum 'Alan Bloom'
Geranium sanguineum 'Cedric Morris'
Geranium 'Ann Folkard'
Helleborus foetidus
Helleborus foetidus 'Wesker Flisk'
Helleborus orientalis
Helleborus orientalis 'Dusk'
Helleborus orientalis Party Dress series
Hemerocallis 'Black Ruffles'
Heuchera villosa 'Autumn Bride'
Iris reticulata 'J. S. Dijt'
Iris 'Cozy Calico'
Iris 'Ecstatic Night'
Iris 'Pansy Purple'
Iris 'Ruffled Velvet'
Liatris borealis
Liatris graminifolia
Liatris spicata
Liatris spicata 'Kobold'
Lobelia ×gerardii
Lobelia ×gerardii 'Vedrariensis'
Lobelia ×speciosa 'Compliment Purple'
Lychnis coronaria
Penstemon 'Port Wine'
Pinellia pedatisecta
Pinellia tripartita
Primula vulgaris 'Double Burgundy'

Pulsatilla halleri
Pulsatilla pratensis
Pulsatilla vulgaris
Tricyrtis formosana
Tricyrtis hirta
Tricyrtis hirta 'Miyazaki'
Tricyrtis 'Kohaku'
Tricyrtis 'Lemon Glow'
Trillium cuneatum
Trillium cuneatum 'Eco Silver'
Trillium decipiens
Trillium erectum
Trillium sessile
Trillium stamineum

GREEN OR CHARTREUSE

Geum triflorum var. *campanulatum*
Hakonechloa macra
Hakonechloa macra 'Alboaurea'
Helleborus foetidus
Helleborus foetidus 'Wesker Flisk'
Helleborus orientalis Party Dress series
Heuchera americana
Heuchera 'Amethyst Mist'
Heuchera 'Bressingham Bronze'
Heuchera 'Chocolate Veil'
Heuchera 'Dale's Selection'
Heuchera 'Palace Purple'
Heuchera 'Pewter Veil'
Heuchera 'Plum Pudding'
Heuchera 'Smokey Rose'
Heuchera 'Whirlwind'
Veratrum viride

Fragrant Flowers/Foliage

The following perennials have fragrant flowers or leaves. Fragrance is an intensely personal thing. Some people believe a flower is marvelously scented, while other noses may detect a fetid odor for the same bloom.

Allium giganteum
Anemone sylvestris
Campanula lactiflora
Clematis heracleifolia
Dianthus caryophyllus
Dianthus gratianopolitanus
Hemerocallis fulva
Hosta sieboldiana

Ipheion uniflorum
Iris louisiana
Iris reticulata
Lilium auratum
Lilium regale
Lupinus polyphyllus
Narcissus hybrids

Phlox divaricata
Phlox paniculata
Primula bulleyana
Primula denticulata
Primula japonica
Primula pulverulenta
Primula vulgaris

Santolina chamaecyparissus
Santolina virens
Thymus praecox
Thymus pseudolanuginosus
Thymus serpyllum
Thymus vulgaris
Trillium luteum

Ground Covers

All plants cover the ground, but some plants do so more aggressively. The following plants, which generally spread by tubers, stolons, or runners, can be used to cover large areas reasonably quickly. As in all discussions, where you live—where the ground is!—will influence what plants you should select to cover the ground.

Achillea millefolium
Adiantum pedatum
Ajuga genevensis
Ajuga reptans
Asarum canadense
Astilbe chinensis
Astrantia major
Bergenia cordifolia
Bergenia purpurascens
Brunnera macrophylla
Campanula portenschlagiana
Campanula poscharskyana

Ceratostigma plumbaginoides
Dianthus deltoides
Epimedium grandiflorum
Epimedium ×perralchium
Epimedium ×rubrum
Epimedium ×versicolor
Geum rivale
Lamium galeobdolon
Lamium maculatum
Lysimachia japonica
Lysimachia nummularia

Macleaya cordata
Patrinia triloba
Patrinia villosa
Phlox divaricata
Phlox stolonifera
Phlox subulata
Polemonium reptans
Pulmonaria angustifolia
Pulmonaria longifolia
Pulmonaria saccharata
Ranunculus bulbosus

Ranunculus ficaria
Sedum acre
Stachys byzantina
Thymus praecox
Thymus pseudolanuginosus
Tiarella cordifolia
Viola labradorica
Waldsteinia fragarioides
Waldsteinia lobata
Waldsteinia parviflora
Waldsteinia ternata

Plant Height

Plant height varies tremendously with the climate in which you garden. Heat, cold, sun, shade, rainfall, and soils affect the mature height of any plant. While the absolute heights may differ from region to region, the relative heights in the following lists should be the same in most areas of the country.

One Foot or Less
Adiantum pedatum
Ajuga genevensis
Ajuga reptans

Allium karataviense
Anemone blanda
Anemone coronaria
Anemone sylvestris

Aquilegia flabellata
Arisaema sikokianum
Artemisia schmidtiana 'Nana'
  ('Silver Mound')

Aruncus aethusifolius
Aruncus 'Southern White'
Asarum arifolium
Asarum canadense

One foot or less, continued
Asarum splendens
Asarum yakushimanum
Athyrium nipponicum
Baptisia minor
Bergenia ciliata
Bergenia cordifolia
Bergenia purpurascens
Brunnera macrophylla
Campanula carpatica
Campanula portenschlagiana
Campanula poscharskyana
Cerastium buisseri
Cerastium tomentosum
Ceratostigma plumbaginoides
Ceratostigma willmottianum
Colchicum autumnale
Colchicum byzantinum
Colchicum speciosum
Coreopsis auriculata
Coreopsis auriculata 'Nana'
Coreopsis rosea
Corydalis cheilanthifolia
Corydalis flexuosa
Corydalis lutea
Crocus chrysanthus
Crocus speciosus
Crocus vernus
Dianthus deltoides
Dianthus gratianopolitanus
Disporum sessile
Epimedium grandiflorum
Epimedium ×*perralchium*
Epimedium ×*rubrum*
Epimedium ×*youngianum*
Euphorbia myrsinites
Geranium ×*cantabrigiense*
Geranium cinereum
Geranium sanguineum
Geum rivale
Hakonechloa macra
Hepatica acutiloba
Hepatica americana
Hepatica nobilis
Hepatica transsilvanica
Hosta venusta
Hosta hybrids

Ipheion uniflorum
Iris danfordiae
Iris reticulata
Lamium galeobdolon
Lamium maculatum
Linum flavum
Linum perenne
Lychnis ×*arkwrightii*
Lysimachia japonica
Lysimachia nummularia
Mertensia asiatica
Mertensia virginica
Narcissus bulbocodium
Narcissus cyclamineus
Oenothera berlandieri
Oenothera drummondii
Oenothera missouriensis
Oenothera speciosa
Patrinia triloba
Patrinia villosa
Penstemon smallii
Phlox divaricata
Phlox stolonifera
Phlox subulata
Pinellia pedatisecta
Pinellia tripartita
Polemonium reptans
Polygonatum humile
Polygonum affine
Primula denticulata
Primula veris
Primula vialii
Primula vulgaris
Pulmonaria angustifolia
Pulmonaria longifolia
Pulmonaria rubra
Pulmonaria saccharata
Pulsatilla halleri
Pulsatilla pratensis
Pulsatilla vulgaris
Ranunculus bulbosus
Ranunculus ficaria
Ranunculus repens
Saponaria ocymoides
Sedum acre
Sedum kamtschaticum
Sedum reflexum

Sedum spathulifolium
Sedum spurium
Silene caroliniana
Silene polypetala
Silene regia
Silene uniflora
Silene virginica
Sisyrinchium angustifolium
Sisyrinchium idahoense
Stachys byzantina
Stylophorum diphyllum
Stylophorum lasiocarpum
Thalictrum ichangense
Thalictrum minus 'Adiantifo-
   lium'
Thymus praecox
Thymus pseudolanuginosus
Thymus serpyllum
Thymus vulgaris
Tiarella cordifolia
Trillium catesbaei
Trillium cernuum
Trillium cuneatum
Trillium decipiens
Trillium discolor
Trillium erectum
Trillium grandiflorum
Trillium luteum
Trillium sessile
Trillium stamineum
Trillium vaseyi
Uvularia grandiflora
Uvularia perfoliata
Uvularia sessilifolia
Verbena canadensis
Verbena peruviana
Verbena tenuisecta
Veronica austriaca
Veronica incana
Veronica prostrata
Viola cornuta
Viola cucullata
Viola labradorica
Viola pedata
Waldsteinia fragarioides
Waldsteinia lobata
Waldsteinia parviflora

Waldsteinia ternata

One to Three Feet
Acanthus mollis
Acanthus spinosus
Achillea filipendulina
Achillea millefolium
Achillea ptarmica
Achillea sibirica
Allium christophii
Anemone coronaria
Anemone tomentosa
Aquilegia alpina
Aquilegia caerulea
Aquilegia canadensis
Aquilegia chrysantha
Aquilegia vulgaris
Arisaema candidissimum
Arisaema ringens
Arisaema sazensoo
Arisaema sikokianum
Arisaema sikokianum × *A. ta-
   kedae*
Arisaema triphyllum
Aster novae-angliae
Aster novi-belgii
Astrantia major
Astrantia maxima
Athyrium filix-femina
Baptisia sphaerocarpa
Baptisia tinctoria
Baptisia viridis
Centaurea cyanus
Centaurea dealbata
Centaurea hypoleuca
Centaurea montana
Chrysanthemum coccineum
Chrysanthemum ×*koreanum*
Chrysanthemum pacificum
Chrysanthemum ×*superbum*
Coreopsis grandiflora
Coreopsis lanceolata
Coreopsis verticillata
Crocosmia hybrids
Dahlia hybrids
Delphinium nudicaule
Dianthus barbatus

Dicentra eximia
Dicentra formosa
Dicentra spectabilis
Digitalis grandiflora
Digitalis lutea
Digitalis ×mertonensis
Digitalis purpurea
Disporum sessile
Disporum sessile var. flavum
Dryopteris erythrosora
Dryopteris filix-mas
Dryopteris marginalis
Echinacea pallida
Echinacea paradoxa
Echinacea purpurea
Eryngium giganteum
Eupatorium coelestinum
Euphorbia characias
Euphorbia dulcis
Gaillardia ×grandiflora
Gaura lindheimeri
Geranium endressii
Geum chiloense
Geum triflorum
Helleborus foetidus
Helleborus niger
Helleborus ×nigristern
Helleborus orientalis
Hemerocallis dumortieri
Hemerocallis fulva
Hemerocallis minor
Hemerocallis hybrids
Heuchera sanguinea
Heuchera villosa
Hibiscus moscheutos
Hosta montana
Hosta sieboldiana
Hosta hybrids
Hypericum androsaemum
Hypericum calycinum
Hypericum 'Hidcote'
Iris ensata
Iris fulva
Iris hexagona
Iris louisiana
Iris nelsonii
Iris xiphium

Kalimeris pinnatifida
Liatris borealis
Liatris spicata
Lilium hybrids
Linum usitatissimum
Lobelia siphilitica
Lobelia tupa
Lunaria annua
Lunaria rediviva
Lupinus polyphyllus
Lychnis chalcedonica
Lychnis coronaria
Lychnis flos-cuculi
Lycoris albiflora
Lycoris aurea
Lycoris radiata
Lycoris squamigera
Lysimachia ciliata
Lysimachia ephemerum
Mertensia sibirica
Monarda didyma
Nepeta ×faassenii
Nepeta govaniana
Nepeta nervosa
Oenothera fruticosa
Osmunda cinnamomea
Osmunda claytoniana
Papaver nudicaule
Papaver orientale
Papaver rhoeas
Papaver somniferum
Penstemon barbatus
Penstemon cardwellii
Penstemon confertus
Penstemon digitalis
Penstemon pinifolius
Phlox paniculata
Platycodon grandiflorus
Polemonium carneum
Polygonatum odoratum
Primula bulleyana
Primula florindae
Primula heladoxa
Primula japonica
Primula pulverulenta
Ranunculus aconitifolius
Ranunculus asiaticus

Rehmannia angulata
Rehmannia elata
Rudbeckia fulgida
Salvia koyamae
Salvia officinalis
Salvia ×sylvestris
Santolina chamaecyparissus
Santolina pinnata
Santolina virens
Saponaria officinalis
Scabiosa caucasica
Scabiosa columbaria
Sedum aizoon
Silene fimbriata
Sisyrinchium atlanticum
Sisyrinchium striatum
Smilacina racemosa
Stachys macrantha
Stokesia laevis
Symphytum asperum
Symphytum grandiflorum
Symphytum officinale
Tanacetum vulgare
Tradescantia virginiana
Tricyrtis hirta
Verbena rigida
Veronica spicata
Zauschneria californica

Three Feet or More
Aconitum carmichaelii
Aconitum lamarckii
Aconitum napellus
Aconitum reclinatum
Aconitum septentrionale
  'Ivorine'
Allium giganteum
Allium 'Beauregard'
Allium 'Globemaster'
Arisaema consanguineum
Arisaema fargesii
Arisaema japonicum
Arisaema tortuosum
Artemisia ludoviciana
Aruncus dioicus
Aster novae-angliae
Aster novi-belgii

Baptisia alba
Baptisia australis
Boltonia asteroides
Campanula lactiflora
Campanula latiloba
Centaurea macrocephala
Cephalaria gigantea
Chrysanthemum ×superbum
Clematis cirrhosa
Clematis ×durandii
Clematis heracleifolia
Clematis integrifolia
Clematis ×jackmanii
Clematis terniflora
Clematis texensis
Clematis hybrids
Crocosmia hybrids
Dahlia imperialis
Dahlia hybrids
Delphinium elatum
Dianthus caryophyllus
Dicentra scandens
Digitalis lutea
Dryopteris erythrosora
Echinops ritro
Eremurus aitchisonii
Eremurus himalaicus
Eremurus stenophyllus
Eryngium agavifolium
Eryngium alpinum
Eryngium yuccafolium
Eupatorium maculatum
Eupatorium purpureum
Eupatorium rugosum
Euphorbia griffithii
Euphorbia lathyris
Geranium psilostemon
Helenium autumnale
Helianthus ×multiflorus
Heliopsis helianthoides
Hemerocallis hybrids
Hibiscus coccineus
Hibiscus mutabilis
Hosta hybrids
Iris ensata
Iris louisiana
Kirengeshoma palmata

Three feet or more, cont.

Ligularia dentata
Ligularia macrophylla
Ligularia sibirica
Ligularia stenocephala
Lilium auratum
Lilium canadense
Lilium henryi
Lilium martagon
Lilium regale
Lilium hybrids
Lobelia cardinalis
Lobelia ×*gerardii*
Lobelia ×*speciosa*
Lunaria rediviva
Lupinus arboreus

Lupinus polyphyllus
Lysimachia clethroides
Macleaya cordata
Miscanthus sinensis
Miscanthus hybrids
Nepeta ×*faassenii* 'Six Hills Giant'
Nepeta sibirica
Osmunda cinnamomea
Osmunda regalis
Papaver somniferum
Patrinia scabiosifolia
Perovskia atriplicifolia
Phlomis fruticosa
Phlomis italica
Phlomis russeliana

Physostegia virginiana
Platycodon grandiflorus
Polemonium caeruleum
Rodgersia aesculifolia
Rodgersia pinnata
Rodgersia podophylla
Rodgersia sambucifolia
Rudbeckia laciniata
Rudbeckia nitida
Rudbeckia triloba
Salvia guaranitica
Salvia involucrata
Salvia 'Indigo Spires'
Santolina chamaecyparissus
Scabiosa ochroleuca
Symphytum asperum

Symphytum caucasicum
Symphytum ×*uplandicum*
Thalictrum aquilegiifolium
Thalictrum flavum
Thermopsis caroliniana
Thermopsis fabacea
Thermopsis montana
Tricyrtis formosana
Veratrum album
Veratrum viride
Verbena bonariensis
Veronica longifolia
Veronicastrum sibiricum
Veronicastrum virginicum
Zantedeschia hybrids

Interesting Foliage/Fruit

The following plants are often planted for the ornamental value of the foliage and fruit, rather than the flowers.

FOLIAGE

Acanthus mollis 'Holland's Lemon'
Acanthus spinosus 'Spinosissimus'
Achillea 'Coronation Gold'
Adiantum capillus-veneris
Adiantum pedatum
Ajuga reptans 'Atropurpurea'
Ajuga reptans 'Bronze Beauty'
Ajuga reptans 'Burgundy Glow'
Ajuga reptans 'Catlin's Giant'
Ajuga reptans 'Silver Beauty'
Allium karataviense
Artemisia ludoviciana 'Latiloba'
Artemisia ludoviciana 'Silver King'
Artemisia ludoviciana 'Valerie Fennis'
Artemisia schmidtiana 'Nana' ('Silver Mound')

Artemisia 'Huntington Gardens'
Artemisia 'Powis Castle'
Aruncus dioicus 'Kneiffii'
Astrantia major 'Sunningdale Variegated'
Athyrium filix-femina 'Frizelliae'
Athyrium filix-femina 'Linearis'
Athyrium filix-femina 'Minutissimum'
Athyrium nipponicum 'Pictum'
Athyrium nipponicum 'Ursala's Red'
Bergenia ciliata
Bergenia purpurascens
Brunnera macrophylla 'Langtrees'
Brunnera macrophylla 'Variegata'
Canna 'Bengal Tiger' ('Pretoria')

Canna 'Cleopatra'
Canna 'King Humpert'
Canna 'Panache'
Canna 'Tropicana' ('Phaison')
Canna 'Pink Sunburst'
Canna 'Stuttgart'
Disporum sessile 'Variegatum'
Dryopteris erythrosora
Dryopteris filix-mas 'Barnesii'
Dryopteris filix-mas 'Polydactyla'
Dryopteris marginalis
Eupatorium rugosum 'Chocolate'
Euphorbia characias 'Ember Queen'
Euphorbia dulcis 'Chameleon'
Gaura lindheimeri 'Corrie's Gold'
Hakonechloa macra
Hakonechloa macra 'Alboaurea'
Hakonechloa macra 'Aureola'

Heuchera villosa 'Purpurea'
Heuchera 'Amethyst Mist'
Heuchera 'Bressingham Bronze'
Heuchera 'Chocolate Veil'
Heuchera 'Dale's Selection'
Heuchera 'Palace Purple'
Heuchera 'Smokey Rose'
Heuchera 'Whirlwind'
Hosta montana
Hosta montana 'Aureomarginata'
Hosta sieboldiana
Hosta sieboldiana 'Frances Williams'
Hosta venusta
Hosta 'Antioch'
Hosta 'Blue Cadet'
Hosta 'Bright Lights'
Hosta 'Francee'
Hosta 'Gold Edger'
Hosta 'Invincible'
Hosta 'Red Neck Heaven'

Hosta 'Royal Standard'
Hosta 'Spritzer'
Hosta 'Sum and Substance'
Hosta 'Sun Power'
Kalimeris yomena 'Variegata'
Lamium maculatum 'Beacon Silver'
Lamium maculatum 'Chequers'
Lamium maculatum 'White Nancy'
Lysimachia ciliata 'Purpurea'
Lysimachia japonica 'Minutissima'
Lysimachia nummularia 'Aurea'
Macleaya cordata
Mertensia asiatica
Miscanthus sinensis 'Adagio'
Miscanthus sinensis 'Arabesque'
Miscanthus sinensis 'Cabaret'
Miscanthus sinensis 'Malepartus'
Miscanthus sinensis 'Morning Light'
Miscanthus sinensis 'Silberfeder' ('Silver Feather')
Miscanthus sinensis 'Strictus'
Miscanthus sinensis 'Variegatus'
Miscanthus sinensis 'Yaku Jima'
Osmunda claytoniana
Penstemon digitalis 'Husker Red'
Phlox paniculata 'Norah Leigh'
Phlox stolonifera 'Variegata'

Physostegia virginiana 'Variegata'
Polemonium caeruleum 'Brise d'Anjou'
Polygonatum odoratum 'Variegatum'
Pulmonaria longifolia
Pulmonaria longifolia 'Bertram Anderson'
Pulmonaria longifolia subsp. *cevennensis* ('Little Blue')
Pulmonaria rubra 'David Ward'
Pulmonaria saccharata
Pulmonaria saccharata 'Benediction'
Pulmonaria saccharata 'Berries and Cream'
Pulmonaria saccharata 'Excalibur'
Pulmonaria saccharata 'Highdown'
Pulmonaria saccharata 'Mrs. Kittle'
Pulmonaria saccharata 'Mrs. Moon'
Pulmonaria saccharata 'Sissinghurst White'
Pulmonaria saccharata 'Spilled Milk'
Pulmonaria 'Roy Davidson'
Ranunculus ficaria 'Brazen Hussy'
Ranunculus repens 'Susan's Song' ('Buttered Popcorn')
Salvia officinalis 'Icterina'
Salvia officinalis 'Purpurescens'

Salvia officinalis 'Tricolor'
Santolina chamaecyparissus
Santolina virens
Sedum reflexum
Sedum reflexum 'Blue Spruce'
Sedum spathulifolium 'Cape Blanco'
Sedum spurium 'Fuldaglut'
Sedum 'Atropurpureum'
Sedum 'Mohrchen'
Sedum 'Vera Jameson'
Sisyrinchium striatum 'Aunt May'
Stachys byzantina
Stachys byzantina 'Countess Helene von Stein'
Stachys byzantina 'Primrose Heron'
Stachys byzantina 'Sheila Macqueen'
Symphytum 'Goldsmith'
Symphytum officinale 'Variegatum'
Symphytum ×*uplandicum* 'Variegatum'
Thalictrum flavum 'Glaucum'
Thymus vulgaris 'Silver Posie'
Tiarella cordifolia 'Oakleaf'
Tiarella 'Brandywine'
Tiarella 'Ink Blot'
Tiarella 'Snowflake'
Tiarella 'Tiger Stripe'
Tricyrtis 'Lemon Glow'
Trillium cuneatum 'Eco Silver'
Trillium sessile
Uvularia grandiflora

Uvularia grandiflora 'Sunbonnet'
Veronica austriaca subsp. *teucrium* 'Aurea'
Yucca filamentosa 'Bright Edge'
Yucca filamentosa 'Gold Band'
Yucca filamentosa 'Golden Sword'

FRUIT

Baptisia alba
Baptisia alba 'Pendula'
Baptisia australis
Baptisia minor
Baptisia sphaerocarpa
Baptisia tinctoria
Baptisia viridis
Clematis ×*durandii*
Clematis integrifolia
Clematis ×*jackmanii*
Clematis terniflora
Clematis texensis
Clematis hybrids
Euphorbia lathyris
Geum triflorum
Geum triflorum var. *campanulatum*
Hypericum androsaemum
Hypericum androsaemum 'Albury Purple'
Kirengeshoma palmata
Lunaria annua
Lunaria annua 'Variegata'
Lunaria rediviva
Osmunda cinnamomea

Native Plants

The following plants are native to the United States.

Aconitum reclinatum
Aquilegia caerulea
Aquilegia canadensis
Aquilegia chrysantha
Arisaema triphyllum
Asarum arifolium
Asarum canadense
Aster carolinianus
Aster divaricatus
Aster novae-angliae
Aster novi-belgii
Astilbe biternata
Baptisia alba
Baptisia australis
Baptisia minor
Baptisia sphaerocarpa
Baptisia tinctoria
Baptisia viridis
Boltonia asteroides
Clematis texensis
Coreopsis auriculata
Coreopsis grandiflora
Coreopsis lanceolata
Coreopsis rosea
Coreopsis verticillata
Dicentra eximia
Dicentra formosa
Dryopteris marginalis
Echinacea pallida
Echinacea paradoxa

Echinacea purpurea
Eryngium yuccafolium
Eupatorium coelestinum
Eupatorium maculatum
Eupatorium purpureum
Eupatorium rugosum
Gaillardia ×grandiflora
Gaura lindheimeri
Geum triflorum
Geum triflorum var. campan-
 ulatum
Helenium autumnale
Helianthus angustifolius
Helianthus giganteus
Heliopsis helianthoides
Hepatica acutiloba
Hepatica americana
Heuchera americana
Heuchera villosa
Hibiscus coccineus
Hibiscus moscheutos
Iris fulva
Iris hexagona
Iris louisiana
Iris nelsonii
Liatris borealis
Liatris graminifolia
Liatris spicata
Lilium canadense
Lobelia cardinalis

Lobelia siphilitica
Mertensia virginica
Monarda didyma
Oenothera berlandieri
Oenothera drummondii
Oenothera fruticosa
Oenothera missouriensis
Oenothera speciosa
Osmunda cinnamomea
Osmunda claytoniana
Osmunda regalis
Penstemon barbatus
Penstemon cardwellii
Penstemon confertus
Penstemon digitalis
Penstemon pinifolius
Penstemon smallii
Phlox divaricata
Phlox paniculata
Phlox stolonifera
Phlox subulata
Physostegia virginiana
Polemonium reptans
Rudbeckia fulgida
Rudbeckia laciniata
Rudbeckia nitida
Rudbeckia triloba
Silene caroliniana
Silene polypetala

Silene regia
Silene virginica
Sisyrinchium idahoense
Smilacina racemosa
Tiarella cordifolia
Tradescantia virginiana
Trillium catesbaei
Trillium cernuum
Trillium cuneatum
Trillium decipiens
Trillium discolor
Trillium erectum
Trillium grandiflorum
Trillium luteum
Trillium sessile
Trillium stamineum
Trillium vaseyi
Uvularia grandiflora
Uvularia perfoliata
Uvularia sessilifolia
Veratrum viride
Verbena canadensis
Viola labradorica
Viola pedata
Waldsteinia fragarioides
Waldsteinia lobata
Waldsteinia parviflora
Yucca filamentosa
Zauschneria californica

Sun/Shade Tolerance

Perennials do not "like" sun or shade but tolerate conditions of sun or shade in varying degrees. Most species that tolerate heavy shade also tolerate dappled or partial shade. Plants that tolerate full sun seldom do well in heavy shade and vice versa.

A quick and dirty guide to determining the amount of sun or shade in a garden location: On a sunny day, with your back to the sun, hold a piece of white paper in your right hand, place your left hand about six inches in front of the paper. If a sharp shadow falls on the paper, consider the area in full sun; if a fuzzy shadow occurs, consider the area in partial shade; and if no shadow can be detected, then you are in heavy shade. Obviously, the amount of shade at a given location in the garden changes with the track of the sun. An area of full sun is generally considered five hours or more of direct sun; one in heavy shade is less than one hour; and partial shade/sun is somewhere in between.

Heavy Shade

Adiantum capillus-veneris
Adiantum pedatum
Ajuga reptans
Arisaema candidissimum
Arisaema consanguineum
Arisaema fargesii
Arisaema japonicum
Arisaema ringens
Arisaema sazensoo
Arisaema sikokianum
Arisaema sikokianum × *A. ta-kedae*
Arisaema tortuosum
Arisaema triphyllum
Asarum arifolium
Asarum canadense
Asarum splendens
Asarum yakushimanum
Athyrium filix-femina
Brunnera macrophylla
Disporum sessile
Dryopteris erythrosora
Dryopteris filix-mas
Dryopteris marginalis
Epimedium grandiflorum
Epimedium ×*perralchium*
Epimedium ×*rubrum*
Epimedium ×*versicolor*
Epimedium ×*youngianum*
Hepatica acutiloba
Hepatica americana
Hepatica nobilis
Hepatica transsilvanica
Hosta montana
Hosta sieboldiana
Hosta venusta
Hosta hybrids
Osmunda cinnamomea
Osmunda claytoniana
Osmunda regalis
Pinellia pedatisecta
Pinellia tripartita
Viola pedata

Partial Shade/Sun

Acanthus mollis
Achillea ageratum
Aconitum napellus
Adiantum capillus-veneris
Adiantum pedatum
Ajuga genevensis
Ajuga reptans
Allium 'Globemaster'
Anemone blanda
Anemone sylvestris
Anemone tomentosa
Aquilegia alpina
Aquilegia caerulea
Aquilegia canadensis
Aquilegia chrysantha
Aquilegia flabellata
Aquilegia vulgaris
Arisaema candidissimum
Arisaema consanguineum
Arisaema fargesii
Arisaema japonicum
Arisaema ringens
Arisaema sazensoo
Arisaema sikokianum
Arisaema sikokianum × *A. ta-kedae*
Arisaema tortuosum
Arisaema triphyllum
Aruncus aethusifolius
Aruncus 'Southern White'
Aster divaricatus
Astilbe ×*arendsii*
Astilbe biternata
Astilbe chinensis
Astilbe chinensis var. *taquetii*
Astilbe simplicifolia
Astrantia major
Astrantia maxima
Athyrium filix-femina
Athyrium nipponicum
Baptisia alba
Bergenia ciliata
Bergenia cordifolia
Bergenia purpurascens
Brunnera macrophylla
Campanula portenschla-giana
Campanula poscharskyana
Canna 'Stuttgart'
Cerastium buisseri
Cerastium tomentosum
Clematis cirrhosa
Clematis heracleifolia
Clematis integrifolia
Colchicum autumnale
Colchicum byzantinum
Colchicum speciosum
Corydalis cheilanthifolia
Corydalis flexuosa
Corydalis lutea
Dicentra eximia
Dicentra scandens
Dicentra spectabilis
Digitalis grandiflora
Digitalis lutea
Digitalis ×*mertonensis*
Digitalis purpurea
Disporum sessile
Disporum sessile var. *flavum*
Dryopteris filix-mas
Dryopteris marginalis
Epimedium grandiflorum
Epimedium ×*perralchium*
Epimedium ×*rubrum*
Epimedium ×*versicolor*
Epimedium ×*youngianum*
Eupatorium coelestinum
Euphorbia dulcis
Euphorbia lathyris
Euphorbia myrsinites
Geranium cinereum
Geranium endressii
Helleborus foetidus
Helleborus niger
Helleborus ×*nigristern*
Helleborus orientalis
Hepatica acutiloba
Hepatica americana
Hepatica nobilis
Hepatica transsilvanica

Partial Shade/Sun, cont.

Heuchera sanguinea
Heuchera villosa
Hosta montana
Hosta sieboldiana
Hosta venusta
Hosta hybrids
Iris tectorum
Kalimeris yomena
Kirengeshoma palmata
Lamium galeobdolon
Lamium maculatum
Ligularia dentata
Ligularia macrophylla
Ligularia sibirica
Ligularia stenocephala
Lobelia cardinalis
Lobelia siphilitica
Lobelia ×speciosa
Lobelia tupa
Lunaria annua
Lunaria rediviva
Lysimachia ciliata
Lysimachia japonica
Lysimachia nummularia
Mertensia asiatica
Mertensia sibirica
Mertensia virginica
Nepeta govaniana
Osmunda cinnamomea
Osmunda claytoniana
Osmunda regalis
Penstemon digitalis
Penstemon smallii
Phlox divaricata
Phlox stolonifera
Pinellia pedatisecta
Pinellia tripartita
Polemonium reptans
Polygonatum humile
Polygonatum odoratum
Polygonum affine
Polygonum bistorta
Primula bulleyana
Primula denticulata
Primula florindae

Primula heladoxa
Primula japonica
Primula pulverulenta
Primula veris
Primula vialii
Primula vulgaris
Pulmonaria angustifolia
Pulmonaria longifolia
Pulmonaria rubra
Pulmonaria saccharata
Ranunculus ficaria
Ranunculus repens
Rehmannia angulata
Rehmannia elata
Rodgersia aesculifolia
Rodgersia pinnata
Rodgersia podophylla
Rodgersia sambucifolia
Salvia koyamae
Sedum ternatum
Silene fimbriata
Silene polypetala
Silene regia
Silene virginica
Smilacina racemosa
Stachys byzantina
Stylophorum diphyllum
Stylophorum lasiocarpum
Symphytum asperum
Symphytum caucasicum
Symphytum grandiflorum
Symphytum officinale
Symphytum ×uplandicum
Thalictrum aquilegiifolium
Thalictrum ichangense
Thalictrum minus 'Adianti-
    folium'
Tiarella cordifolia
Tricyrtis formosana
Tricyrtis hirta
Trillium catesbaei
Trillium cernuum
Trillium cuneatum
Trillium decipiens
Trillium discolor
Trillium erectum

Trillium grandiflorum
Trillium luteum
Trillium sessile
Trillium stamineum
Trillium vaseyi
Uvularia grandiflora
Uvularia perfoliata
Uvularia sessilifolia
Veratrum album
Veratrum viride
Viola labradorica
Viola pedata
Waldsteinia fragarioides
Waldsteinia lobata
Waldsteinia parviflora
Waldsteinia ternata

Full Sun

Acanthus mollis
Acanthus spinosus
Achillea filipendulina
Achillea millefolium
Achillea ptarmica
Achillea sibirica
Aconitum carmichaelii
Aconitum lamarckii
Aconitum napellus
Aconitum reclinatum
Aconitum septentrionale
    'Ivorine'
Allium christophii
Allium giganteum
Allium karataviense
Allium 'Beauregard'
Allium 'Globemaster'
Anemone coronaria
Anemone sylvestris
Anemone tomentosa
Artemisia ludoviciana
Artemisia schmidtiana
Aruncus dioicus
Aruncus 'Southern White'
Aster carolinianus
Aster novae-angliae
Aster novi-belgii
Aster tataricus

Baptisia alba
Baptisia australis
Baptisia minor
Baptisia sphaerocarpa
Baptisia tinctoria
Baptisia viridis
Boltonia asteroides
Campanula carpatica
Campanula lactiflora
Campanula latiloba
Campanula portenschlagiana
Campanula poscharskyana
Canna hybrids
Centaurea cyanus
Centaurea dealbata
Centaurea hypoleuca
Centaurea macrocephala
Centaurea montana
Cephalaria gigantea
Cerastium buisseri
Cerastium tomentosum
Ceratostigma plumbaginoides
Ceratostigma willmottianum
Chrysanthemum coccineum
Chrysanthemum ×koreanum
Chrysanthemum pacificum
Chrysanthemum ×superbum
Clematis ×durandii
Clematis heracleifolia
Clematis integrifolia
Clematis ×jackmanii
Clematis terniflora
Clematis texensis
Clematis hybrids
Coreopsis auriculata
Coreopsis grandiflora
Coreopsis lanceolata
Coreopsis rosea
Coreopsis verticillata
Crocosmia hybrids
Crocus chrysanthus
Crocus speciosus
Crocus vernus
Dahlia imperialis
Dahlia hybrids
Delphinium elatum

Delphinium nudicaule
Dianthus barbatus
Dianthus caryophyllus
Dianthus deltoides
Dianthus gratianopolitanus
Echinacea pallida
Echinacea paradoxa
Echinacea purpurea
Echinops ritro
Eremurus aitchisonii
Eremurus himalaicus
Eremurus stenophyllus
Eryngium agavifolium
Eryngium alpinum
Eryngium giganteum
Eryngium yuccafolium
Eupatorium coelestinum
Eupatorium maculatum
Eupatorium rugosum
Euphorbia characias
Euphorbia dulcis
Euphorbia griffithii
Euphorbia lathyris
Gaillardia ×grandiflora
Gaura lindheimeri
Geranium ×cantabrigiense
Geranium endressii
Geranium psilostemon
Geranium sanguineum
Geum chiloense
Geum rivale
Geum triflorum
Hakonechloa macra
Helenium autumnale
Helianthus angustifolius
Helianthus giganteus
Helianthus ×multiflorus
Heliopsis helianthoides
Hemerocallis dumortieri
Hemerocallis fulva
Hemerocallis minor
Hemerocallis hybrids
Hibiscus coccineus
Hibiscus moscheutos
Hibiscus mutabilis
Hypericum androsaemum

Hypericum calycinum
Hypericum 'Hidcote'
Ipheion uniflorum
Iris danfordiae
Iris ensata
Iris hexagona
Iris louisiana
Iris nelsonii
Iris reticulata
Iris tectorum
Iris xiphium
Kalimeris pinnatifida
Kniphofia hybrids
Liatris borealis
Liatris graminifolia
Liatris spicata
Ligularia dentata
Ligularia macrophylla
Ligularia sibirica
Ligularia stenocephala
Lilium auratum
Lilium canadense
Lilium henryi
Lilium martagon
Lilium regale
Linum flavum
Linum perenne
Linum usitatissimum
Lobelia cardinalis
Lobelia ×gerardii
Lobelia siphilitica
Lobelia ×speciosa
Lobelia tupa
Lunaria annua
Lunaria rediviva
Lupinus arboreus
Lupinus polyphyllus
Lychnis ×arkwrightii
Lychnis chalcedonica
Lychnis coronaria
Lychnis flos-cuculi
Lycoris albiflora
Lycoris aurea
Lycoris radiata
Lycoris squamigera
Lysimachia ciliata

Lysimachia clethroides
Lysimachia ephemerum
Macleaya cordata
Miscanthus sinensis
Miscanthus hybrids
Monarda didyma
Narcissus bulbocodium
Narcissus cyclamineus
Narcissus hybrids
Nepeta ×faassenii
Nepeta ×faassenii 'Six Hills
   Giant'
Nepeta govaniana
Nepeta nervosa
Nepeta sibirica
Oenothera berlandieri
Oenothera drummondii
Oenothera fruticosa
Oenothera missouriensis
Oenothera speciosa
Paeonia hybrids
Papaver nudicaule
Papaver orientale
Papaver rhoeas
Papaver somniferum
Patrinia scabiosifolia
Patrinia triloba
Patrinia villosa
Penstemon barbatus
Penstemon cardwellii
Penstemon confertus
Penstemon digitalis
Penstemon pinifolius
Perovskia atriplicifolia
Phlomis fruticosa
Phlomis italica
Phlomis russeliana
Phlox paniculata
Phlox subulata
Physostegia virginiana
Platycodon grandiflorus
Polemonium caeruleum
Polemonium carneum
Polemonium foliosissimum
Polygonum affine
Polygonum bistorta

Pulsatilla halleri
Pulsatilla pratensis
Pulsatilla vulgaris
Ranunculus aconitifolius
Ranunculus asiaticus
Ranunculus bulbosus
Ranunculus ficaria
Ranunculus repens
Rehmannia angulata
Rehmannia elata
Rudbeckia fulgida
Rudbeckia laciniata
Rudbeckia nitida
Rudbeckia triloba
Salvia guaranitica
Salvia involucrata
Salvia officinalis
Salvia ×sylvestris
Salvia 'Indigo Spires'
Santolina chamaecyparissus
Santolina pinnata
Santolina virens
Saponaria ocymoides
Saponaria officinalis
Scabiosa caucasica
Scabiosa columbaria
Scabiosa ochroleuca
Sedum acre
Sedum aizoon
Sedum kamtschaticum
Sedum reflexum
Sedum spathulifolium
Sedum spurium
Silene caroliniana
Silene uniflora
Sisyrinchium angustifolium
Sisyrinchium atlanticum
Sisyrinchium idahoense
Sisyrinchium striatum
Stachys macrantha
Stokesia laevis
Thalictrum aquilegiifolium
Thalictrum flavum
Thermopsis caroliniana
Thermopsis fabacea
Thermopsis montana

Full Sun, continued
Thymus praecox
Thymus pseudolanuginosus
Thymus serpyllum
Thymus vulgaris
Tradescantia virginiana
Tricyrtis formosana

Tricyrtis hirta
Verbena bonariensis
Verbena canadensis
Verbena peruviana
Verbena rigida
Verbena tenuisecta

Veronica austriaca
Veronica incana
Veronica longifolia
Veronica prostrata
Veronica spicata
Veronicastrum sibiricum

Veronicastrum virginicum
Viola cornuta
Viola cucullata
Yucca filamentosa
Zantedeschia hybrids
Zauschneria californica

Sprawling Habit/Vines

The following vines or plants tend to sprawl if not provided with support. Large sprawling plants can be trained to grow through and over small shrubs or can be supported by neighboring plants.

Campanula portenschlagiana
Campanula poscharskyana
Clematis cirrhosa
Clematis×durandii

Clematis heracleifolia
Clematis×jackmanii
Clematis terniflora
Clematis texensis

Dicentra scandens
Euphorbia myrsinites
Geranium psilostemon

Geranium 'Ann Folkard'
Oenothera speciosa
Silene polypetala

Evergreen/Winter Interest

Although much of the country is covered with snow in the winter, some plants still provide winter interest in the form of architectural features, seed heads, and persistent foliage.

Ajuga genevensis
Ajuga reptans
Asarum arifolium
Asarum splendens
Asarum yakushimanum
Bergenia cordifolia
Bergenia purpurascens
Clematis cirrhosa
Dryopteris erythrosora
Dryopteris marginalis

Epimedium grandiflorum
Epimedium×perralchium
Epimedium×rubrum
Helleborus foetidus
Helleborus niger
Helleborus×nigristern
Helleborus orientalis
Hepatica acutiloba
Hepatica americana

Hepatica transsilvanica
Heuchera americana
Miscanthus sinensis
Phlomis fruticosa
Phlomis russeliana
Phlox stolonifera
Phlox subulata
Pulmonaria angustifolia
Pulmonaria longifolia

Pulmonaria saccharata
Ranunculus repens
Sedum acre
Sedum kamtschaticum
Sedum spathulifolium
Sedum spurium
Sedum 'Autumn Joy' ('Herbst-
    freude')
Tiarella cordifolia

Flowering Season

As far as a plant is concerned, the seasons depend on environmental changes such as soil warming, day and night temperatures, photoperiod, and frost—not calendar dates, as we are used to thinking. A spring-flowering plant simply means it is early to flower, not that it flowers in March, April, or even May. The flowering calendar offered here is therefore relative.

SPRING

Acanthus mollis
Acanthus spinosus
Achillea ageratum
Achillea millefolium
Adiantum capillus-veneris
Ajuga genevensis 'Pink Beauty'
Ajuga reptans
Allium christophii
Allium giganteum
Allium karataviense
Allium 'Beauregard'
Allium 'Globemaster'
Anemone blanda
Anemone coronaria
Anemone sylvestris
Aquilegia alpina
Aquilegia caerulea
Aquilegia canadensis
Aquilegia chrysantha
Aquilegia flabellata
Aquilegia vulgaris
Arisaema candidissimum
Arisaema consanguineum
Arisaema ringens
Arisaema sazensoo
Arisaema sikokianum
Arisaema sikokianum × *A. takedae*
Arisaema tortuosum
Arisaema triphyllum
Aruncus aethusifolius
Aruncus 'Southern White'
Asarum arifolium
Asarum canadense
Asarum splendens
Asarum yakushimanum
Astilbe ×*arendsii*

Astilbe chinensis
Astrantia major
Astrantia maxima
Baptisia alba
Baptisia australis
Baptisia minor
Baptisia sphaerocarpa
Bergenia ciliata
Bergenia cordifolia
Bergenia purpurascens
Brunnera macrophylla
Centaurea montana
Cerastium buisseri
Cerastium tomentosum
Chrysanthemum coccineum
Coreopsis auriculata
Corydalis cheilanthifolia
Corydalis flexuosa
Corydalis lutea
Crocus chrysanthus
Crocus vernus
Dianthus barbatus
Dianthus deltoides
Dianthus gratianopolitanus
Dicentra eximia
Dicentra spectabilis
Digitalis purpurea
Disporum sessile
Disporum sessile var. *flavum*
Epimedium grandiflorum
Epimedium ×*perralchium*
Epimedium ×*rubrum*
Epimedium ×*versicolor*
Epimedium ×*youngianum*
Euphorbia characias
Euphorbia myrsinites
Geranium cinereum
Geranium endressii
Geranium sanguineum

Geum chiloense
Geum rivale
Geum triflorum
Geum triflorum var. *campanulatum*
Helleborus foetidus
Helleborus niger
Helleborus ×*nigristern*
Helleborus orientalis
Hepatica acutiloba
Hepatica americana
Hepatica nobilis
Hepatica transsilvanica
Heuchera sanguinea
Ipheion uniflorum
Iris danfordiae
Iris reticulata
Iris tectorum
Iris xiphium
Lamium galeobdolon
Lamium maculatum
Lobelia cardinalis
Lobelia ×*gerardii*
Lobelia siphilitica
Lobelia ×*speciosa*
Lobelia tupa
Lunaria annua
Lunaria rediviva
Lupinus arboreus
Lupinus polyphyllus
Lychnis ×*arkwrightii*
Lychnis flos-cuculi
Lysimachia japonica
Lysimachia nummularia
Mertensia asiatica
Mertensia sibirica
Mertensia virginica
Narcissus bulbocodium
Narcissus cyclamineus

Narcissus hybrids
Nepeta ×*faassenii*
Nepeta ×*faassenii* 'Six Hills Giant'
Nepeta govaniana
Nepeta sibirica
Oenothera berlandieri
Oenothera missouriensis
Oenothera speciosa
Osmunda cinnamomea
Osmunda claytoniana
Osmunda regalis
Paeonia hybrids
Penstemon barbatus
Penstemon smallii
Phlox divaricata
Phlox stolonifera
Phlox subulata
Pinellia pedatisecta
Pinellia tripartita
Polemonium reptans
Polygonatum humile
Polygonatum odoratum
Polygonum affine
Polygonum bistorta
Primula bulleyana
Primula denticulata
Primula florindae
Primula heladoxa
Primula japonica
Primula pulverulenta
Primula veris
Primula vulgaris
Pulmonaria angustifolia
Pulmonaria longifolia
Pulmonaria rubra
Pulmonaria saccharata
Pulsatilla halleri
Pulsatilla pratensis

Spring, continued

Pulsatilla vulgaris
Ranunculus asiaticus
Ranunculus bulbosus
Ranunculus repens
Saponaria ocymoides
Saponaria officinalis
Scabiosa caucasica
Scabiosa columbaria
Sedum acre
Sedum aizoon
Sedum aizoon var. auranti-
 acum
Sedum kamtschaticum
Sedum reflexum
Sedum spathulifolium
Sedum spurium
Sedum ternatum
Silene caroliniana
Silene polypetala
Silene regia
Silene uniflora
Silene virginica
Smilacina racemosa
Stachys byzantina
Stachys macrantha
Stylophorum diphyllum
Stylophorum lasiocarpum
Symphytum asperum
Symphytum caucasicum
Symphytum grandiflorum
Symphytum officinale
Symphytum ×uplandicum
Thalictrum aquilegiifolium
Thalictrum flavum
Thalictrum ichangense
Thalictrum minus 'Adi-
 antifolium'
Thermopsis caroliniana
Thermopsis montana
Thymus praecox
Thymus pseudolanuginosus
Thymus serpyllum
Thymus vulgaris
Tiarella cordifolia
Trillium catesbaei

Trillium cernuum
Trillium cuneatum
Trillium decipiens
Trillium discolor
Trillium erectum
Trillium grandiflorum
Trillium luteum
Trillium sessile
Trillium stamineum
Trillium vaseyi
Uvularia grandiflora
Uvularia perfoliata
Uvularia sessilifolia
Veratrum album
Veratrum viride
Verbena peruviana
Verbena tenuisecta
Veronica austriaca
Veronica austriaca subsp.
 teucrium
Veronica incana
Veronica longifolia
Veronica prostrata
Veronica spicata
Viola cornuta
Viola cucullata
Viola labradorica
Viola pedata
Waldsteinia fragarioides
Waldsteinia lobata
Waldsteinia parviflora
Waldsteinia ternata

SUMMER

Acanthus mollis
Acanthus spinosus
Achillea ageratum
Achillea filipendulina
Achillea millefolium
Achillea ptarmica
Achillea sibirica
Aconitum carmichaelii
Allium giganteum
Anemone sylvestris
Anemone tomentosa
Arisaema candidissimum

Arisaema consanguineum
Arisaema fargesii
Arisaema japonicum
Artemisia ludoviciana
Artemisia schmidtiana
Aruncus dioicus
Aster divaricatus
Astilbe ×arendsii
Astilbe biternata
Astilbe chinensis
Astilbe chinensis var. taquetii
Astilbe simplicifolia
Baptisia tinctoria
Baptisia viridis
Boltonia asteroides
Campanula carpatica
Campanula lactiflora
Campanula latiloba
Campanula portenschlagiana
Campanula poscharskyana
Canna hybrids
Centaurea cyanus
Centaurea dealbata
Centaurea hypoleuca
Centaurea macrocephala
Cephalaria gigantea
Chrysanthemum ×superbum
Clematis ×durandii
Clematis heracleifolia
Clematis integrifolia
Clematis ×jackmanii
Clematis texensis
Clematis hybrids
Coreopsis grandiflora
Coreopsis lanceolata
Coreopsis rosea
Coreopsis verticillata
Crocosmia hybrids
Delphinium elatum
Delphinium nudicaule
Dianthus caryophyllus
Dicentra scandens
Digitalis grandiflora
Digitalis lutea
Digitalis ×mertonensis
Echinacea pallida

Echinacea paradoxa
Echinacea purpurea
Echinops ritro
Eremurus aitchisonii
Eremurus himalaicus
Eremurus stenophyllus
Eryngium agavifolium
Eryngium alpinum
Eryngium yuccafolium
Eupatorium rugosum
Euphorbia dulcis
Euphorbia griffithii
Euphorbia lathyris
Gaillardia ×grandiflora
Gaura lindheimeri
Geranium ×cantabrigiense
Geranium endressii
Geranium psilostemon
Geum triflorum
Geum triflorum var. campan-
 ulatum
Helianthus ×multiflorus
Heliopsis helianthoides
Hemerocallis dumortieri
Hemerocallis fulva
Hemerocallis minor
Hemerocallis hybrids
Hibiscus coccineus
Hibiscus moscheutos
Hosta montana
Hosta sieboldiana
Hosta venusta
Hypericum androsaemum
Hypericum 'Hidcote'
Ipheion uniflorum
Iris ensata
Iris fulva
Iris hexagona
Iris louisiana
Iris nelsonii
Kalimeris pinnatifida
Kalimeris yomena
Kirengeshoma palmata
Kniphofia hybrids
Liatris borealis
Liatris graminifolia

Liatris spicata
Ligularia dentata
Ligularia macrophylla
Ligularia sibirica
Ligularia stenocephala
Lilium auratum
Lilium auratum var. *platy-*
  phyllum
Lilium canadense
Lilium henryi
Lilium martagon
Lilium regale
Linum flavum
Linum perenne
Linum usitatissimum
Lobelia cardinalis
Lobelia ×gerardii
Lobelia siphilitica
Lobelia ×speciosa
Lobelia tupa
Lychnis chalcedonica
Lychnis coronaria
Lycoris albiflora
Lycoris aurea
Lycoris squamigera
Lysimachia ciliata
Lysimachia clethroides
Lysimachia ephemerum
Macleaya cordata
Monarda didyma
Nepeta ×faassenii 'Six Hills
  Giant'
Nepeta nervosa
Oenothera drummondii
Oenothera fruticosa
Paeonia hybrids

Penstemon cardwellii
Penstemon confertus
Penstemon digitalis
Penstemon pinifolius
Perovskia atriplicifolia
Phlomis fruticosa
Phlomis italica
Phlomis russeliana
Phlox paniculata
Physostegia virginiana
Platycodon grandiflorus
Polemonium caeruleum
Polemonium carneum
Polemonium foliosissimum
Primula bulleyana
Primula florindae
Primula heladoxa
Ranunculus aconitifolius
Ranunculus ficaria
Rehmannia angulata
Rehmannia elata
Rodgersia aesculifolia
Rodgersia pinnata
Rodgersia podophylla
Rodgersia sambucifolia
Salvia guaranitica
Salvia involucrata
Salvia koyamae
Salvia officinalis
Salvia ×sylvestris
Salvia 'Indigo Spires'
Santolina chamaecyparissus
Santolina pinnata
Santolina virens
Saponaria officinalis
Scabiosa caucasica

Silene fimbriata
Sisyrinchium angustifolium
Sisyrinchium atlanticum
Sisyrinchium idahoense
Sisyrinchium striatum
Stokesia laevis
Thalictrum aquilegiifolium
Thermopsis fabacea
Tradescantia virginiana
Veratrum album
Veratrum viride
Verbena bonariensis
Verbena canadensis
Verbena rigida
Verbena tenuisecta
Veronica spicata
Veronicastrum sibiricum
Veronicastrum virginicum
Yucca filamentosa
Zantedeschia hybrids
Zauschneria californica

FALL
Aconitum carmichaelii
Aconitum lamarckii
Aconitum napellus
Aconitum reclinatum
Aconitum septentrionale
  'Ivorine'
Anemone tomentosa
Aster carolinianus
Aster divaricatus
Aster novae-angliae
Aster novi-belgii
Aster tataricus
Boltonia asteroides

Canna hybrids
Ceratostigma plumbaginoides
Ceratostigma willmottianum
Chrysanthemum ×koreanum
Chrysanthemum pacificum
Clematis terniflora
Colchicum autumnale
Colchicum byzantinum
Colchicum speciosum
Crocus speciosus
Dahlia imperialis
Dahlia hybrids
Eupatorium coelestinum
Eupatorium maculatum
Eupatorium purpureum
Eupatorium rugosum
Helenium autumnale
Helianthus angustifolius
Helianthus giganteus
Heuchera villosa
Hibiscus mutabilis
Lycoris albiflora
Lycoris aurea
Lycoris radiata
Miscanthus sinensis
Miscanthus hybrids
Rudbeckia fulgida
Rudbeckia laciniata
Rudbeckia nitida
Rudbeckia triloba
Salvia involucrata
Salvia 'Indigo Spires'
Santolina chamaecyparissus
Tricyrtis formosana
Tricyrtis hirta

U.S. Department of Agriculture
Hardiness Zone Map

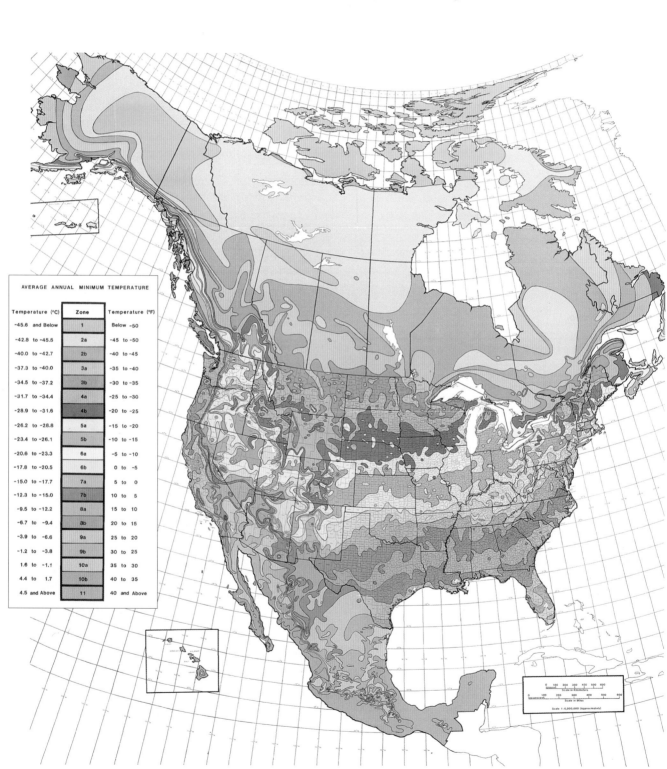

Index of Species and Cultivars

319

Index of Common Names